THE LASTING SUPPER:
Letters for Deconstruction

By

David Hayward
(nakedpastor)

ISBN-13: 978-1535100526

To Lisa, my partner in deconstruction.

ACKNOWLEDGMENTS

I want to thank my wife Lisa for encouraging me to do this.

I want to thank our kids, Joshua, Jesse, and Casile, for being with me in this.

I want to thank Phyllis Mathis, John La Grou, Pat Green, Eric Lawrence for joining me in making this.

I want to thank my editor, Amy Leibowitz, for helping me with this.

Finally, I want to thank the members of The Lasting Supper for walking with me through this.

FORWORD

Deconstruction - such an interesting word. To deconstruct an idea is to reduce it to its component parts and then question the assumptions that led to its existence. To deconstruct a faith system is to call into question the tenets of one's beliefs. But it's not only that. To deconstruct a faith system is to realize that all the tenets of one's beliefs are just that - tenets. Ideas. Constructs of the mind.

It's nice to have a tidy word to describe this, to explain why the earth under our feet seems to be shaking uncontrollably or to help steady ourselves when it feels like our heads are going to explode before we die and go to the hell we're starting to think does not exist anymore. It's nice to have a word to hold onto.

Categories are nice too. Before sociologist Josh Packard coined the term *Dones* to describe those of us who have left institutional Christianity for a variety of important reasons, we've been stuck with unhelpful labels such as *Backsliders*, *Heretics*, or *Apostates*. *Done* is better. Much better.

I myself am a *Done*. I am a practicing psychotherapist, having been so for nearly 30 years now. I have also been a leader in the evangelical/charismatic wing of the Christian church in America, serving as a small group leader, intercessor, prophet, prayer minister, teacher, elder, and pastor. Since 1972, I have immersed my soul, my work, my passion and my identity in what I simply called The Church. I was a true believer.

And then I started to deconstruct.

In my case the word deconstruction is a euphemism that belies a decade-long period of disillusionment, heartbreak, grief, loneliness, anger, spiritual vertigo, shame, and fear. It's better described as a prolonged period of internal thrashing, kicking against the fetters, bulldozing my most strongly held beliefs, launching myself into the spiritual unknown.

Deconstruction, indeed. More like *nuclear winter*.

I started walking alongside other devastated deconstructionists, personally and professionally. With my friend Kathy Escobar, I wrote and facilitated an online class for people like me, providing a space for others to thrash around in relative safety. I continue to counsel individuals for whom the word deconstruction could never begin to describe the emotional, spiritual, and relational devastation they experience as a result of their changing faith.

Along the way I met David Hayward, the Naked Pastor. I had loved his cartoons for years, always impressed by his insight, his wry sense of humor, and his willingness to confront the foibles of modern church systems.

He told me the story of his own deconstruction and his subsequent exit from the ministry. And then he told me about his online community, The Lasting Supper.

At last, I thought, a place for us.

Whatever you want to call us—Nones, Dones, Faith Shifters, or Spiritual Orphans—there is one thing we have in common—loss.

Loss of certainty, community, relationships, position; loss of vision, purpose, even identity. But after listening to the stories of hundreds of church leavers, I believe the deepest pain we feel is the loss of connection, a place to belong.

David Hayward knows this. He feels it. In the age of pastors-as-CEOs, pastors-as-dictators, pastors-as-TV-personalities, or worse, pastors-as-chief-abusers, David has always been a real live pastor-as-shepherd-and-carer-of-souls. David knows that true spiritual growth often means breaking out of the boxes we try to keep God in. It means risking the comforts of certainty to become spiritually independent.

He also knows that you can't lead beyond the boundaries if you've never gone there yourself. You can't comfort the broken-hearted if you own heart remains unfazed.

But most importantly, David Hayward knows you can't create a healthy thriving community with an ego-driven agenda. We've all had enough of that.

David Hayward is the real deal, uniquely qualified to create a home for the Nones, the Dones, and the spiritual refugees.

The Lasting Supper is like nothing I have ever known. It's the thing I've always believed was possible, but was never able to create. It's a place where people can be themselves, believe what they want, and support each other in their own path of development, in all kinds of circumstances.

Through online resources, forums, a Facebook group, interest-driven sub-groups, virtual pot lucks, and the weekly letters you are about to read, The Lasting Supper provides a little bit of what our hearts have always longed for - a place to be ourselves, messy as we are, and be accepted.

Not just anyone can hold a space like The Lasting Supper and help it thrive. It takes a certain kind of soul. A unique gift mix. A lifetime of experience. A willingness to be vulnerable, make mistakes, and make things right.

And so much more.

But that's David—one born for such a time as this.

So I am honored to introduce you to these letters, the epistles from the heart of The Lasting Supper. May they feed you, comfort you, encourage you, and bring you hope.

Because as tidy as the word sounds, deconstruction is not for the faint of heart.

Phyllis Mathis

INTRODUCTION

I first read David's blog nakedpastor somewhere around 2007. Here was this guy, head pastor of a Canadian church, wrestling publicly with not only his faith but religion in general. David's online religious criticism, salted with his own artwork and cartoons, echoed what many of us had been experiencing for years—a disconnect between love and religion.

I think David calls himself the *naked pastor* because, unlike most, he would rather be naked than clothed in fantasy. As George Bernard Shaw wrote, "The reasonable man adapts himself to the world; the unreasonable one persists in trying to adapt the world to himself. Therefore all progress depends on the unreasonable man." David is not a reasonable man. He is living more from his imagination than his memory.

Internet guru Clay Shirky says, "Institutions will try to preserve the problems to which they are the solution." We watched as David wrestled publicly with entrenched problems of institution—what few religious professionals would talk about even privately. Those in religious employment—theological professors, clerics, religious writers and publishers—do not challenge publicly their livelihood with doubts and flat-out disbelief. Such a posture, for most, would bring immediate dismissal, ravaging their families and life dreams. Reasonable people don't do this.

David's clash with institution accelerated and, in 2010, reached critical mass. He courageously abandoned his paid clerical position and started a new life focused on artwork, cartooning, online community, and a unique arc of existential commentary. David's virtual presence gathered momentum and attracted a growing global community of conversational readers. Two years later, he created an online-hybrid interactive community called *The Lasting Supper*. Many readers became supporters of, and participants in, *TLS*. Not surprisingly, *TLS* has attracted many people with life trajectories not unlike David's: questioners, revolutionaries, anarchists, artists, change agents, institutional refugees. The community pretty much runs itself. No credentials are required. It's a safe place for dangerous ideas and challenging perspectives. Hundreds of members are now active, both on Facebook and a dedicated *TLS* website. I'm not an active participant, but I've spent a fair bit of time observing. The honesty goes deep, and it's clear that a lot of good people have been previously shredded and discarded by some form of toxic institution. There is gut-level storytelling and catharsis and healing at work here, unlike any other hybrid community I've seen. As the tag line says, "Come hungry, and help yourself."

David is what I would call a "super-connector." In the business world, there are specialized local-virtual (hybrid) community structures created to "super-connect" people globally (*e.g.,* Thousand Network). *TLS* is a similar connective environment, not for business branding, but for personal growth. It's a place to re-learn freedom and independent thinking. I say "re-learn" because we're all born with a natural independence and curiosity—childlike attributes that are too easily snuffed out by unhealthy environments.

David says that *Lasting Supper* members are as diverse as the conversations that unfold: academics, atheists, agnostics, church members, ex-church members, artists, seekers, clergy, ex-clergy, writers, poets and more. In its diversity and reach, *TLS* beautifully reflects an old Eastern Orthodox saying, "It is not our task to provide easy answers to every question, but to make us progressively aware of a mystery." Hard questions are encouraged, and easy answers are quickly dismantled. As political theorist Ludwig Borne said, "Getting rid of a delusion is better than getting hold of a truth."

Writing from a Nazi prison cell, not long before his execution in 1945, the esteemed theologian Dietrich Bonhoeffer admitted that the old paradigm had run its course, that the "time of religion" is over. He observed that we are becoming "radically religionless." He writes positively, "We are moving toward a completely religionless time; people as they are now simply cannot be religious anymore."

The Lasting Supper is a kind of prototype, a living embodiment of Bonhoeffer's prophetic pen. A colorful diversity of men and women—

from many countries, from very different backgrounds and experiences, of different generations, each with unique goals and desires—coming together in a religionless community experiment, all seeking more authentic and free-spirited expressions and experiences of life, healing, growth, hope, value, meaning, and most importantly, love. Half a century ago, philosopher Paul Tillich saw this coming, calling it the "latent" or "hidden" community; groups and individuals organizing with generative humanitarian purpose but without the factional trappings of identity politics, divisional creeds, or inherited dogma.

The visionary Buckminster Fuller said, "You never change things by fighting the existing reality. To change something, build a new model that makes the existing model obsolete." *TLS* is one of the *new models*. David and community are not seeking approval from anyone's dominant paradigm. They are busy creating a new paradigm. Unlike old institutional community models, *TLS* reflects the collective wisdom of all participants rather than the narrow agenda of a few. Thomas Paine said, "My country is wherever liberty lives." To many, *TLS* is a place where liberty lives and thrives.

What is the future of *TLS*? I'm confident that hybrid communities will continue to grow and flourish over coming generations. Anything that allows people to reach beyond previously isolated belief-tribes by definition broadens our collective understanding of who "WE" are, even if we don't necessarily recognize it at the time. And anything that truly expands our awareness and understanding of the broader human condition must, over time, increase the light we all desperately need.

John La Grou

Dear Reader: Before you begin reading my letters to The Lasting Supper community, I want to explain the structure of the book. I write a letter to the community about once a week. Over the four years we've been together, I've obviously written quite a few. When I decided to collect them into this book, I had a hard time deciding whether I should put them in some kind of thematic order, or sections, or just leave them in the chronological order in which they were written. I chose the latter because I believe there is a flow to them. As the community changed, so did the issues I felt needed to be addressed. So the first one in this book was written in the spring of 2012 when TLS began, and the last one was written in the spring of 2016. I hope you find good food here at The Lasting Supper. When you're finished the book, perhaps you'll consider joining us at www.theLastingSupper. com. And now for the first letter...

DON'T LET ANYONE RUSH YOUR GRIEF!

Don't let anyone rush your grief! You've left the church. That's heavy! Grieve it. Feel it to the full. Go ahead and deny that it hurts. Then bawl your eyes out once in a while. Get angry. Get frustrated. Think about going back then change your mind again. Get depressed. That's the best way to let it pass and finally find peace.

Grieving is an important and necessary step after any kind of loss. You have to grieve when you lose your favorite pen. You have to grieve when you lose your loved one. Of course they are on a different scale, but grief is a part of the process of responding to loss. Any kind of loss.

Is there an appropriate length of time for grief? I don't think so. But let's take me for an example. I lose my favorite pen. I can't find it. It seems there's nothing I can do to get it back. It's gone. Forever. My response has been everything from denial, bargaining, anger, depression, to hopefully and finally a sense of peace. After all, I can go back out and buy another one. Maybe that grieving response took...I don't know...15 minutes.

But what if I lose a loved one? The same stages of grief apply, but they will take longer. It will take a much longer time for me to eventually and hopefully reach the stage of peace. But this depends on a lot of factors too. How close was I to this loved one? Were we living together? For how long? How dependent was I on this person? How much did they mean to me? Were we estranged when we were separated? And so on. You might grieve for a year. Or maybe 10 years with the occasional reversions on anniversaries, etc. Who knows?

We grieve when we leave the church. Even if we left volitionally or were forced to leave. Whatever the circumstances, we must allow ourselves time to grieve. If you only went one month to church just to observe and then left, your grieving might not take as long. But what if you went to church for 50 years, were deeply involved in its life, and then were asked to leave or you felt you simply could no longer stay? How long should grieving take then? A week? A month? A year? Five years? A lifetime?

I would suggest having someone to talk to so you can walk through it in a healthy manner, whatever that is. It is possible to get stuck in grief, stalled in depression, broken down in sorrow. Having someone to talk to could jumpstart you to make your grief manageable and help you progress towards a joyful life.

But don't let anyone tell you how long you have to grieve. Take as long as you want. I remember just a few months after a devastating church split, some people who were strong supporters finally left the church because I wasn't healing fast enough. But I couldn't speed it up. And you might know me well enough by now that I just couldn't fake it. I was grieving. It took me a long time to get over that. Some might argue I'm still not over it.

I left the church a couple of years ago under strained conditions. I'm still grieving, but no one's rushing me now. I'm talking with someone. I'm getting better. At my own pace. I'm going to be fine. I see joy coming.

You can too. Don't rush the grief. Let it come. Feel it to the full. This is the best way to let it pass. And it will. Eventually. And you will be happy again.

MY Z-THEORY IN ONE PAGE

This dream ended over thirty years of theological and intellectual anxiety for me and brought a lasting peace of mind that I enjoy to this day. I hope it helps you in your own journey. My goal is to write a book explaining this theory in more detail.

In 2009 I had a dream that relieved my theological anxiety and brought peace:

"There is a huge waterfall. Oceans of water pour over the rim of the cliff. The water tumbles down and explodes at the bottom. The deluge spreads over the land covering and consuming everything."

Let me analyze what I felt this meant when I dreamed it.

"There is a huge waterfall. Oceans of water pour over the rim of the cliff."

We can't see above the rim, but we can guess that it is an infinite source. There is no proof. Only evidence. We can't even say it exists. We just know it must be. It is.

This is That-Which-We-Call-God, the Absolute, the Source, Wholly Other, Nirvana, Allah, Yahweh, the Unknowable, the Frontier, the closeted, the Undiscovered.

"The water tumbles down and explodes at the bottom."

This is the evidence we have of what is above the rim. The infinite and invisible is now finite and visible. This is the revelation of the Wholly Other, the exposure, the incarnation of the mystery, the transmission of truth, the manifestation of the unknown, the discoveries of science. It is the encounter and reception of the unknown now known, the mysterious now perceived.

This is what we call the Christ, the Torah, the Buddha, scientific discovery, revelation, the condescension, the incarnation, the transmission, the embodiment, the coming down and the coming out.

"The deluge spreads out over the land covering and consuming everything."

This is the realm of time, history and culture. This is where spirit and nature meet. It is the manifestation of the good in the muck of the human story. It is forgiveness, reconciliation and love that find expression in community. Where truth, justice and love abide, this is the working of spirit in the turmoil of history.

This is what we call the spirit, the application of the revelation, the discovery, and the made-known. This is the historical impact in the mess and beauty of this world. This is community, unity, peace and justice in the midst of suffering. Here scriptures are written that try to point to what's been revealed and seen. It spreads throughout the earth filling and fulfilling all living things, binding all together as one.

This trinitarian structure describes reality that everyone shares. No one has exclusive rights. Though our language articulates our own vantage points, they all describe the same thing from a superficial to a complex level.

We are all in the same world experiencing the same world, and we each perceive and interpret this through our own paradigms and world views, and we each articulate our understanding through our own words and languages.

ALBINO COUGARS AND WHALES OF THE DEEP

Good morning, my dear friends. And I do call you friends because that's what you are. You are providing me with a deep sense of connection and understanding, as well as happiness. You've made a huge difference in my life. I hope everyone on The Lasting Supper feels the same way. I know many of you do because I hear this from you in personal emails to me.

Which, by the way, is something I do with the members of TLS. I get lots of messages every day from people everywhere. But when I get an email or message from a member of TLS, I pay special attention and spend extra time with you. I'm investing far more time and energy into the members of TLS because I consider it my community. As I know you do as well. So feel free to talk with me. That's what I'm here for.

I want to continue talking about the z-theory in smaller parts. Last week, I gave a one-page summary of the z-theory and discovered, to my delight, that it was very beneficial to many of you. I hope it provides the same peace of mind and spirit that it has provided me. Let's talk about the first part in a little more detail.

Here's what I wrote about the first part:

"There is a huge waterfall. Oceans of water pour over the rim of the cliff."

We can't see above the rim, but we can guess that it is an infinite source. There is no proof. Only evidence. We can't even say it exists. We just know it must be. It is.

This is That-Which-We-Call-God, the Absolute, the Source, Wholly Other, Nirvana, Allah, Yahweh, the Unknowable, the Frontier, the closeted, the Undiscovered.

So from a Christian perspective, this is That-Which-We-Call-God. I emphasize that this is what is *above* the rim. We cannot see it. It is invisible to us. This doesn't make it any less real or more real, but it certainly makes it improvable. If this was all there was, I would call this unsubstantiated. This is where many Christians stumble and fall.

I remember many years ago when I was trying to explain my Christian faith to a friend who had become an atheist. If you read posts from nakedpastor from years ago to the present, you can certainly see my development. My conversations with my atheist friend were years ago when I was still standing in theological certitude. But he kept pressing me because I felt so certain about the existence of God yet couldn't seem to provide enough substantial proof to settle his mind. No matter how much I talked about my personal journey, my deeply held beliefs, even my own intense spiritual experiences, nothing I could say provided the proof he needed to restore his belief and faith. These conversations were always frustrating to me because deep down, I knew he was right. There is no proof.

I explain it this way: Let's say a good friend of mine, someone I trust and believe completely, has never in his life lied to me. He comes back from deer hunting one day all excited because he tells me he saw a cougar in the woods. There are strong rumors where I live in New Brunswick that there are cougars here. Some people claim to have seen them. It's yet to be proven. But my trustworthy friend is excitedly telling me he really did see one. Not only was it a cougar, but it was an albino cougar! I'm looking at him in disbelief. Did he get a picture? No! But he did get a picture on his cell phone of what looks like a partial paw print. Hm. Interesting. Ya, maybe I can see a partial print. Not sure though. He tells me that as he was walking along a deer trail he saw some movement far ahead on the path. A flash of white. When you're deer hunting this usually means you saw the warning flash of a white-tailed deer's tail. He says he crouched down and clicked the safety off on his rifle, raised it and looked through his scope in the direction of the white flash looking for movement or the straight line of a deer's back. Eventually he saw slight movement. And then... he couldn't believe his eyes... there 100 yards up the path looking straight at him was a white cougar! He says they locked eyes for about 15 seconds and then, in a flash, he was gone. In fear and trepidation but with unrelenting curiosity, he walked slowly up the path to where the cougar stood. He bent down and found a partial print and took a picture of it. At the same time, he says, he heard the blood-curdling scream of the cougar. His hunting day was over. He returned to tell me this unbelievable tale.

What do I do with it? I believe my friend believes he saw what he saw and heard what he heard. But do I believe there is an albino cougar in the woods a few miles up the road? I'm not sure what to do with this information. My friend's not irrational or prone to exaggeration. But this is just too spectacular a story. I'm not sure what to do with it. He never provided me with any proof, just an incredible but unsubstantiated story. His testimony. But it couldn't be used in court as proof of the presence of cougars in New Brunswick. Especially albino ones!

This is how many people feel about people's stories about God. There seems to be lots of evidence. So many scriptures, Christian and otherwise, provide testimonies about this God. Some people claim to have seen, heard or felt something. Many of these people are completely rational and not prone to lying. But it all comes down to testimony. Word of mouth. Feelings. Intuitions. Insights. The fact that these testimonies come to us from all around the world and down through thousands of years with uncanny similarities is impressive, but it all comes down to testimonies. No proof.

We are standing at the bottom of the falls looking up. We know that there must be something up there. Next week I'll talk about how the water tumbling down gives us excellent clues as to what is actually above the rim. But for now all we can share are our strikingly similar testimonies of what is up there. Christians, Jews and Muslims like to call this God, Yahweh, or Allah and that it is heaven up there, or paradise, or infinity. Or Buddhists call this nirvana or bodhisattva or Buddhahood or Compassion or Nothingness or The All. Or Hindus might call it God or gods or the Infinite or Eternal. Or scientists might call this the Unknown, the not-yet-disclosed, beyond the present frontiers of scientific discovery. Or perhaps a quantum physicist might call it the Source, the Really Real, or the Unified Oneness, or just Reality. Perhaps philosophers and mystics could call it the One or Oneness, or the Archetypal, or Uncaused Cause. I could go on and on with descriptors… words that attempt to describe what this unnamable infinite source may be… testimonials and theories, sometimes from wise and intelligent men and women and sometimes from people whose ideas don't make sense to us. But they are all pointing to the same Mystery with different methods and language, all of them insufficient to prove but sufficient enough to give evidence and even give us serious pause.

This is why I claim it isn't necessary for me to reject my Christian heritage or education or language to simply adopt another. In fact, I incorporate all languages into mine because it fills mine out to make sense for me and to help me articulate to others what I mean. I no longer worry about how people label me because I do not label myself. I do believe there are better insights and languages I could use in my testimony than others.

I have a friend who, when I asked her what the "unknown" is for her, told me that she loves to go out on her husband's fishing boat and look for whales. For her, whales symbolize all that is Good, Mysterious, Powerful, Gracious, Eternal and Loving. Looking for, waiting for, longing for, and sighting a whale is full of mystical profundity that makes her feel One with All Things. Sighting a whale is all she needs to be at peace with herself and know that everything is right with the world. That's her language. Although I indeed have personally experienced her metaphor for Mystery and Oneness, it's not sufficient for me. But it is for her and provides the same value for her as mine does for me. This is why I feel no anxiety to reject one paradigm for another one that simply functions in the same way in attempting to describe the indescribable.

As I always say, my home is in Christianity but I have cottages everywhere. I feel peace about this and am free of theological anxiety about it.

I hope this makes some sense to you and helps you.

SIMPLE Z-THEORY DIAGRAM

The "All" "God"?
(what we can't see, the infinite, what we don't know)

The "Appearance" "Jesus"?
(what is revealed, discovered, made known, realized, learned, manifested...)

The "Actualization" "Spirit"?
(the actualization of love, justice, etc., in the human collective)

Hopefully this will help some of you understand my z-theory better. It is based on a waterfall dream I had a few years ago that left me the impression it graphically depicted the structure of reality. I suggest this diagram can be used by all religions and world-views.

So as I try to explain to my Christian friends, this is why I rarely, if ever, use the word "God", or demand that people believe in the man "Jesus" and the bible as sole source of truth, or that the "Holy Spirit" of Christianity holds dominion over how we talk about the human collective, including the church. I always try to avoid exclusivity and the presumption of privilege that comes with that.

Therefore, a Buddhist could say the All is Nirvana or the Buddha nature; the Appearance is the Buddha, Siddhartha, including the Sutras; and the Application is the Sangha, or the community.

An Atheist could say the All is undiscovered scientific realities; the Appearance is human discoveries of these realities; and the Application is the use of these discoveries for the betterment of the human collective and the earth.

On and on we could go.

So at the same time, even though the All, like water over the falls, fills all things, somehow it is at the same time separate, an infinite source, so that we are at once full of "God" or the All, while at the same time the All does not lose itself, its objectivity, its "Wholly Otherness."

I'm offering this paradigm to us, the members of TLS, as a way to understand how, even though we are very diverse in our beliefs and world-views, we can all find ourselves within this construct and thus our unity.

ZERO TOLERANCE FOR BULLYING!

One of the most important aspects of community is strong moderation.

If you are not involved with the community, make sure someone is. With my online community, I am not only involved, keeping an eye on things, but I have facilitators who love the community and care about its health.

With an online community, diversity must be at or near the top of the list of values. Why? Because this reflects how people really are, not as we wish them to be. So there's bound to be conflict that has to be moderated and mediated.

But there's another factor that presents itself from time to time, and that's bullying. We allow all kinds of disagreements, questions, challenges, swearing, even anger, but never bullying. We have zero tolerance for that because it suddenly makes the room unsafe, members afraid, and the community destructible. When someone displays bullying, they are immediately removed. I try to dialog with them because I don't want them to feel condemned forever. I would like them to seek help and maybe return. But the priority is the community. Even with over 300 members, an online bully can decimate the morale of the room with one simple post. Sometimes a bully can ruin community to the point where it can take months to recover. So moderation is key.

I recently had to deal with an online bully. The community was shocked. But those who were victimized were grateful. Because there was confusion that this popular person was removed... some knew why and some didn't... I felt it necessary to write a post explaining it. Here it is:

"As many of you already know, I had to ask one of our members to leave yesterday. There have only been a few who've been asked to part ways since the inception of TLS, and I think that's a pretty good record. In all these cases it came down to one behavior that we cannot tolerate on TLS: bullying.

"We can ask questions. We can disagree. We can swear. We can talk about anything. We can get depressed. We can get faithless. We can get angry. We can even say something that is unintentionally hurtful to another. As long as we can be informed, challenged, corrected, educated, and opened for change. In a community context, trying our best to live together is crucial.

"But bullying is the intentional harming of another. And we must have zero tolerance for that. Even if the person is angry for understandable reasons, they have no right to inflict harm or damage another person.

"My advice to them is always the same: 'We had to remove you from the room because you were hurting people. Please get some help, and when you feel you are better and can function in a healthy way in a community without harming others, then please write to me and we'll talk about you returning to the community so that we can try it again.'"

Zero tolerance for bullying!

I hope this gives you guys confidence in how hard we work to keep TLS safe.

Thanks!

FINDING, USING, AND KEEPING THE HELP

Some time ago I wrote a post about the importance of using help when we need it. I received several requests for me to write something about actually finding good help. So this lap-letter is about finding, using and keeping the help.

Finding:

A few years ago when I left the ministry, I felt numb for about a year. I didn't know it at the time, but I was in shock. After about a year, my wife Lisa finally pointed out to me how unwell I actually was. I thought I was okay because I wasn't feeling any pain. In fact, I thought I'd never felt better.

The truth is that I wasn't feeling anything. I was emotionally shut down.

I was in a state of spiritual stupor. I was, as Lisa put it, dead. Numb. She insisted I get help immediately. She insisted because I was in danger and putting us in danger. I was breaking things, metaphorically, in my life, including my relationship with Lisa. Reluctantly, I finally admitted to myself that maybe, just maybe, I wasn't well and needed professional help.

I didn't know what to do. I didn't want to look for a counselor locally because I have a bit of a reputation around here as the nakedpastor, which is part of the reason why I ended up where I was. There was no one I could trust. Plus, there was no one I could trust with my story. What kind of counselor out there would understand me... a person who was a Christian, was a pastor for 30 years, involved with craziness of things like the Vineyard and the renewal movement, who loved philosophy, who quit the ministry and drew cartoons critiquing the church because he is still passionate about it, who is accused of being both a nutcase believer or a rampant atheist? Who would get me? I didn't think I could find someone who would get and appreciate my whole story without dismissing parts of it, none of which I could reject and all of which I embraced as essential parts of my journey.

So I put my feelers out. I put in the research. I approached a few people online with whom I'd developed a relationship and perhaps could lead me to someone. Eventually, after a couple of months of searching, a person contacted me with a name. She sounded okay. So I gathered up as much nerve and shed as much pride as I could and approached her, and she graciously agreed to counsel me, mentor me, and coach me by phone since she lives in another country. We started talking. We clicked. We talked maybe every week or so through the worst of it. I paid her. She gets me. We still talk. What a gift that connection was.

Using:

I've had many friends who have taken medication for, say, depression. As soon as they started feeling better they quit. Bad idea! That's the drug working. Don't stop! I determined, under the auspices of Lisa, that I would talk with my counselor every week and not stop until Lisa and my counselor decided I was somewhat healthy again. I wouldn't stop when I thought I was okay because I now realized that I was the poorest detector of the status of my own mental, emotional, and even spiritual health.

When we decide to trust someone, we are essentially putting ourselves in their hands. Like a good doctor, we entrust our body to her and silently agree that we will do as she says until we are whole again. We agree to not interrupt their care because she knows when we are whole again better than we do. That's if she's a good doctor. Do everything they tell you to do. Take their advice. Apply their suggestions. If they're good, they'll work! Use them until the counselor, mentor, coach or spiritual director says, "You can do this on your own from now on. If you need to check in, I'm here for you."

Keeping:

One of the biggest lessons I learned through this whole process is that I, like everyone else I judged, have blind spots. I couldn't see how sick I was. So I carry that forward to assume that I will always have blind spots. When I get rid of one, another one develops or gets discovered. The mind is the trickiest organ on the planet. It will always find a way to protect itself, fortify its defenses, and manufacture a false sense of security. The brain's number one purpose is to keep the organism alive, safe, and sound. It resists death like a cornered wild beast, especially the death of itself and its thoughts. It will fight you for supremacy without mercy. So as soon as I think I'm doing awesome, it's crucial that I check in with people I trust for confirmation.

Did you know that doctors won't do surgery on themselves but will put themselves under the knife of another doctor they respect and trust? Did you know that in many jurisdictions professional counselors are required to have their own counselors? Did you know that even the most advanced monks submit themselves to a confessor? Yes, even Thomas Merton, one of the greatest Christian thinkers and mystics of all time had a spiritual director. Actually, he had several around the world from different religions he used for spiritual direction. Why? Because he wanted to grow, not just be stroked. He wanted transformation, not affirmation. I plan on talking with my coach throughout my life. In fact, I should make another appointment soon.

Find good help. Use good help. And keep good help.

You will be better for it.

YOU ARE YOUR BRAND

I watched an interview on PBS of the fashion designer and humanitarian Kenneth Cole. It was quite fascinating. But he said one thing that really stuck with me. He was asked about branding and how he feels about promoting the Kenneth Cole brand since globally things are changing so rapidly and drastically. His response was something like this...

He said that branding has taken a huge turn. Now, because of the internet, each person is his or her own brand. Each person can decide what their brand looks like and promote it at will for free all over the world. Each person can determine who sees their brand and who doesn't. They can choose their market and audience. So Cole... and I thought this was the cool part... feels that now as a famous brand himself that the best he can do is humbly ask to be invited to contribute to a person's individual brand. He can no longer expect people to promote his brand, but that he might participate in the promotion of each individual's personal brand.

I think Cole has a lot of wisdom here. He recognizes that the world is changing and becoming more and more global and at the same time more and more individualistic. He never complained about this. He just noticed, acknowledged, and embraced it. He even, in a way, respects it and works with it. Of course, he runs a business and wants to succeed in this new, rising culture. But part of his success is his respect for the individual's personal autonomy as well as the influence of the global village.

I immediately applied this to our spiritual selves. Something that TLS promotes is spiritual independence. That is, personal autonomy.

I remember when I first started promoting TLS as a safe space to explore, discover and exercise your spiritual independence, I got a lot of kickback from Christians who felt this was inherently wrong and unbiblical. In their minds, we need to be dependent upon God and be able to depend on each other. The fact is, like a good marriage, it takes two healthy, independent people to come together interdependently rather than co-dependently in order to make the relationship work. It's the same here. I need to be independent. I need to possess my own personal autonomy in order to be mature, healthy and wise.

You are your own brand. Your spirituality is yours. Your religion or philosophy is yours. Your way of being spiritual and living spiritually is yours. And all those ideas and truths and realities and theories, etcetera, are there for you to consider adding to your brand or not. This is not to say that therefore everything is true or everything is not. But it is your right, privilege and responsibility to explore, discover, and exercise what is true. True for you! You might even get lucky and discover things that are true for all. Universally true. All the other brands out there are at your disposal to incorporate into your own personal expression of who you are, a manifestation of your inner self, your own personal brand!

This takes courage to claim and live. But once you do take that step, the courage seems to immediately show up. And once you've been doing it for a while it will be natural and you will wonder why you made yourself live under the expectations and opinions of others.

You'll wonder why you were used to promote someone else's brand rather than your own.

You! You are your brand. Wear it. Be it. Now, let us see it.

THE ART OF FLOATING

I compare the art of living spiritually to the art of floating. Can you float in water? I mean… everyone can float if they know how. What I mean is, do you know how to float in water?

It's very easy. You can look it up. I'm going to give you 3 easy steps:

Shed Heaviness: Don't wear your army boots and goose-down winter coat into the water. Although you can float with clothes on, it's much easier and safer without clothes. Wear a swimsuit. And don't carry things like your family Bible or a concrete block or your mother-in-law. Just you. And don't give up. Did you know one of the key ingredients for survival is hope? Always, always, always hope. Don't give up!

Trust: Technically, everyone can float. That is, everyone is floatable. But you have to trust that you can. No, you don't have to be in the Dead Sea, so full of salt that you can't sink. You can even float in rough water. This is the intrinsic right of all human beings… to be able to float. Trust the water. Trust your mind, your lungs, your body. You aren't going to sink to the bottom of the sea. You can float! Yes, you can!

Relax: The most important skill to acquire for floating is the ability to relax. You actually rest your head back as if you're lying down on a pillow. You let your feet dangle. You fill your lungs with air and breathe shallow. You image a string attached from the sky to your bellybutton pulling it up out of the water. If your feet sink too much stretch your hands behind you over your head in the water to distribute and balance your body weight. Simple as that! Now, float. Relax. You can do this forever.

The same applies to our spiritual lives.

Shed Heaviness: I'm one to talk, but it's true. I'm responsible for my own spirituality and no one else's and no one else is responsible for mine. I'm going to shed everything that is not necessary and keep only that which is. I don't need a huge Bible. I'm not going to wear concrete boots because I'm guilty and deserve to die. I'm not going to allow the negative voices of others to pull me down. I'm going to always hope because I deserve to live, and to live well.

Trust: I'm allowed to float! I'm allowed to be happy. It's my human right to live and be happy doing it. I'm not going to drown because I'm a bad person, an unintelligent person, or a sinful person. I remember the days when I was terrified Jesus was going to come back while I was in a movie theater or some other pleasurable pastime, or that the sins of my fore-fathers would be visited upon me, or that I had some kind of demon for some kind of reason. No! I'm a person who deserves to live and be happy, so I'm going to float. I'm just going to trust that. Thank you.

Relax: Oh my, I was raised uptight. Spiritually I was wound so tight you could hear my spirit whining in the wind. I was raised to be anxious and fearful. I was raised to be obsessed with my spiritual condition, to be self-absorbed in my faith and fixated on the condition of my relationship with the Lord. This is the kind of anxiety that will make me sink. No. Instead, I'm going to just relax. I'm going to lay my head back like on a pillow. I'm going to imaging my body being pulled up to heaven. I'm going to imagine my lungs full of fresh air. I'm going to do this forever. I'm going to relax. I mean, doesn't the Bible say that we are a Sabbath people? Yes!

Relax. Go swimming and try it. Just float. Shed heaviness. Trust. Relax.

Now go live life and try it. Just float. Shed heaviness. Trust. Relax.

SOMETIMES PAIN IS A GOOD THING

I've been thinking about pain…most recently this morning when I ran six kilometers in the snow and ice. I wanted to share with you guys why I think pain is sometimes a good thing.

Now, to be clear, pain is sometimes a signal that something is being violated. You've all heard that the one of the major problems with leprosy is that when there is nerve destruction, we can no longer feel when a part of our body is being damaged. So with no feelings in our fingers they can be seriously harmed without us knowing it. I've experienced this myself in the extreme cold of Canada. For some stupid reason I was outside on a very cold day without my gloves and cleaning off a car and then quickly grabbing an armload of wood to bring in for the wood stove. After I dropped the wood in the wood box I noticed my fingers, now numb with cold, were cut and bleeding. I was rougher on them than I would've been if I had feeling in my fingers. So pain is an excellent indicator that something is wrong or something is being harmed. But I don't want to talk about this kind of pain.

The kind of pain I want to talk about today is the kind that indicates progress is being made. Like when the feeling started returning to my frost-bitten fingers, it was excruciatingly painful. But it was a good sign that I hadn't permanently killed the nerves and that my fingers would be restored to normalcy soon. Or when I was running this morning, it hurt. It hurt a lot. But it was a sign that progress was being made in my health. My lung capacity was increasing, my muscles were stretching and building, my blood was flowing and toxins were leaving my body. I heard a comedian once say that he tried exercise once but he found that it hurt his muscles, caused his heart rate to escalate, his breathing to become irregular, and he broke out in sweats. So he stopped. But this kind of pain is good. It means we are getting healthier.

I love the vulnerability and honesty of the members of TLS who are so willing to share their pain with the rest of us. Seriously, I take it as a complete honor to be invited into your lives. It shows an incredible amount of trust. I don't take it lightly. So I want to encourage those of you who are experiencing pain right now.

If it's the first kind of pain… that something is being violated… then it is necessary to find ways to stop it. Not the pain but the cause. Unless of course something that should be violated is being violated… like something harmful that is being removed from our spiritual selves, our beliefs, our feelings or thoughts.

But if it's the second kind of pain, perhaps you can take courage that you are actually getting healthier spiritually. You know, if we ignored our spiritual health like we sometimes ignore our physical health, then

19

there might be a sense of reprieve from pain. But it would also be a sad indicator that we're not attending to something that really is important. When we experience existential, emotional, spiritual or intellectual pain, perhaps it's good. Perhaps your heart is increasing its capacity to hold more love. Maybe your ability to think outside the box and more broadly is stretching. Perhaps the lifeblood of your whole self is flowing more freely throughout your entire self as it integrates. Perhaps unhealthy, damaging, limiting or toxic beliefs are leaving your mind and spirit. This is a good pain.

Sometimes the motto is true spiritually as well: no pain no gain.

IT'S OKAY TO HIDE

It's okay to hide.

I did a sculpture a few years ago. I call it "Shelter". It is made out of Brazilian soapstone. There is a small, smooth, beach pebble resting in a hole in the side of this large stone. To be honest, sometimes I would like to be that little pebble hiding away in an impenetrable fortress… safe, secure, and untouchable.

Do you ever feel that way?

Here's a more important question: How do you feel about that feeling?

Have you been taught that it is escapist? That you should stay engaged at all times with those you love? That to retreat is cowardly? That you need to be available at all times, especially when you are needed?

I remember this story about Jesus. Early in the morning he sneaks away by himself. After a while his disciples are frantically looking for him. He's done this many times before. The first time he did this that we know of he was just a boy. His parents lost him during a trip. They found him in the temple talking with the elders. Not this time. This time they find Jesus in the desert. Peter freaks out and tells Jesus that there are people who need to see him and people he needs to help. No, Jesus says, let's go this way. No more cities. Let's do villages from now on. We'll take the back roads.

Moses would sneak away and hide too. People freaked out. David would sneak away and hide. People freaked out. Jeremiah would sneak away and hide. People freaked out. Jesus. Paul. John. I could include the Buddha, Mohammed, Gandhi, Krishnamurti, and on and on and on. When they made time to be alone, everyone around them freaked out. Their managers lost it.

But here's the thing: not one of these people did this because it was warranted by scripture or by some expectation or rule. They did it simply because they wanted to or needed to. They did it out of the freedom of meeting their own needs and desires.

You don't need divine approval. You don't need scriptural support. You don't need ecclesiastical permission. You don't need a nod from your peers or parents or partner. Authorization is not required.

You don't need permission. You don't need forgiveness. You owe nobody an explanation. You owe nobody an apology.

You have the right to hide.

So…go hide! Ready or not, here I come!

STOP WORRYING ABOUT WHAT YOU BELIEVE

Good morning my friends! (I'm always aware when I say good morning that it might not be morning where you are or when you read this because you guys are all over the world, but oh well!)

It's a bright day and the snow is brilliantly blinding. I went for a five kilometer run this morning. I wanted to run ten but at -20°C I couldn't feel my legs after a while and my feet started to feel weird. So I cut it short.

While I was running I thought about how I was going to address this issue today: fear. So today I want to talk about "Stop worrying about what you believe."

I think the first question we need to ask ourselves is where did this belief come from? For example: the existence of hell. If you believe in hell, where did this belief come from? Do you believe it because you were taught to believe it? I mean, has this idea of hell been drilled into your belief system since infancy? I know it has for me. I've never met anyone yet who came to a conclusion on their own, completely separate from all religious thought, that there was a literal hell. This is a theological, religious idea that has been passed down from generation to generation. What do we do with this idea that's become a key component in the fabric of our thinking? It's so enmeshed in our thought patterns. How do we extricate it?

I don't know about you, but I can't simply dismiss something I've believed my whole life with a single thought. Again, the idea of the final judgment and punishment by hell... I can't read Rob Bell's book Love Wins and say, "Oh! There's no hell! La-la-la-la-la!" No! Why would I replace one adopted belief for another? I'm going to test everything for myself. One of my favorite ideas is that the best way to solve a problem is not by skirting around it but by going through it. So I investigate, for myself, all the ideas about final judgment and hell and fit this into the larger puzzle of history, religious developments, and textual criticism, as well as compassion, grace, and forgiveness. Stir in some wisdom too. I've come to the conclusion, personally, that the final judgment and hell are metaphors used to motivate us, either through fear of punishment or desire for reward, to be and do good. In other words, they were developed and are used to control us. I've come to that on my own. I'm not sure when I stopped being afraid of the last judgment and hell, but I'm not afraid anymore.

Well... I'll be honest. Once in a while a terrifying thought will race through my mind, but I immediately recognize it as a phantom memory. It's not real. I want to share with you what really helped to remove the worry about what I believed.

I personally don't think Jesus ever threatened people with judgment for what they believed. Jesus was not a professional theologian. He was a mystic and a teacher. He was most concerned with what people said and did, not what they thought or believed. Even his parables are all concerned with right action, not right belief. Of course, I'm sure he would have agreed that what we believe leaks out in what we do. But I think he would have laid emphasis that if a person's fruit is good, then the root is good. If the water is good, then so is the spring. Remember the parable of the sheep and the goats? The religious people stand at the judgment bragging about how they've been missionaries for Jesus, preaching and casting out demons in his name. They've got the lingo and the liturgy. But where is the love? The others who don't even recognize Jesus ("When did we visit you…?"), who don't have the lingo or the liturgy, are praised. Why? Not for religious beliefs or religious deeds, but for simple, human acts of kindness… giving a cup of water, visiting people in prison, clothing the naked. Remember the Roman centurion who is considered good by everyone and Jesus praises him in front of the others? I'm sure his theology wasn't in line with the religious expectations of his day. So why are we so hung up about what we believe when Jesus didn't seem to be?

So I believe what I believe. I just notice it. That's all. I don't believe in a literal existence of a physical hell. But I do believe it is a powerful mythological metaphor that can teach us something important, like perhaps understanding that our actions could have lasting consequences and we should try to be aware of this. I don't believe in supernatural stuff. Bigfoot. UFOs. Aliens. Ancient gods who visited the earth and left archeological remains behind to perplex us. Magic. Faith healing. Now I examine this because some weird and unexplainable things have happened in my life that seem to be miraculous. I also know a lot of people I trust who believe some of these things. So I don't believe some of these things loosely. I'm not willing to die over them. I also don't think I'm going to be eternally judged for not believing or believing in them.

At some point in our journeys we have to become independent. We have to get to the place where we help ourselves. Confidently! Perhaps if we remove the fear and worry about what we believe, that in the end even if there is a judgment that what we think or believe is not on the table, perhaps then we will feel free enough to believe what we've come to believe.

HOW TO RESPOND TO DISAPPOINTMENT AND HURT

I ran six kilometers today and got passed by three youngsters talking away like they were relaxing on a beach. I gave them a go though. I fantasized that they were just starting when I was just finishing. They passed me right when I returned to the bottom of my driveway. I guess I'm a little competitive. I decided to feel good about myself even though they were faster.

What was nice though was that the sun was warmer today. It felt like spring was in the air.

In today's letter I want to talk about noticing how we respond. I'm going to share one of the important lessons I've learned from my own experience. My hope is that this will help you in your own unique journey.

How I do anything is how I do everything. I've noticed that I have a particular way of responding to things, a particular way of doing things. My way! One could look at how I respond to things and say, "Typical!" It is because how we do anything is how we do everything. Particularly I want to talk about the way I respond to disappointment and hurt. The way I respond to these is the way I always respond to these, no matter the source.

Let me explain. If I feel disappointed by someone or hurt by them, perhaps my response might be to pull away from that person and distance myself from them. If the disappointment is slight from someone I really love, like Lisa, perhaps I will only pull away a small distance and only temporarily. If the disappointment or hurt is from someone who is a friend or an acquaintance or someone I dared to trust, perhaps I will pull far away and totally remove that person from my life. Maybe I will even reject them entirely forever.

About thirty years ago, my spiritual director Sister Marie noticed something about me. Lisa and I had gone through a very difficult time in our young marriage and in the church where I was an assistant minister. Please note that this was during a time when I had a very certain belief in God and a very concrete faith. But because my life was a mess at this time, I let all my spiritual passions and practices fade away and I drifted far away from the God I knew and loved. Sister Marie brought this to my attention one day by looking me straight in the eye and asking, "So, why do you run away from God whenever life gets rough?"

I've learned how to rationalize. I can *theologize* it and say that the God I believed in was insufficient and therefore false and I had to run away from it to find the true God. Or I could *psychologize* it to say that I had to distance myself emotionally from something I was attached to that was unreliable and untrustworthy in order to find That Which I Could Truly Trust. Or I could philosophize it to say that there really is no god and I was learning how to wean myself off of this illusory attachment in small doses. Whatever. These are all coping mechanisms. The real issue is what is going on inside me.

It dawned on me at that young age that perhaps I have such an idealistic view of life and such a magical view of God that when something goes wrong I get angry and reject God.

But at the bottom of it all was that this is how I deal with disappointment and hurt. Always. I run away. I close myself off. I distance myself emotionally, spiritually, even physically, from that which disappoints me or even threatens to disappointment me in the future. Whether it's God or Lisa or a bank. I might even demonize the one who disappointments me to justify my rejection of them.

If I go even deeper though, I can perhaps see that inside of me there's a small boy who is insecure and afraid, who lives in an uncertain and scary world, who knows that people can and will disappoint him, hurt him, and even reject him. So maybe I harden my heart to protect myself from these things even potentially happening. Perhaps I am not experiencing true love at its deepest and most carefree level because I'm always on guard, waiting for the next sting of disappointment and the next infliction of hurt.

But… and this is key my friends… what I've also learned is that it is enough to notice this. It is enough to know that this is how I respond to the world and people. I am aware. I didn't use to be. But Sister Marie pointed this out to me many years ago. It was a revelation. Have things changed? Sure. Somewhat. But I can still find this frightened small boy hiding in the dark corners of my heart.

However, this is the other thing that Sister Marie taught me because her response to that revelation was perfectly gracious. When she said, "So, why do you run away from God whenever life gets rough?", I was dumbstruck. I just stared at her because I knew she was right. Even though I thought I was somewhat spiritually and emotionally mature, I responded in very childlike ways to disappointment and hurt. I was speechless. So she very gently said, "David. David. It's okay. It is good that you see this. Now, what do you feel when you see this small boy inside of you? Will you love him?" I wept. I weep now as I type this.

She reminded me of Paul's bold assertion in 1 Corinthians 4:3… "I care very little if I am judged by you or by any human court; indeed, I do not even judge myself."

I just notice that this is how I respond to disappointment and hurt. Noticing it is what matters. That's the important thing. I don't judge myself. I don't beat myself up over it. I just notice it. This is enough. And I'm learning how to embrace this small, frightened boy and beckon him out into the light of a safer world.

Because how I do anything is how I do everything.

Same for you.

SPIRITUAL BIRTH COACHING

Good morning my friends.

Today I want to talk about our roles as spiritual birthing partners.

Three of my most graphic memories are the birthing of our three children. For all three of our kids Lisa and I went to prenatal birthing lessons. Lisa gave birth to all three naturally without any medication or intervention. I was glad to be coaching and not delivering because, well, I don't like the idea of being physically torn apart for 20+ hours. Lisa performed excellently. I think I performed excellently as her coach.

What were my responsibilities? There were basically three ways I supported Lisa:

Emotional: It was my job to keep encouraging Lisa. I was her cheerleader. Everyone knows that if you can keep your spirits up it can relieve stress and even physical pain. It was exhausting work being positive and uplifting during her labor, but it worked. Especially for the first time, convincing her that she could do this was my mantra to her. Trying to keep her outside of her head and her pain was my full time job. Even though there were times I was crying watching her in pain, I knew that my pain was secondary to hers and it was my responsibility to support her through hers.

Physical: When our first was being born, Joshua took over 20 hours of labor to come into this world. Lisa paced the floors of the hospital while I rolled behind her in a wheeled office chair rubbing her back since that's where she experienced most of the labor pain. I remember her turning around once in a while telling me to hurry and keep up with her. I held her hands. I wiped her brow with a cool cloth. I fed her ice… her particular craving at that time. Then during the actual birthing I had to coach her when not to push and when to push, even mimicking for her how to breathe when she was entirely focused on the pain and pushing.

Advocacy: I had to make sure Lisa had all the resources she needed and fetch them when she couldn't. It was me who called the nurses. It was me who told the interns to stop trying to persuade her to take medications, a drip, or even laughing gas. It was me who demanded that they find a birthing bed NOW because the regular hospital bed wasn't made for birthing and wasn't working. Going to get more ice or juice or food, guarding the bathroom door, keeping our families at bay, and telling the staff that we would wait for our own doctor stuck in a snowstorm on the way to the hospital. These were some of the things I had to do. Although most of the staff was amazing, some nurses weren't very nice. Advocating for her was one of the more important tasks.

It is the same spiritually. This is why I love facilitating TLS. It's like being a spiritual birthing coach. I'm not the only one of course, because many of you perform this same function in the lives of other members… giving each other emotional, physical, and advocacy support.

The emotional support we give one another is so gratifying to give and to receive. We all know how painful transitioning can be, and having support around us cheering us on is invaluable and sometimes even necessary. It is good to hear when we are in the thick of our pain that we are going to make it.

The physical support we give one another, metaphorically speaking, is also crucial. Helping one another to relax, to give a cup of refreshing water in the form of encouragement, suggesting to one another not to rush it, but also giving people permission to push when the time comes, is amazing to watch. Even sending books, money, messages, or letters to one another is the kind of physical support many people lack, crave and need.

The advocacy support is necessary as well. I love watching how you guys advocate for each other. You know what people, books, or resources to suggest at the right time. You know when to suggest to someone when they should demand their rights, when to ask for help, and when to cry out for proper treatment. Saying to someone that they have the right to advocate for themselves and that you've got their back is more than just helpful. It is liberating! All these things are so critical for our spiritual births.

What I've discovered is that I seem to always be giving birth. I find TLS continually helpful in getting me to the next stage. Even though I had a kind of birthing when I started TLS, I'm also experiencing a kind of spiritual birthing now, and I so appreciate your support emotionally, physically, and in advocacy. It makes it easier. It really does.

We're all a mix of people having babies and at the same time being birthing coaches for each other. My goodness! Look how far you've come! Look at all the beautiful babies that are being born. In your own life!

So! Here's to more spiritual births! And here's to spiritual birthing coaches!

YOU ARE ALLOWED TO FEEL YOUR FEELINGS

Good day my good friends!

Many years ago when I was continuing my education in theology and ministry, I took a course called Clinical Pastoral Education. This course is designed to prepare pastors for ministry in clinical settings such as hospitals. It was a fascinating though intense course that lasted for many months full-time in a hospital, with a mixture of classes and practicums.

The director was the Protestant chaplain of the hospital. He was a good teacher. I remember one week he taught us all about emotions. He had us try to name feelings from things people said. He would say something... quote a palliative care patient, for example... and we had to define the emotion being expressed. He also had us try to analyze each other's emotions. Finally, he had us attempt to describe our own emotions... the way we were feeling at any certain time.

At first glance, many people might think this is easy. But surprisingly, for many it is not. Most of us are horribly deficient in the skill of being able to name an emotion. In other words, our emotional intelligence is low. This could be for a number of reasons, the most common ones being that we were taught and trained how to judge, condemn, and suppress our emotions. Later we were groomed to be ashamed of them and punish them.

Especially if they were negative in nature!

I have learned that our feelings are just feelings. Emotions exist. They simply are. Period. There is nothing wrong with them.

Right here I will make an announcement: *you are allowed to feel what you feel.*

I encourage you to *understand* what you feel. *Name* your emotions. Try to *define* and *describe* how you feel. *Write* them down. *Share* them with someone.

Maybe you don't know how.

There are emotion charts available online. Look them up and study them. I've found them very helpful.

I encourage you to feel. Get in touch with your feelings. Define them. Talk about them. Write them. Feel them. This doesn't mean you have to act on them. But you are allowed to feel them. In fact, you DO feel them.

I claim it is healthiest to embrace them.

MY MIND IS THE PROBLEM

Hi my friends.

A couple of weeks ago I sent out a letter with a one-page summary of what I've called the z-theory. I will remind you of the dream that prompted the z-theory:

There is a huge waterfall. Oceans of water pour over the rim of the cliff. The water tumbles down and explodes at the bottom. The deluge spreads over the land covering and consuming everything.

Then last week I sent our Sunday letter with an explanation of the first part... the water over the top of the rim... that which we cannot see. I've heard back from many of you that you found it very helpful. Thanks so much for your responses. I appreciate it.

So this week I want to describe the second part, that is, the water pouring down over the rim. This is the part we can finally see. It is the oceans of water tumbling down.

"The water tumbles down and explodes at the bottom."

This whole visible part of the waterfalls is the most spectacular. It is a spectacle! To us it is the overwhelming, thunderous evidence that there is an unlimited supply of water above the rim. It substantiates the unsubstantial. Perhaps if we were primitive and superstitious we could believe there was a water-god up there spewing water out of his mouth. We don't know because we cannot see it. But now, even though we haven't seen it, we are less superstitious. We can fairly guess it is a huge river infinitely fed with rain, mountain snows, springs, and lakes, which are in turn fed by rain, mist and dew. But for now all we see and smell and taste and hear and even feel is this great downpour of water.

This is the evidence we have of what is above the rim. The infinite and invisible is now finite and visible. This is the revelation of the Wholly Other, the exposure, the incarnation of the mystery, the transmission of truth, the manifestation of the unknown, the discoveries of science. It is the encounter and reception of the unknown now known, the mysterious now perceived.

This is what we call the Christ, the Torah, the Buddha, scientific discovery, revelation, the condescension, the incarnation, the transmission, the embodiment, the coming down and the coming out.

I remember long ago when Lisa and I were dating we went to visit my dad's family in California. They all lived in Long Beach and Lakewood. I had a cousin there. Lisa and I were in Bible College, and my cousin had lots to talk about. She'd experienced a lot of pain in her own family and in her life.

Although everybody down there seemed to be Christian, she couldn't believe everything that she was being taught. She wasn't sure she believed in God, Heaven, and Hell the way it was told. She was going through a huge intellectual change at such an early age.

I remember how deeply affected I was by this. I loved her so much, not just as a cousin but as a friend. She was a person who'd suffered so much and just couldn't believe pat answers. She rejected a simplistic faith. Perhaps she was considered rebellious. I remember how tormented I was over the logical conclusion that she was going to Hell because of her lack of faith. How can this be? How can a God who claims to be Love throw such a person in Hell forever just because she didn't think according to what was considered correct? I was angry and confused and very emotionally involved with this intellectual problem. I was 21 years old.

Now, add to this intellectual problem the bigger picture that there are good Jews, Muslims, Buddhists, Hindus, atheists, agnostics, Nones, you name it, along with my cousin. Are all these good people going to Hell even though God is love? As you can see, I was sinking deeper into an intellectual quagmire.

What the fundamentalist mindset does is simply draw the line and say, "Yes, you're going to Hell. Period!" Simple. Done! And shut your ears and shut down your brain to keep out conflicting data. Or, if you are at all intellectually curious, you will try to make sense of this. I chose the latter.

I look back to that time as a huge turning point for me.

Although I was to remain in the church for decades following this and even be a minister within it, my encounter with my cousin and the conundrum she caused changed my life and flung me into this quest to try to understand these two conflicting truths. Not just conflicting, but contradictory: 1. God is Love, and 2. You're going to Hell if you're not a certain kind of believer… preferably a Bible-believing, born again, conservative, fundamentalist evangelical. This is an impossible equation.

Thus began my search to understand something that is simply not understandable. It took me a very long time to come to the obvious conclusion that I cannot see or define what is above the rim. I cannot see it or describe it. That is, God. All I have to go by is the waterfalls pouring down. That is, all the testimonies that claim to describe and define it.

The tradition I was in was Christianity. It claims to have not only the best description of what is God, but the only valid one. This is Jesus. Therefore, you have to fully subscribe to this Jesus in some way to be connected to "God". You had to completely agree with Christianity's definition of God, that is "Jesus", in order to be saved and go to Heaven. Of course, there are as many varieties of this Jesus as there are religions in the world. It doesn't make it any easier, does it?

Then you have the Bible that is the document, the holy book, that Christianity calls "The Word", which obviously reflects "Jesus", the "Word become flesh". So there you have the package, the witness, the physical manifestation of what we call God. I spent years and years and years studying this bible. I got my B. A. in college in Bible and Theology, and then I got my Masters in Biblical Theology, studying Greek, Hebrew and even Aramaic… all the original biblical languages. And then I started PhD studies in New Testament and started learning theological French and German so I could read the important theologians who expounded the Bible and their several theologies. I did all this so that I could understand this book that talked about Jesus. I was still stuck looking at the waterfalls from a strictly Christian perspective.

I spent something like 30 years studying my brain out trying to understand this huge problem. I studied Judaism. I studied Buddhism. I studied Hinduism. I studied Islam. I studied all kinds of spiritualities and mystics. I studied science and atheism. You name it… I studied it! I meditated. I talked with Buddhist masters, philosophers, scholars, etcetera, all in an attempt to understand this problem. I tried to find everything that was similar to Christianity in other religions, philosophies and spiritualities. For example, I found so many similarities to what the Buddha taught and what Jesus taught. I found the same with Mohammed and Jesus. I was driving myself crazy because I always came back to the same required place: Jesus was the only way to God. Even if you were a Buddhist that talked like Jesus, if you didn't believe in Jesus, too bad! Again, the problem was I was still looking at the waterfalls from a Christian perspective only. I did this for over 30 years!

I gave up.

I went to sleep.

Then I had the dream of the waterfalls in May of 2009, and I woke up with a peaceful mind. I finally saw that what I thought was the problem wasn't the problem. I was the problem! My mind was the problem! I was believing my own thoughts! I finally saw that my mind was limiting. My perspective, my viewpoint, my paradigm, was the issue. I finally saw that my perspective was a Christian one and that I was looking at the revelation of what is invisible with Christian eyes. As soon as I saw that my eyes were the problem peace came to my mind. Theologically, stillness came and it has never left.

I now knew that the Buddhists describe their perspective on reality with Buddhist eyes, Jews with Jewish eyes, Muslims with Muslim eyes, Hindus with Hindu eyes, atheists with atheist eyes, and so on. We are all seeing and experiencing the same thing through our own filters. This suddenly gave me a profound respect for all perspectives and allowed me to humble myself with my Christian perspective to sit among all other perspectives on the same level. Sure, I do believe there are more sufficient ways to explain Reality and less sufficient ways, more insightful and less insightful, more mature and less mature, more superstitious and less superstitious, more helpful and less helpful, more honest and less honest. But we are all perspectives experiencing the same Reality.

Some like to say, "All paths lead to the same place!" Now we might say, "There aren't many paths, just one path with different experiences and thoughts about this one path!" Or even better, "There is no path!"

We are all already there.

THE Z-THEORY PART 3

How are you guys? I think about you every day and hope you are all well. We had a massive snow storm here, lost our power for several hours, got it back, then lost our internet for a few more. We are just getting ready now to go out for breakfast with some friends.

This is the third installment of my z-theory letters. I had the privilege of explaining it to a friend of mine the other night, and she got excited about it. So I feel I'm on to something helpful.

The first part is the top of the waterfalls that we can't see… the invisible.

The second part is the water coming down… the invisible made visible.

Today I'll talk briefly about the third, the bottom part… how the water spreads over all the land, covering and consuming everything. It's the applicable. This is the world and the human race. All that is. This is where we find ourselves. All of us. Together. On the same level. We are one.

Some people claim to have seen over the rim, seen the invisible. Some believed them and founded religions upon these people. Others believed the testimonies of these people and became their disciples.

Others believe that certain outstanding individuals must have seen over the rim. This isn't to say that nothing is above the rim. This is to say that what is above the rim is invisible and that all we have are testimonies of those who claim to have seen it or claim to have had what is up there revealed to them. Moses' claim that no one has seen God and lived comes to mind.

So here we all are on the same floodplain. Even though there are a vast variety of religions and sects within these religions and schools of thought and philosophies, I believe we are all the same. We are one. We all see the same thing and experience the same thing. What separates us is our paradigms, our worldviews, our adherence to these views, and our languages and words we use to articulate them. Thoughts! This is all that separates us. Actually, it doesn't separate us, but we believe it does.

I think you all get this. This is why on The Lasting Supper we can have amazing conversations from a variety of different perspectives while respecting each other, hearing each other, and not trying to convert each other. We are neither offensive nor defensive because we understand that we are essentially one, experiencing and seeing the same thing, but from our own angle.

I got a message from one of our members. Here's a quote:

"I like the empathy that people have for one another. It's been very nice to have people ask how my daughter is doing or my husband when he was sick. They message me etc. It's nice to know that outside of church, authentic community can happen. I get that it's online - whatever - losing my church community has been painful... TLS has eased the blow a bit..."

The care and respect you guys show to each other in spite of differences is what I call harmonious living.

I love it. I hope you do too.

HUMILY. HONESTY. HARMONY.

I love hearing from our newest members. Just today a new member said, *"This is my first opportunity to check out the Lasting Supper community and all I can say is, I may have just found my real church…"*.

So we're heading into another storm. I guess here in the Maritimes this winter our storms only work on weekends.

My waterfalls analogy for Reality continues to provoke interesting responses from people. After doing a lot of thinking about it one day, I realized that the three categories… the top of the falls over the rim… the waterfall itself… and the water spreading over the floodplain… can be broken down into three neat theological "postures" that I think are necessary today.

Here they are:

Humility: If we can admit that we haven't seen what's over the rim, then that demands humility about the Unknown.

Honesty: We all see the manifestation of the Unknown, all from different angles, that requires us being honest about our own insufficiencies as well as our solidarity with all others who observe. We need to be honest about what our religion proposes, as well as other schools of thought, including science.

Harmony: Once we are humble about what we do not know and honest about what we do know, then we can perhaps see the harmony in, and live harmoniously with, all things.

Take a peak around. I know some of you are testing the waters and lurking while you build some confidence to chime in. I totally understand.

Humility, honesty, and harmony take some getting used to.

EX-PASTOR

The sun is shining. The ice has broken up in the river and the moving river shines with light. My mug is full of coffee. Lisa is getting the table ready for our Easter dinner. Our boys are still in bed and our daughter is still at University in Ottawa. We'll see her in about a month. I hope you guys are having a good day.

First of all, here's a bit of housekeeping. Our planned Hangout didn't work Friday night. We experienced technical difficulties. Those who managed to sign in joked about how it was the devil foiling our plans. Others joked that maybe it was God preventing a bad thing from happening. Your lightheartedness and sense of humor, your graciousness, made it easier for me to put the failure behind us. So we've rescheduled it.

For Christians it's Easter morning. The dream I had of the waterfalls continues to flesh itself out for me. I wrote this the other day on nakedpastor:

"The Easter story declares that we live in a new reality. Everything has changed. Behold, it is a new creation! A new reality! A new way of being! It is the true fulfillment now in time of the Emanuel promise… God with us… God no longer 'up there' high above separate in the heavens but now among us, with us, in us, through us, as us, the All in all, the through all things reconciling all to the All. There is no longer "us" and "God", for all is reconciled and all is one.

"As I explain in my z-theory, the story of the incarnation announces the end of God's inapproachable transcendence. The Christian story of Easter declares that the God of Beyond has died on the cross and, through the Holy Spirit, is now the human community as the struggle for human equalities and freedoms, the impulse for harmony."

It is important to mention that with this theory, we are not tempted to merge all religions into one, for each one has the right to exist and contribute its own uniqueness to the vast and diverse tapestry of the human community. This is why we can respect, protect, and appreciate the vast diversity we witness and experience in the world. It is also why we appreciate the wonderful variety of personalities and opinions and ideas on The Lasting Supper. I just love how, say, people with radically different philosophical positions can engage in civil conversation. I hear a joke coming on: "A ex-pastor, an atheist, and a Buddhist nun walk into The Lasting Supper…" And it all works out because we're not jerks.

Here's a response to my post:

"I'd just like to say, that I didn't come to TLS cuz it was some slick shit. I came, curious at first, but stayed because I too was feeling disqualified, invalid, illegitimate, even ashamed. I had been called recalcitrant by my pastor/boss in front of my peers. I've prayed that tag off myself many times, but it's stuck deep. Anyways, I love the DIY feel of TLS, I love the vulnerable sharing. I hear my own recalcitrance resonating in this place. Thanks for being real."

Who doesn't want that?

LIVING WHERE YOU CANNOT SAY NO

Sit down.

I went to church this morning. My friend who is a Soka Gakkai International Buddhist was speaking at the local Unitarian Universalist Church. She invited me to come.

She did an excellent talk… so gentle, inviting and kind. Gracious. I love listening to her and learning from her.

The other day a friend sent me an article that really meant a lot to me. It's called "The Man Who Never Says 'NO'". It's about Adam Grant, a professor at the University of Pennsylvania. I found it fascinating because he is a pioneer in the field of motivation and productivity. I've been reading studies lately indicating that money, rewards, and other incentives don't make people more productive or happy at work. In fact, when people find meaning in their work and experience a sense of fulfillment, they'll do the same work for free! Of course, everyone recognizes the danger in this: employers could easily take advantage of a worker's altruism and monopolize their resources for lower pay.

What I found meaningful about this however is how important it is to find something that is meaningful for you. I've finally found what I love doing: writing and drawing about spirituality and creating safe spaces for communities. And what these all boil down to is helping people with spirituality. I love validating and encouraging people. I love walking along with people on their way and being a support. I'm passionate about it! It's what makes me tick and makes me happy. Of course, just like Adam Grant has to do, I have to know where my boundaries are. But outside that fair boundary I just won't say no.

So I want to encourage you to find your passion. What is it that makes you tick? What do you love? What would you do even if you never got paid for it? In what way can you contribute to the world or make a difference where you are?

I really love Adam's story. I think he's found his passion.

I've found mine. I hope you find yours.

WHAT I'VE LEARNED FROM BEING MARRIED TO LISA

We've had sunshine for 2 days in a row now. I don't know what to do with myself. I know! I'll have another cup of dark roast, listen to some Renaissance Church music, and write you guys my letter!

Let's talk about relationships. Something I've learned as Lisa and I approach our 33rd anniversary on May 4 is that it isn't compatibility that keeps us together. It's love. That's it!

Lisa and I are very different. We are different in the small ways, like she is more introverted and I'm more extroverted. She is not prone to vices like smoking and drinking and driving fast, whereas I am. I like coffee. She likes Dr. Pepper. I am easily distracted. She is not. She says toe-may-toe and I say toe-mah-toe. Just kidding! But you get my point. Our personalities are different and it shows up in all kinds of small ways. Those kinds of differences are fairly easy to navigate.

We are also very different spiritually. We started out more alike. We were two young Pentecostal kids who met at a Pentecostal Bible college in Springfield, Missouri.

Theologically we were very much on the same page. Over the years we experienced more growth individually and in our relationship. We matured. We grew wiser. Lisa found her unique style of being spiritual, being a whole person, and I found mine. Now, 33 years later, we are still in the same book but are on very different pages. But that's okay, because we've learned something very important about relationships: it's not compatibility that keeps us together, but the breadth and depth and width and height of our love for each other. As we matured, our hearts expanded to embrace not only all of the other as she actually is, but as she also may be now and in the future. Lisa not only loves me as I am, but loves whatever I will choose to become. This includes our spiritual differences. Love demands… yes, demands… that my heart is large enough to include all of Lisa, both known and unknown, even if something she believes is different from what I believe. This doesn't mean we don't have occasional tension, disagreement, and discussion. But it does mean we always figure out a way to figure it out. We navigate as we go.

I know some of you have experienced a breakup in a relationship because your partner could not accept your spirituality. They could not imagine a way to live together with you when you did not agree with them theologically.

We can see this same dynamic at work on TLS. We all come with a vast variety of spiritualities. Each and every one of us is on our own theological page. But one of our most crucial values as a community is that we are first of all here to respect and listen to one another. What do we do with another TLS member who is vastly different in their experiences and beliefs? We widen our hearts, respect them, and listen. It's not always about who did what. Most often it's about what we do to process our own stuff in healthy ways, as well as not carrying someone else's offense.

I'm confident we'll figure things out as we go.

RUNNING, BLEEDING, AND WATERFALLS

So Lisa got up at 5am to get ready to go to work. I finally dragged myself out of bed at 6am in time to see her off. I had a tall glass of water and an espresso, donned my running gear, and took off. I ran 17 kilometers, which is 10.5 miles. I did it in 105 minutes.

But when I was running back home I passed other runners going the other way and a couple of cyclists. A few of them looked at me strangely. Some people are weird, I thought. I never know if a cyclist is going to say hi. But most runners do. Not today. Strange looks. When I got home and looked down at my shirt, this is what I saw: two bloody stains on my nipples.

Yes! My nipples were bleeding. Nice! I've told Lisa that my shirts chafe. Today I guess it went on so long they decided to bleed. Lisa says I could wear a sports bra. Funny! Or those nipple pads she wore when she was nursing our babies. Right! Or round bandages. What a joker!

Empathetic nurse. Not! I don't want to go topless because I'm hairy enough I might be mistaken for an animal and shot. This is a problem. I don't know what to do. Later I found out that they actually make a special gel and pads for runners' nipples. Okay!

That got me thinking about the z-theory. Actually, no it didn't, but how am I going to segue into the z-theory from bleeding nipples?

Remember my dream of the waterfalls that represents a picture of reality? In my mind it is a unifying picture of the structure of reality. Above the rim is the mystery we can't see, the infinite source, the fountain of all being. The falls is the revelation, the incarnation of this mystery. It is the invisible made visible. Then the water that hits the earth and spreads out over it is the application of the mystery and it's revelation upon humanity and the earth. It is the assimilation of the mystery discovered. It is its benefit.

Someone recently shared a story with me about how their friend lost their job and their friend said God would fix it. He replied that he didn't believe that in the same way. His friend asked how he would say it. After a while he just realized he was being over-sensitive and particular about words. I get this!

I claim that saying something like "All paths lead to the same place" is problematic. I'd rather say there is no path. There is no other place. We are all already there. We are all, I claim, caught up in this waterfalls picture of reality. We are all experiencing the same thing. Everyone! Every religion and philosophy is experiencing the exact same thing. Only we are experiencing it through our own worldviews and are articulating it through our own languages. There is a very complex and wonderful unity of all things and connectivity between them that we are all in the midst of, doing our best to understand and explain it.

So, we can get to a point where we don't get caught up in making sure everyone adopts the same worldview or employs the same language to explain it as we do. When someone uses the word "God", I may or may not know what he means, but I know what I mean when I think of or say that word. It is just a matter of perspective and speech. That's all. I can let people believe and say what they do without freaking out over whether or not they're saying it like I would. Because I can guarantee they aren't! Or, when someone says, "I believe in Jesus", I know what they mean, but in my mind I know what I mean... that "Jesus" represents for me the whole part of the waterfalls falling over the rim and crashing to the earth... the revelation of all mysteries, the discovery of the unknown, the incarnation of all the Source, the

43

exposure of the ground of all being. That's what this means to me. Everyone experiences this. Christians call it the Christ.

Now, time to wash my shirt.

TENTS AND TEMPLES

Early in the Old Testament the Israelites traveled through the wilderness before they finally settled. They used tents. They worshipped in a tent called a tabernacle. Everything was, necessarily, portable and temporary. Provisional. Uncertain. Disposable.

When they finally settled in the land they built a temple. Gone was uncertainty. Now everything was fixed and permanent, an establishment eliminating all other options.

I encourage spiritual tenting. Not spiritual templing! I encourage us to resist replacing old beliefs with new ones. I believe when we do this we are only preparing ourselves for the same painful deconstruction down the road.

Anita Moorjani, in *Dying to be Me*, says,

"From my point of view, strongly held ideas actually work against me. Having concrete beliefs limits my life experiences because they keep me locked into only what I know, and my knowledge in this world is limited by my physical senses. Being comfortable with uncertainty, on the other hand, opens me up to all possibilities. Ambiguity is wide open to infinite potential."

It is a more eastern approach to wisdom and goes against our instinct to stop and build. But I think it's very wise. It's a tent approach, not a temple approach.

At least try it for a while. Eventually you will realize that you have a peace that you are in the truth rather than anxiously fretting that the truth is in you. It is a beautiful way to live. Krishnamurti said "Truth is a pathless land." I like that.

TLS is more like a tent than a temple. In fact, it doesn't matter where you are, you can check in on your mobile.

SO… let's go tenting! Tenting in the desert! Camping in the wilderness!

THE SUN SHINES ON ALL OF US THE SAME

One of the benefits of the z-theory for me is that it made my suspicion that we are all united, that we are all one, a different kind of certainty in that it looks and feels like peace. That's because it is! It helped me to really see that in spite of our individuality and diversity, we are all deeply connected.

Everything everybody experiences is universal. The way we experience it is particular and sometimes tribal.

What this means is that everyone in the world lives in the same world and experiences the same things. The sun shines on all of us the same. The rain falls on all of us the same. But how we experience these things and how we understand them and describe them is different, unique, and individual. If we can get others to see things our way, then we develop tribes that equalize and normalize our interpretation of reality.

Quite frequently I'll get a message from a member of TLS saying something like, "You know, I'm still a believer, and I'm not sure I fit in at The Lasting Supper." Right on the tail of that I'll get a message from another member, "You know, I'm an atheist and I'm not sure I fit in at The Lasting Supper." I always write them back assuring them that they fit in. I'm not just trying to retain members. I really do believe we all fit.

Here's why:

Many of us have never experienced unity in diversity before. Our unity

45

is not based on compatibility of beliefs. It is based on a respect for the journeys of others, even if they are different from ours, because we acknowledge what I wrote above: they are simply understanding and describing the very same thing I experience, only through their own matrix and language. So when one person talks about their love for Jesus and another talks about their rejection of the divinity of Christ and another questions the reliability of the historicity of Jesus, we all respect the other because we understand that we are all doing our own best with what we are experiencing with the personal tools each of us has at our disposal. I love Lisa even though we don't believe the same things. What keeps us together is that we respect each other's journeys, trusting that we will discover and know what is best for ourselves. It is a kind of love that is without fear.

Each one of us brings our own history, psychology, intellect, emotions, desires, fears, etcetera, to the experience. I deeply respect yours. And I trust you'll respect mine. That's been my experience so far.

This is what makes such communities like TLS so remarkable.

BEING ASKED QUESTION YOU CAN'T OR WON'T ANSWER

I ran eight kilometers today. As usual I met cyclists. I don't understand them. I say hi to all of them, but maybe one out of ten will say hi back. We live in the Maritimes of Canada… one of the friendliest places in the world. Everybody says hi to everybody. Canadians even apologize to everybody for nothing at all. Super nice. So when I'm running and automatically say hi to a cyclist and they ignore me, first I look down to make sure my nipples aren't bleeding through my shirt, then I wonder if there's something else wrong with me or if they have earbuds in and didn't hear me and I should've waved or if I have super bad breath; then finally I just realize it's them. For some reason when you go from two legs to two wheels you become a jerk. I'll have to ask my cycling friend what's up with that. There must be a code I'm not aware of.

It's the same with motorcycles. I have my license and had a bike until

I watched a pickup truck back up over mine in a parking lot. But motorcyclists are strange too. Cruisers don't wave at crotch-rockets. And Harleys don't wave at anybody except Harleys. There's a code.

So, I just wave at everybody. I'm going to be nice. How they handle my niceness is their problem. Not mine.

It's the same when someone asks you a question. Most often they are exposing something about themselves. In fact, questions are usually self-revealing statements only cloaked in curiosity. It's not about you at all. It's about them.
I can tell right away if it's a genuine question arising out of curiosity and a desire to know or if it's a question designed to slot me somewhere in the categorical mind of the questioner.

I take time to answer the curiosity ones. For example, a good friend of mine recently asked me if I believe in God. I knew this question came from a genuine desire to try to understand something. I answered her as best I could, and it was helpful all around. These questions are worth investing in because they not only help the questioner but they help me learn how to articulate what I believe to be true in clearer ways.

I don't take time to answer the ones that intend to slot me, categorize me, or correct me. They're traps!

Jesus was an expert in the question. It takes intentional thought and practice to get good at it. And courage! But we must because we are going to be questioned a lot. Many of you already are!

1. The first thing I often do is deflect. I change the topic. "Do you believe in miracles?" I answer, "This coffee is great!" Or, "Hey, speaking of miracles did you hear about that guy who can hold his breath for 22 minutes?" Or I speak about serendipitous moments that have happened in my life, but that I've never ever in my life seen a physical healing of any significance. I have received the exact amount of money I've needed in just the nick of time in my mailbox. I can talk about that.

2. Once in a while Jesus did take time to answer the question arising from genuine curiosity. Like Nicodemus in John 3. Jesus knew he was serious because he came to him alone and at night. Nicodemus also knew the two-fold nature of a question: I am genuinely curious, but my asking Jesus this question is revealing something about me I don't want my peers to know. So Jesus spent time answering his question.

3. Jesus most often answered with a question. For example, when the Pharisees asked him by what authority he was doing what he was doing, he said, "First answer me a question and I'll answer yours. What John the Baptist did... was that from heaven or from men?" They couldn't answer because even though they hated John and believed he was of men, they knew the people loved him and felt he was from heaven. So they couldn't answer or there'd be a riot.
I do this a lot. Recently a person asked me if I felt the Bible was true. I asked, "Is anything in the Qur'an true?" "Yes, some things I guess." I asked, "Where does all truth come from?" He said, "God." I asked, "Then are you saying that the Qur'an is true?" That ended that conversation.

4. Many questions, like from our parents or other concerned ones like friends, arise from fear. Maybe your parents think that you have to believe a certain way to go to heaven, and because you no longer think that way they're genuinely afraid you are going to hell. So they ask you questions hoping that you will answer them correctly, proving to them that you are okay and will live together with them forever in heaven.

The pressure to just answer to their liking may be incredible. I have a friend who frequently asks me very basic theological questions because she is terrified for me. But I think she is unconsciously afraid for herself as well. When she does ask me a question like, "Well, what do you do with Jesus?" I simply say, "I know this is hard for you. I know you're afraid. I do realize that I've changed a lot. But I assure you I've never been happier. I am at peace. I'm on a journey that is not only exciting and terrifying like a roller-coaster, but necessary and fulfilling. I mean, it's tough, but it's good for me. I just know it. Trust me. Really, I'm okay. And if you want to come with me, I'm here for you."

There's many ways to answer questions. These are just some. And I think, as evidenced by this letter, that it is okay to be prepared.

So here's my final question to you: What have you tried?

ON BEING A SPIRITUAL REFUGEE

Finally we have some sunshine. Lisa was off this morning, so we went with a friend to breakfast. I got my usual: 2 eggs over easy, link sausage, potatoes grilled with onions, white toast with blueberry preserves, and coffee. It's my one sinful meal of the week, and I love it!

They offer healthier choices at this restaurant. But they are so much more expensive. Just like the grocery store. Healthy food is far more costly. I eat healthy most of the week. This is my time to sin, and sin boldly!

I've been invited out for supper after Lisa goes back to work, so I'm going to skip lunch. I gladly accepted the invitation because when Lisa's working and since we have an empty nest, I sometimes go days on end without being with another person. It gets very lonely sometimes. I'm an E/INFP, so I can stand long periods without another person, like a hermit. But when I want company, sometimes there's none to be had. An invitation is rare but welcomed.

I didn't choose this isolation. But it certainly is a ramification of my choices. I chose to submit no longer under the spiritual authority or dominion of others. I sued for my own spiritual independence. I wanted to walk my own spiritual path and find my own spiritual land. I feel this is everyone's right and responsibility.

The ramification of that is that those in authority and the mainstream they dominate told me, essentially, that I was no longer a citizen of their country. I had, I was informed, betrayed my own citizenship. My passport to their established spiritual domain was revoked. I'm denied access and privileges unless I surrender my rights.

It wasn't me who told me I was no longer welcomed at the church I left. It wasn't me who unfriended me on Facebook. It wasn't me who cut off all communications with my former colleagues and friends. It wasn't me who banished myself into a spiritual no-man's land to fend for myself.

No! I took a stand, and the crowd that used to surround me gradually dispersed.

The friend we went to breakfast with this morning has decided to no longer go to church. And this person also suddenly feels alienated and isolated. It wasn't that this person chose this, but they did choose to be able to make decisions for their own spiritual health. Another spiritual refugee!

Many of you know exactly what I'm talking about.

You are lonely not because you are a loser or an unfriendly person or unpleasant or anything of that sort. You are lonely because you made a wise and healthy choice! And like healthy food, it costs you extra. It is harder to live by. You can eat what everybody else is eating, but you instinctively know that this is not best for your spiritual health. You can join where everyone else is joining, but you know you would have to surrender too much.

We are like spiritual refugees. But, I'm afraid we can't have it any other way if we choose independence.

So we take moments during the week to pop in to the refugee center, TLS, to have a drink, meet up with other refugees, get encouragement, gather more resources, and to strengthen our resolve that we not only made the right decision, but that we will stick by it.

Peace, my independent friends!

KNOWTICE YOUR LIFE!

I know I misspelled "notice", but I wanted to combine it with the word "know". Works for me! To notice is to know. To know is to notice.

I got up early this morning… 5am… to be with Lisa before she left for work at the hospital. She's a nurse in palliative care. She's my hero.

So, I spent the morning like I do most mornings. First thing: put on some clothes. Second thing: put on some music. Third thing: put on some coffee. Fourth thing: put on my artistic and thinking cap. Fifth thing: create!

I've been thinking about this letter for a while. I wanted to encourage you all to claim ownership of your life, as many of you already are.

Religion dictates how you are to be spiritual. It provides you with all the theology, beliefs, rituals, prayers, disciplines, rules, liturgies, etcetera to achieve its ends and benefits. That's how I was raised. I know that's how many of you were raised as well.

I needed to notice my own life. Somewhere along the way I began to realize that I preferred to be spiritually independent. I wanted to pay attention to my own needs and wants. I remember the first time I took the personality test. It blew my mind. It was like I was acquainted with myself, but now I felt that I was finally formally introduced to myself.

Then I embraced myself. This is me! This is how I am. It was cool to realize that I'm not a weirdo. I finally felt validated and valued. In fact, I felt a good measure of healthy pride in who I am. All my so-called quirks and weaknesses and oddities and strengths and skills and assets were an essential part of me. I not only noticed myself. Now I embraced myself. What a liberating and exquisite feeling!

From here I could now cultivate myself. Care for myself. When I was taking my Diploma of Ministry at McGill University in Montreal, one of my instructors said to me one day, "You know David, you have a very mystical side that you should pay attention to. It would probably help you if you took time every day to meditate, with candles and incense or whatever. I just want to encourage you to nurture that part of yourself." It blew my mind that someone would care about me like that. But more importantly, it was a powerful affirmation of my unique spirituality. I didn't have to follow protocol or expectations or tradition. I could custom fit anything that would nourish myself.

I want to clarify something. Some people balk at the term spiritual independence. They would prefer I use interdependence. But I claim that spiritual independence comes first. It's like a good marriage. It is important for each partner to be a healthy person. Then they can enter into a relationship and work together to make it a healthy and interdependent one. Otherwise, if unhealthy people enter into a relationship, there is the danger of it becoming codependent. We don't want that!

Be spiritually independent! Don't be dictated to. Determine for yourself what's best for you.

OUR RELATIONSHIPS AND RIGOUR

I was taking my dog Abby for a walk along our road that follows the river. It was foggy but the sun eventually prevailed. What a strange sight and sensation walking through fog when the sunlight is trying to pierce through. I could see the small particles of mist in the air, dancing before the oncoming warmth. And this against spider webs sprayed across the trees. It was gorgeous.

Guys a few houses down from me are doing their roof. I felt a great sense of accomplishment having done mine in just two days with my two sons Joshua and Jesse this week, and I still feel the echoes of pain in my body. I almost wanted to shout out, "Did mine in 2 days!" But I resisted.

I posted this on Facebook last night, so you might've already seen it.

It was very late. Lisa was at work and my boys were out. I was alone. I was drinking Sam Adams Boston Lager. I felt like a smoke so I grabbed a small cigar and went out on my back deck. The sky was clear and the stars were shining. All was quiet. But in the distance, wafting through the air, was the faint sound of a woman singing, like a lullaby, and it was oh so lovely. It was so moving, so beautiful, so mystical. In a subtle way this experience made me feel instantly at one with all things, and I swam in a kind of serenity. It changed my mood, opened my heart and mind, and I felt at peace.

Our secret Facebook page was alive last night (please ask for an invite if you're a member of TLS and not on there yet). One of our members, who is now our official post-master since whenever he posts something he gets a ridiculous amount of comments, suggested we all get together. One day!

This got me thinking about the quality of our relationships in TLS. One of the most powerful values TLS delivers is that people realize that if we're okay, then they're okay. That is, many people who've taken the incredible risk of being spiritually independent can feel very weird, strange, and different. Then they meet up with the likes of us and they realize that they're okay. They're perfectly fine. They're not alone. They're not foolish. They're totally okay. They learn to be self-validating.

Here's the thing though: if we were all cultish or unintelligent or ignorant, then this couldn't happen. If you meet up with people who are on the same page as you but are endeavoring to be bravely intelligent and brutally honest then you will feel that, instead of getting worse, you're actually getting better. You're progressing. You're maturing!

That's why I so appreciate the rigorous thought and honesty that is happening on TLS. It keeps us real with ourselves and with our relationships with one another.

So, I want to thank you. You guys are amazing.

I AM STILL ME AND YOU ARE STILL YOU

I completed a painting this week. I have normally done very moody, atmospheric and even melancholic. But I got to the point where I was feeling trapped and stuck. I've never been able to do abstract because it seemed against my nature. I always applied thought to what I was doing. But with this abstract, I never thought at all. I just painted in a sort of unconscious flow. I was terrified. It was fun. I like it.

Many people would say to me, "You've changed!" But have I? Have I really? Or have I just changed clothes?

I'm still me. You're still you.

I've thought about this a lot over my lifetime. I have kept a journal for over 30 years now. Needless to say, but I have scores of black journals taking up shelves in my bookcases.

It is often alarming and depressing for me to read them. I'll tell you why. I read entries from, say, twenty years ago, and even though I feel I've gone through significant changes, I'm still same person I was back then. I totally recognize myself as exactly the same person. It's true! Even though I have gone in and out of the church, into and out of ministry, gained and lost friends, moved hither, thither and yon, changed my mind and changed my theology, lost a reputation as a pastor and gained a reputation as a radical, I am still, surprisingly, the same guy I was twenty years ago, twenty-five years ago, fifty years ago. I'm still me! What am I supposed to do with this?

My reaction to this realization used to be: "What? I'm still struggling with the same old issues?" And then I'd ramp up my efforts to finally rid myself of them. But after a while I caught on to the trick my mind was playing on me. I had to accept the fact that what I was writing in my journal now would be read by the new and improved me twenty years from now whereupon I would exclaim in frustration: "What? I'm still struggling with the same old issues?" My self-improvement was an illusion!

So now I've adopted a new way of reacting to this realization that I'm still the same old me: "I value this person who refuses to go away. There is something resilient and worthwhile about this person who has survived intact all these years. I will love and respect him."

Of course, we are all changing on the surface. We adapt. We tweak. We compromise. We evolve. We even undergo dramatic transformations. But is the "we" that experiences these things somehow still there, in all his, her or their essential life? When I say, "I'm going to change!" who is the "I" who says that and is going to change this "I"? Is there even a "me" at the center? Is there even an "I"? Do we have a soul? This question has baffled us for millennia.

This is why I love reading your stories. Most of you have been through incredible experiences from as far back as you can remember. Still, you were thrust into all these experiences and are still here and talking about it with a ravishing self-respect and even love.

You are sharing your resilience with us. And we thank you for it.

THE COSTLY COST OF CHANGE

It's been a lovely weekend here. It's thanksgiving weekend in Canada. The weather's been beautiful. I've had a couple cups of coffee. Lisa's gone to work for the day. Feeling a bit lonely as well as a residue of sadness.

Can I be really vulnerable with you guys today? I trust you. So I'll give it a shot.

I've told the story of running into an old friend and how different he treated me than when I was a pastor and in the church. I told you I'd tell you about it today. So I want to share my story that, for many of you, is your story.

I've known this guy for many years. He was involved in the leadership of another church. We would meet for coffee and have great conversations. He's younger than me and said he valued me as a mentor. He would look to me for encouragement, support, and advice. I've been through a great deal and have lots of experiential wisdom that he appreciated. I shared my struggles with him as he did his with me. I'm that way anyway… an open book.

When I left the ministry and the church, though, I abruptly lost all contact with him and many others. In my naiveté I presumed our friendship would continue. I tried three times to get together with him. After the third try I ran into him walking through the mall. You know that cold, stiff voice that many people have when they're emotionally distant from you? That's how he talked to me. It was obvious he had no intentions of maintaining our relationship. Fine. But when it rains, it pours.

Last night Lisa and I went to a party. This guy was there. We ran into each other again and he said that maybe we could chat. Okay, I said. So when I noticed he was alone, I took the opportunity to go over and talk with him. But he had the distant and unavailable switch on. Still. I knew within two seconds that this was going nowhere. We talked about superficialities for a few minutes. I tried to engage on a deeper level as I would a friend, but when I lost eye contact with him and he got fidgety, I saved him the discomfort. I politely said it was good to see him again, then moved on.

It's moments like these that remind me of the cost of change.

I changed. I admit it. I really did change. It wasn't overnight. I changed over time, evidenced by my progressively honest blog posts. But I suppose, like an elastic band, I stretched it too far and it snapped. I think it snapped when I quit being a pastor and left the church. I mean, people watched me stretch and stretch and stretch the elastic, testing the limits of my freedom and independence, until I wanted it truly.

Then it snapped. I would have kept stretching it as far as it would go. I claim it snapped at their end. Or they cut it. Or maybe it was mutual.

I accept the blame for wanting to be independent and achieving it. I don't accept the blame for ending relationships because of it.

When you change it forces those around you to change. I must change. Be transformed by the renewing of your mind! So I renewed my mind. I changed my mind. And its ramifications were transformations in my life. It forced people around me to change. Including my closest friends and even family.

I'm not angry with him. I don't think he was being mean or cruel. He just didn't know how to relate to me anymore. He lost the sense of who I am. Sure, if he cared enough he could find out and rediscover that sense. But that would require more of him than he is willing to invest. Or maybe it requires more currency than he has. Like the book I always recommend for relationships, Passionate Marriage by David Schnarch, a relationship is like a crucible. You can't enter into it without both parties changing. But if one is unwilling to change, then it will break or at least dramatically diminish its quality. One will bail… emotionally and ultimately physically.

Could I go back? Sure. But I won't because I must be true to myself first. Experiences like this remind me about how important and necessary change is.

But with these kinds of costs, it must be a pearl of great price.

WEYLU'S. FARM LIFE. AND THE GOD BOX

I got up early today to see Lisa off to work. The first thing I did was make myself a coffee. Then I turned on my stereo to listen to music. Then I sat down to draw my cartoon for the day. After Jesse got up, I made us Mexican omelets. Then I took Abby for a walk. Now I'm sitting down to write you our weekly letter.

Let's talk about God.

Many years ago I met up with a very good friend of mine in Boston. We hadn't seen each other in years. We lived together in seminary, studying biblical theology. He'd gone through some pretty horrible experiences lately. On this particular day, as we sat in one of my favorite Chinese restaurants, Weylu's, he told me he'd come to this conclusion:

"Either God is everywhere or God is nowhere."

At the time I agreed. Now I would augment that a little. Actually, I now believe that those two apparently opposite statements say the same thing. They are the opposite sides but of the same coin.

Did you know that the Buddha never denied the existence of the soul? But neither did he affirm it. This is what is called the middle way.

Another person I read with fascination is Byron Katie, especially her book *Loving What Is*. I've also read her biography. Never does she deny the existence of God. Never does she affirm it. When she uses the word "God," it's always held loosely and almost always as a convenient word to describe something mysterious or to connect to a listener who believes in God. For her, what *is* is God, or God is what is. For her, Reality is God, because Reality rules. It just is. Neither here nor there!

This is how I approach all ideas about God. I do not deny it. I do not affirm it. These are the same thing appearing as opposites. I'm cool with that.

I've struggled with the concept of God since I was a child. I remember waking up one night terrified of death. I got up in the dark and went out to my mom and dad and sat on my dad's lap. But they had company and couldn't really attend to me. I didn't even really know what to say or ask. I was just very afraid. We lived on a farm, and I saw death on a regular basis. I couldn't get my little head around it. My desire to understand the truth about life and death was ignited. For some reason, even at this very young age, I couldn't believe that there was a God seated in the heavens, separate from the world in which I live. A good God. Death. It did not compute. I intuitively knew there wasn't a simplistic answer.

Over time, verses like these: "For in him we live and move and have our being" (Acts 17:28); and "God was in Christ reconciling the world to himself" (2 Corinthians 5:18); and "Christ is the All in all" (Colossians 3:11); and "… so that God may be the All in all" (1 Corinthians 15:28) helped things make sense to me. Jewels like these, buried in a deeply diverse extended metaphor, provided a matrix within which to make sense of my world. My concept of God was breaking free of every box that was handed to me until I finally realized that no box would suffice. So I threw out the boxes. Burned them. There is no box!

Did God get burned in the process? This I can't answer, or won't. Now, when I feel I must refer to "God", I usually say "That-Which-We-Call-God". That is as close as I can get to a description of what we're talking about.

My waterfall dream that launched my z-theory articulates this by the use of a metaphor: what is above the rim of the waterfalls we cannot see and can only guess at. But what is pouring everlastingly over the falls and spreading all over the earth gives us a pretty good indication that there is an endless, infinite, fathomless source that invades and fills everything and embraces and captures and consumes everything, absolutely everything, and takes it back up into itself so that there is no distinguishing what is and what isn't. With this my mind is at perfect peace and my heart is no longer afraid.

So, as you can see, I've come full circle back to our table at Weylu's. Is God everywhere or is God nowhere? Which is it?

My answer: Yes!

SO I WENT TO CHURCH

So I went to church this morning. Yep. I did.

Unusually, Lisa had the weekend off. So we made plans to go to visit friends of ours who are pastors of a Vineyard church.

We've been friends with them ever since we joined the Vineyard here in 1996 and pastored a Vineyard church. They were always very supportive, encouraging and affirming.

We had a lovely meal of baked salmon with this incredible sauce on it… some kind of teriyaki sauce heavy with soy that she made with tons of mushrooms over top. The mushrooms had this almost burnt flavor to them. We had some micro breweries beer. Drank some great wine. Then late at night he pulled out some single-malt scotches, including a bottle of my absolute favorite, Lagavulin! We talked and talked and talked. What a night. Refreshing.

This morning we went to their church. It was typical Vineyard, with people milling around in everyday clothes, loud worship band playing songs including a couple of Mumford and Sons tunes, kids loud and everywhere, coffee break, and a conversational type of message. I was nervous at first. But I warmed up to it. It was actually nice.

Here are three observations I would like to share:

I felt loved: We met so many people we used to see quite often. They were so kind to us. They were happy to see us. Some people even put on their Facebooks, "David Hayward, the nakedpastor, is showing up at church today!" We were swarmed with nice people… genuinely nice people. I'm always nervous going into a public place because nakedpastor isn't loved by everybody. But these guys love Lisa and me. They really seemed to care and be interested in us. Some people even invited us to come over for a meal and hang out, including some students from the university there. Kids were everywhere. Young people. Some disadvantaged people. Disabled people. All kinds. And there was a real strong sense of mutual love, respect, and community. Even Peter's message was about how we are all not only loved but liked. It was nice to be in the middle of that kind of warmth.

I felt valued: It's strange how paranoid I am sometimes. I'm so used to getting attacked and criticized every day that when someone comes along and says how much they appreciate me, it always surprises me. So many people came up to Lisa and me and were genuinely interested in us. Those who got up to give an announcement or promote a charity got incredible encouragement from the congregation. "Good job!" "You're awesome!" "Thanks so much for doing this! You really are making a difference in the world!" And so on. It was obvious everyone there felt valued equally and therefore had an equal voice in the life of that community. In fact, some students want me to come back and give some more talks at their university. Peter asked me to come back soon to speak to the church again. Wow! I'm not used to that kind of affirmation. It felt good.

I felt stretched: My friend, the pastor, taught. He's always been a very gentle teacher because he's a gentle man. He's always very encouraging, affirming and non-controlling. Sometimes I've thought he's just too nice. But when he was teaching today I was impressed by his ability to ask good questions and pull us all out of our comfortable little worlds. My respect for him grew immensely when he wrote and self-published his book, *Learning to Interpret Toward Love: Actually Embracing People of Different Sexuality*. It has cost him friendships, teaching opportunities, contracts, and respect within the Vineyard and the larger church as well as many members leaving his own church. He felt it was important enough to write and publicize even in the face of incredible risk. So, even though his church community is all loving and affirming, it is also radical and is taking steps to love in radical and even controversial ways. It was cool to feel a part of that in a community of people with different sexualities.

Actually, our friends and Lisa and I talked a lot about community. They were very curious about The Lasting Supper. It turns out that the values he has for community are very much the same as mine were for our last church, and they are very much the same as the values for The Lasting Supper community. It renewed my conviction that we are doing the right thing here.

We love each other. We value each other. We will stretch each other.

WEIRD, WHACKY, AND WONDERFUL PEOPLE. PART 1

My son Joshua runs a business called True Life Training and calls himself a breakthrough expert. I know this language might sound strange to some of you. But, I've gone to several of his events and they have powerfully provoked some pretty major breakthroughs in my own life. I'm grateful for that.

Last weekend he had a booth at a Wellness Expo in a nearby city. Because he was feeling so overwhelmed and burned out I offered to come with him to provide moral support and give him a hand. It was in a huge auditorium with hundreds of booths in a maze of dividers. When I first walked in I was like, oh-oh. It was full of all kinds of spectacular stuff. There were massages, psychics, acupuncturists, crystals, aura-readers, stones, supplements, horse-whisperers, feathers, wands, magic potions, fortune-tellers, meditation, health foods... you name it. It was all there in one huge endless room of magical wonder.

I met fascinating people. I was having a very normal conversation with a woman selling feathers. She works in IT and is obviously very intelligent. Then suddenly she was talking about a ghost she shares her house with, and he has his own feather and how mischievous he is like when he turns off her alarm clock. I talked with another man who is a project manager of an industry. We were having a very normal intellectual kind of conversation when he started talking about his divine mother and forefathers and kings of the atmosphere and purple and archangels. His wife was like, "I don't believe all that. But oh well!" I met another young woman, a university student, who believes she is cleansing the water system of her city through prayer. I met another one who doesn't believe in spirits and all that, but she did believe that by inserting an acupuncture needle in your elbow she could clear your sinuses. I met a man who uses crystals as pendulums to tell if there are spirits in the room. His pendulums were very active yesterday. One woman told me that she sat with the psychic who was there. The psychic said there was some kind of hard object on her bedside table that the spirit of her grandmother was connected to. She said yes, that's true. Her grandmother gave her a stone once and told her to keep it by her bed. Grandma said that whenever she needed her loving presence, then remember she was with her in spirit by looking at the stone and holding it if she wanted. I talked to another business man who believes the earth was populated by gods millions of years ago and there is evidence of this all around the world.

I never batted an eye to any of this.

One of my most interesting conversations was with a young woman. Let's call her Diane. We were part of a group that had supper together at a restaurant, and we were sitting beside each other for a couple of hours. After she learned what I do, she felt free to open up and tell me her story. She said she was raised atheist. She recently moved to that city. She was going through a hard time. She'd met another girl and the girl invited her to her church.

Pentecostal. I'm nodding my head. I know Pentecostal. That's my background! She said she invited God into her heart. She said her life has really changed. Now, instead of having this feeling of cosmic loneliness she feels wrapped in loving arms. She said the pastor told her that he sensed God wanted her to know that he has nothing but love and grace for her, that she was not to judge herself because God wasn't, and that all is well with her soul and to be happy. She was smiling a huge smile when she was telling me all this. She was obviously so happy, content, and positive. She wasn't using Christian lingo because she didn't know it. But I knew what she was talking about. I smiled and said, "Isn't it wonderful to feel this acceptance, this love, and to feel that you are somehow ultimately cared for? I'm really happy for you!" "Yes!" she said. "That's it! I feel that I'm really okay!"

Now, someone could have responded, "You do realize, don't you, that God doesn't have arms? God isn't separate from you somewhere in heaven reaching down to hug you. Or maybe there isn't even a God. I want to warn you that one day you are going to feel abandoned by this very same God and experience a loneliness like you've never experienced before and it could last for years or forever! I would also like to issue a warning about Pentecostals because I was one. They will smother you with love and affection, but enjoy it while you can because… and I don't know when it is… at some point they are finally going to tell you that you need to move out of your boyfriend's apartment, get baptized, stop drinking and smoking, speak in tongues, and obey their particular rules." Someone could have told her that. But no one did.

That's a good thing. I decided a long time ago I validate people. I validate other people's journeys. I am an encourager. I encourage people to be spiritually independent. Diane's journey is a wonderful one. This is one of her chapters. She's a smart woman. She is figuring this out. Right now she's happy, content, loved, and respected, and her life has purpose and meaning. Why rob her of that with depressing news from the future? Perhaps with her smarts, her atheist upbringing, and her open-mindedness, she will avoid some of the traps we fell into. I hope so. Or maybe she'll learn the hard way like we all have and do.

I made new friends. Weird and wacky and wonderful people.

Like me. Like you! Welcome to the world of TLS!

WEIRD, WHACKY, AND WONDERFUL PEOPLE, PART 2

Here's a very recent correspondence between Diane and me.

Diane: So I mentioned to a few people about the healing stones and how I saw a psychic this weekend and people at my church think that people who use this stuff are like evil or this comes from demonic place. It's almost like relying on someone else to heal you when really we are told to rely of god. Part of me thinks it's ok because god must have made these stones. What do you think?

I'm unsure what your opinion is on Christians as of now, but from your cartoons I feel like you're a type of Christian who doesn't follow the rules… a non-typical Christian of some sort. I'm curious what your belief is. I don't feel like I completely agree with most Christians and have a hard time labeling myself as one lately.

ME: Yes I am a non-typical Christian. I identify as "Christian" because that's my roots and my home, so to speak. I tell people "My home's in Christianity but I have cottages everywhere." That means I appreciate truth no matter where it's found or where it presents itself.

Most religions demand complete 100% devotion to their own set of doctrines and rules. This obviously isn't surprising to you. You apparently have a mind of your own and want to use it. You are intellectually curious and that is a good thing. But many people find that threatening and dangerous. You must follow your own heart.

I believe we all experience the same things but perceive these through our own world-views and impute our own stories to these experiences and then use our particular words and languages to articulate them. Once one realizes this then you can be comfortable and confident with where you're at but respect others where they're at too. You can take what's true and reject what isn't without fear.

Labels are dangerous because they attempt to describe the contents thoroughly and finally. But I believe we are fluid beings. You are. I am. The label today won't be the label tomorrow. Sometimes I'm a believer, sometimes an atheist, sometimes agnostic, sometimes confused! I don't care. I love me and embrace all of what I am. I have a healthy inner believer and a just as healthy inner atheist. I'm fine with that. Others might not be, but that's their problem, not mine. It's their fear that demands I label myself to make them feel more comfortable and know how to relate to me. But relate to me, not what I believe.

That's the way I look at it. Does that help?

Diane: Ok, you're making me feel better. Thanks! The people at my church make it sound like the psychic wasn't even a real person, like she was an evil spirit in a body, trying to trick me. I don't feel like healing stones do any harm to anyone. If I put good intensions towards these other forms of healing, then why couldn't it be a good thing?

Christians seem to have such closed minds. It seems they think they know all the rights and wrongs, but it's just all opinions. Why are they all separated into Baptist, Pentecostal, etc., and yet they all think their individual group is the right way? I don't think there's a perfect way of living.

I just won't tell my Christian friends what else I'm up to. I don't feel like having debates with people. I respect their belief but it's becoming clearer that it's not for me. It's like a cookie cutter belief… no room for me to even use my own brain, if that makes sense.

I appreciate your reply. I feel like we share an understanding of the subject. It's nice to have someone like that. I'm still searching for questions and finding my own answers to things though. It's a fun process!

I think she nailed it! Don't you?

JUST HAVING A SAFE PLACE IS MAGIC

I want to share with you guys what happened at my house last night.

An LGBTQ advocate friend of mine arrived with a vanload of representatives from the LGBTQ community. There were seven of them all together. I sent out an open invitation on my Facebook because I no longer know many people in this area and wasn't even sure who would come. However, there were over 20 of us stuffed into my living room. We ordered in pizza, and people brought wine.

I was so nervous because this was the first official meeting I've had of this nature since I left the church in the spring of 2010. But almost immediately after starting, I felt comfortable and even in my element. The discussion was deep, honest, tearful, and funny. I thought they would only stay a few hours, but they were here almost 6 hours! It was a powerful time.

Can I just share with you some of my observations from the evening?

I need to get out more. I do all my work online basically, with nakedpastor, TLS, and my art. I paint, draw, write and work… all at home, all alone every day of the week. There is absolutely no reason for me to see people. I'm borderline introvert and extrovert, so I'm very comfortable living the life of a hermit. But when I want to see people I really want to see people. So last night I concluded that my suspicions are probably right on: I need to figure out a way to meet with people on a regular basis. I want to hang out with real flesh and blood people once in a while and to experience the same level of community I used to at my last church and what I do on TLS. I want to be with people in the flesh.

The conversation was about community. It seems like a lot of people have heard of The Lasting Supper. Right now we are at about 330 members. They all seemed to have heard of TLS. Wendy asked me how we do community. As I was answering and we were discussing it, I realized that this is the primary value, the key asset of TLS… community! It isn't something I deliver. It isn't something I create. It is something you and I make day by day. It isn't easy. As we know, it is very hard work. There are triggers everywhere, and sometimes I feel like we are tiptoeing arm in arm through a minefield. We do our best not to hurt each other, but inevitably we find ourselves trying to patch each other up. But that's community. It isn't like we are trying to get through all this stuff to be community. This is what community does! We're already it! Welcome home!

People hunger for the right to be. The people who were at my house last night—visitors as well as locals—all hunger for a safe place just to be their authentic selves without judgment and fear of rejection. I was overwhelmed with the level of struggle everyone was experiencing. Many last night shared things they admitted they normally wouldn't have, but they felt safe enough to. It convinced me that this alone is the power of authentic community. There's no promise of fixing anyone. There are no expectations we have for people to meet. There are no goals to reach. There is no vision to fulfill. Simply being given space to be is the transformative element! Like a farmer who clears away all the impediments for a plant, that's all authentic community does—it makes space. The result is people will experience profound transformation. And it isn't transformation into something else. It is simply transformation from a confined person to a free one. You're the same. Just blossomed. That's the work. It's as simple as that.

I genuinely thank you guys for teaching me so much about community. I came into TLS thinking I knew quite a bit about community already. But I'm still learning, and the learning curve is steep. But what a ride! Thank you.

What's next? I don't really know. I do know that I will continue to promote TLS as a safe place. I'm thankful for you all.

RESIST THE CLUMP AND EMBRACE THE MIXOLOGY

I'm at my son Josh's event on Transformational Teaching where he coaches entrepreneurs how to break through personal and practical barriers to public speaking and presenting their passion to others. It's cool and I'm enjoying it. I love going to these also because I meet interesting people.

I met a guy last night. He's a financial planner, and we had a good long conversation about our businesses, our passions, and our personal visions. He's an interesting guy who is very intelligent and personable. Once he discovered what I did, he opened up about his own spirituality. He isn't a Christian and doesn't go to church. But he was aware of the Alpha Course. He also likes listening to "Dr. Dino", a creationist who believes in the young earth theory, who teaches a literal interpretation of the Bible, and who believes there are dinosaurs living in remote, unexplored swamps in Africa. When I told this guy that I don't like the Alpha Course and that I think Dr. Dino is interesting but wrong, he was totally offended. Even though he's not a believer himself, he believed that because I associate with Christians that I should believe everything every Christian says. I should love the Alpha Course and I should respect Dr. Dino's opinions and even hold to them. He was completely baffled and abruptly ended the conversation.

This isn't at all unusual to me. Many Christians lump all Buddhists into one, and if one Buddhist says, "I don't like the Dalai Lama!" we are ready to pummel them because, well, it's the Dalai Lama! Or believers lump all atheists into one, so that if a believer sees two atheists disagreeing over the value of Richard Dawkins, he interprets this to mean that all atheists are therefore wrong because they can't even agree.

In the face of the world's attempts to gel us all into a clump, I stand in its face and say, "I will be me!" I refuse to conform. Even though sometimes I may identify as a Christian, I am determined to upset your stereotype of what you think that is. Even though sometimes I may identify as an atheist, I am going to screw with your head because I will crash your categories of what it means to be an atheist.

This is what TLS promotes: you have the right to be uniquely you with all your weird mixology. I am, and I'm proud of it. I am the weirdest concoction I've ever met. Many of you are as well. And I just love watching so many of you learning to acknowledge, embrace and express your unique mixture of who you are!

In fact, I believe we all have the same ingredients but with just our own unique blend and mixture. And our recipe's secret, even to ourselves!

Peace out you wonderful mixtures!

OH-OH I WENT TO CHURCH AGAIN

So Lisa and I went to church this morning. Let me tell you about it.

There is an elderly woman Lisa used to take care of. But once Lisa started university several years ago, she had to quit.

We've stayed in touch and we visit them once in a while. They go to a local Anglican Church that is considered higher Anglican. That is, there's more liturgy, symbols, and formality than most. So we decided we would go today.

It's an old church building with vaulted ceilings, wooden beams, and stained glass. It is the second Sunday in Advent. There were lots of candles, lots of men and boys in robes. There were a few women in robes as well. There was a choir. There was a lot of rising, sitting, and kneeling, lots of singing, prayers read and said. There were large crosses and candles paraded around. The gospel in gold was carried with great care to the center of the church from where it is read in an exalted manner. The sermon was about 10 minutes long, preached by a female divinity student. She read her very well ordered message. Then there was Eucharist. It was all very sober and serious. The whole service lasted 90 minutes. We were informed that it was longer than usual.

It was a very traditional, orthodox, Christian service. The summary of the law was said. The Lord's Prayer was said. The Nicene Creed was said. The hymns were traditional. The sermon was orthodox.

While I was experiencing the service I had a few powerful feelings flow through me that I want to tell you about.

The first is **nostalgia**. It has been years since I attended a traditional Christian church service. I had been attending church all my life until three and a half years ago. I was actually baptized in the Anglican communion as an infant. So it was deeply moving to be in that context again. It evoked pleasant emotions. I remember that even though I'd experienced a lot of terrible things in the church, there were a lot of good things I'd experienced as well. Of course, this is one of the reasons I still believe in the church and love it and passionately speak about it all the time. To be able to find a church where you can enjoy the good that it offers without having to put up with abuse, manipulation, control, and anti-intellectualism is a good thing. If you find such a church or community, be thankful.

The second is **community**. I pretty much live as a hermit. Funny thing is, for many years I wondered if I should have been a hermit. The problem was I was married to a very young Lisa at the time, and it nearly broke up our marriage. I know the meaning of be careful what you pray for, because now I spend almost all my time alone. I'm totally okay with solitude. But I do like being with people when I want to be. So this morning I really enjoyed sitting next to the elderly couple. They were so kind to us. It felt good, beneficial, and something worth enjoying.

The third thing is **theology**. I realized as we were saying all these orthodox words and doing all these orthodox movements that every person in that room assigns to and solicits from these words and movements different meanings. I saw, in a flash, what I dreamed a few years ago, that all these words and movements are symbols, and that some see these symbols as an attempt to articulate a mystery in tangible terms, whereas others believe they are not symbols at all but factual realities. I suddenly felt what I know for certain… that one person who believes God literally became a human baby in order to rescue the human race can sit next to someone who considers this story a beautiful metaphor describing reality in symbolic and mythological terms, and these two people can be totally united as one because, in reality, they are experiencing the same thing but only understanding it and articulating it through their own unique matrices. This is where the knowledge and sense of true unity comes from… not from something that must be attained through theological agreement, but from something that is already attained and which good theology attempts to communicate.

As you can see, a lot can happen in 90 minutes. It was a rich experience. Perhaps it wasn't what the officiators intended. But I was still inspired and edified, and my hard heart, my rigid mind, and my stubborn spirit was again gently broken to love the whole world and all that is in it. I emphasize "gently" because not once did I feel violated. And this is a good thing.

DO YOU EVER FEEL THE FEAR?

I did a cartoon this morning about Noah's ark since it's coming up in the news lately. Plus because of the new Noah movie coming out with Russell Crowe, I suppose.

When I was growing up I was fascinated with Noah's ark. I loved animals. I loved the Bible stories. My dad read a lot of books about Noah's ark and other archeological interests around the Old Testament. I even remember reading *Chariots of the Gods* and watching documentaries on all these archeological and historical curiosities. I even heard stories something like *Whale Caught Off Coast of Greenland With Man Found Inside Still Alive After 2 Days*. Or, how dinosaur bones are a hoax. Or, how dinosaurs were killed by the flood. I was very interested in these kinds of things.

One summer my mom and dad and us five kids all squeezed into a Datsun station wagon and drove from Toronto to Los Angeles to see my dad's family. On the way we stopped off at the Grand Canyon. In one day I walked from the rim all the way down to the Colorado River then back up again. On the way down, Dad was showing me the lines in the rock where Noah's flood rose to, which explained why there were sea fossils in the rock at these levels. It made complete sense to me and made my belief in the Bible sure.

Then I read a book sometime during my teens that the literal translation of Jonah and the whale is not whale, but fish. Jonah was swallowed by a great fish, not a whale! Well, that didn't make sense to me. Apparently I could figure a man could live inside an oxygen-breathing mammal that came to the surface for air, but not a fish. That made no sense at all.

Then in college, I learned about the synoptic gospels and how they are radically different from each other and John radically different from all of them. Wait a minute!

Then in seminary, I read *The Silence of Jesus* by James Beech, and my whole belief in the Bible as the inerrant word of God crumbled forever.

In each of these moments I remember the cold fingers of fear wrapping around my mind. When I think about it now, I know why these were horrible experiences. It's because I was afraid of the fear. The fear is terrifying!

But what was really going on? I think it is that I was trying to protect something that was important to me. In every case it was that the bible was accurate and historically true, and this was a shield for my beliefs and therefore a support for my faith. My fear was if the historical truth was uncovered, then this would threaten all of my beliefs and undermine my faith.

What I found, though, was when I let things go that I knew were no longer true, what was really true to me still remained. I've come to learn that what is most central, important, and true to me does not need lies in order to remain.

Strange, isn't it? It takes so much effort and so much anxiety to sustain one lie in order to protect a more central one.

I used to concede my own independence and allow others to tell me, with their stories, what is true. Now, instead, I have learned to respect my own conclusions about what is true and measure all stories against this. I respect the Bible and its stories and ideas now far more than I used to because I respect it as it is, not as I want it or need it to be.

It is a healthier and happier way to live, and fearless.

MERRY CHRISTMAS 2013

Do you remember that part in the movie *Braveheart* where William Wallace appears to a huge crowd of Scottish soldiers to lead them, but because they've never met him before they doubt that it's him because they've heard he is much taller and fiercer? Wallace says something like, "Yes, and he shoots fire out his arse as well!" And they all laugh. Wallace heard of the legends already building around his reputation even while he was still alive.

The Christmas story wasn't written down until 60 or 70 years after it was said to have happened. There were only stories circulating with perhaps a few scraps of papyrus, nicknamed "Q". Imagine if we tried to give an accurate account of World War II but we only had verbal stories and no surviving written documents! How many versions would be out there? How diversified would the story be? How historically accurate?

The Christmas story, as I understand, percolates down to a few essential components as described by Christian theological ideas and words:

God empties God of God.
God enters humanity and becomes man in the flesh.
When this man dies the Spirit of God comes as promised.
The universal human collective is where God now is by the Spirit.
God is now in all things reconciling all things to God.

If we can appreciate the mythological feel of this structure, we can also appreciate the deep truth that it carries.

When I'm asked if I believe there was a real historical Jesus, at this point I say I believe there was a remarkable man who was an itinerant teacher that died for socio-political reasons and that his followers began to assemble stories, myths and legends around the man to show that he was not only a continuation of the Old Testament but also a radical departure from it.

I believe the man we call Jesus brought a revelation of Reality, lived it, and taught it. I believe Jesus was a graphic rendering of the mystical truth that God is not in heaven on a throne, able and willing to rescue us. That idea had been thoroughly milked in the Old Testament and ultimately, I believe, begged for more.

I think the story of Jesus demonstrated that God is now with us and within us. Jesus himself is said to have promised the Spirit to come after he died, meaning that now, and finally, God is no longer located geographically, neither in heaven or in the temple or in Jerusalem or in one perfect man or in the church, but is a universal and personal presence in all things without exception.

That is my take on the Christmas story. This is why I love it. The vast collection of wondrous stories all point to one remarkably simple but one devastatingly beautiful truth: all this is what we call "God"... you, me, the air we breathe, the environment, all things and the spaces between.

And this is really good news.

I WENT TO CHURCH DRESSED IN MY OWN PARADIGM

I went to church this morning. It is a Vineyard church. The last church I pastored was a Vineyard. Very laid back

.

We know the pastor of this church and many people in his congregation. We are friends. We visit there once in a while because, well, it feels safe. He is completely non-controlling. I don't buy in to everything he says or what they're about anymore. But that's okay. I'm free to do that. And that's what's important.

Right? The freedom to be me amongst others as myself! That's what's important.

There was a lot of God-talk flying around this morning. But I'm cool with that. I'll explain why.

There is a thunderstorm with lightening, wind and rain.

When I was a child I was taught that this was when angels were bowling in heaven and when they lost they cried. I believed it.

Some people are taught that it is when God is wrathful and angrily terrifying and punishing the earth. They believe it.

When we grow up we're taught the scientific explanation. We believe it.

No matter what we believe, we still see the lightening, hear the thunder, and feel the wind and the rain. Essentially we are experiencing the same thing. Add our beliefs to it and it amplifies it, embellishes it, and impregnates it with meaning.

So this morning during church there essentially was worship music, prayer, fellowship and teaching.

I could apply layers to this raw experience.

I could say I went in a sinner, got corrected in the hands of an angry God who disciplined me until I broke, and sent me out in to the world with the command to never do it again and to live right or else.

Or I could say I went in a wandering child of God, that the Spirit in his patient compassion gently eroded away my resistance to him and that through the holy words and intentions he re-yoked my spirit with Jesus. This would be the language they used this morning.

Or I could say that I went in hard-hearted from a rough week, and that through the music, the silence, the sincere prayers and the gentle teaching, my heart slowly softened to the point where I could get in touch again with the openness, compassion and positivity that is the Universe and realigned myself with the source and flow of Life.

Whatever lens through which I experienced this, whatever worldview, whatever paradigm I understood it by or fit it into, or whatever language I use to articulate what occurred, the bottom line is that there was worship music, prayer, fellowship and teaching. And through the course of the hour I felt my hard heart soften, I noticed my mind open to hope, happiness and love, and I left the experience with a new resolve to be the better person that I am.

You see?

I believe we all are experiencing the same thing. But we experience it through our individual *paradigms*. We understand it through our individual *beliefs*. We articulate it through our individual *language*.

This is why I can relate to anyone. This is why I can sit through a Christian service. Or a Muslim one. Or an Atheist one. Or a Buddhist one. Whatever.

Because I see that we are all one and all experiencing the same thing.

She has her paradigm, beliefs and language. I have mine. And you have yours!

MUNDIS' PRAYER

Having grown up in a Christian home and having spent so many years in the church, including the ministry, I came out of the other end of it with very unhealthy attitudes about money and business. It didn't help that I left the ministry bankrupt… literally and metaphorically!

Negative and limiting beliefs about money and business saturated my thinking. So when I left the ministry in 2010, I felt a personal challenge to learn about these things.

What a learning curve! Still on it.

One of our members recommended a book to me, Jerrold Mundis' *Earn What You Deserve: How to Stop Underearning and Start Thriving*. It's an eye-opener for me! Mundis writes that he had been "strenuously an atheist" for all his adult life.

However, at one point later in his life, he decided he wanted to pray. But his religious upbringing was so "murderous" and his rejection of it so "powerful" that he could not bring himself to pray any prayers from any religion. So he decided to create one he thought he could pray without anger, revulsion, doubt or bitterness. You'll have to read this whole section to get the fuller story.

Here is the prayer he came up with. I laughed when I read it, and it made me think that I should send it to you guys. Here it is:

"In the unlikely event there is any motivating force in the universe, in the improbability that it is even remotely aware that the species exists, and in the near impossibility that it has in any way contributed to anything that is good in my life—I am appreciative."

I found it interesting that the core thrust of his prayer is gratitude. I like that!

Great mystics like Meister Eckart and theologians like Karl Barth would agree.

WHAT DO YOU DO WITH ALL YOU WENT THROUGH?

You wouldn't be who you are unless you were who you were.

Also: You wouldn't be where you are unless you were where you were.

(If you haven't had your coffee yet you might want to read those again.)

Even though many people talk about how we grow through stages where we leave one stage behind and move on to the next, I prefer to believe that we grow through phases and carry with us into the next phase what we previously went through.
That is, even though we progress, we subsume all that came before. The phase you are in now carries within it your previous phases. It preserves all the moments as elements in your present state.

I like this idea because it is less mechanistic and more organic. It reminds me of a seed that turns into a corn stalk with many ears of corn: every kernel of corn carries within it the DNA of the seed where it all began. There is a string that connects it all.

Your life is a story with sequential chapters: the chapter you're in now could not possibly be understood without the previous ones.

So how can you apply this to your own life?
What do you do with all the terrible things you experienced, heard, did, inflicted, said, felt, invited, endured, believed, taught, promoted? What do you do with all the manure?

I use imaginative pictures to give my life a story-line that makes sense of who I essentially am and what I've essentially experienced. Stories like this help me see my life as "total" where all the parts are necessary to make the
whole.

Here's what it might look like:

I see myself as a seed, full of life.
I see myself dry up.
I see myself fall from the plant.
I see myself buried into the soil.
I see myself covered with dirt and manure.
I see myself exposed to all the elements.
I see myself die.
I see myself split open.
I see my life pour out.
I see myself transform into something much greater.
I see myself as the plant.
I see myself as very fruitful.
So what I am and what I experience are not the same. But without the experience I wouldn't be what I am. Somehow, my experience, even though it happened unto me, is actually part of me. I neither reject it nor attach to it.

It simply is.

It is my story, manure and all.

DANGERS OF DECONSTRUCTION

What I want to write about today in my weekly "pastoral" letter to you is a kind of a warning. I want to warn you about the dangers of deconstruction.

I've been through it. When I left the ministry and the church four years ago this month, I had no idea what devastation I was about to undergo.

Deconstruction = Devastation.

There's no other way of looking at it. Sorry. It's for good, but getting there can feel bad.

I suppose there are some people who experience a very smooth and serene transition in the deconstruction of their faith and beliefs. But they're rare.

The norm is rocky and stormy.

So I will share with you a few of the dynamics I personally experienced, and still do to some extent.

1. Depression: The first thing I want to warn you about is depression. For the first year after I left the church I thought I was okay. In fact, I thought I was really happy. I felt free for the first time since I could remember. But... and my good wife Lisa pointed this out to me after about a year... I was depressed. I wasn't feeling anything because I was actually numb. Emotionally, I was frozen.

The nasty thing about depression is that it isn't contained. It doesn't restrict itself to one little corner of your brain. It is like campfire smoke that permeates all it touches. It gets into everything and clings to it. No matter what you use to get it out, it still lingers.

This is what may happen to someone who experiences any kind of trauma. We may lock down as a coping mechanism. It is human, natural, and often healthy because it can protect us from something more serious. Freezing emotionally enables us to let the trauma melt in increments and slowly evaporate rather than melting all at once and drowning us in a tsunami of despair forever.

The best thing to do is recognize it. "I'm depressed. I'm in a slump. Emotionally, I am frozen." Just admitting it is the first huge step. Recognize it. Acknowledge it. Embrace it.

Now that you've done that, you can take very certain steps to address it. It took me some good counseling, coaching and spiritual direction, plus the gentle patience of my wife, kids, and friends to guide me out of that slump.

You can do it too. It's just for a season, but you can make sure you weather it well.

2. Confusion: The next thing I would like to warn you about is confusion. When I left the church, the confusion that wrapped itself around my brain was debilitating. I couldn't see the road ahead at all. I was completely blind and in the dark. Not theologically, but practically. I had indeed come to theological peace of mind a year before, but percolating this down into everyday life was a most confusing experience. It orbited around the basic but new question for me, "What am I going to do with my life?"

But I recognized this from times it had happened before. I've personally tested this and now I know it is true: when you let a question abide in your mind, in time the solution will come. I purposely didn't say "the answer will come" because it often isn't like an answer to a math problem. It has happened to me so many times and proven itself to me over and over again that when a deep question of profound importance troubles me, I will just let it stay and do its work. Over time, a peace will come that will resolve the tension in your mind. It might take days, weeks, months or years. But it will come. Promise.

Learning to live with the question is a skill you probably were not taught in the church. But it is a skill you must learn. This does not mean you give up. This does not mean you reject the question. This does not mean you cease your studies. This means you trust the question to unlock itself and reveal the deeper truth you are seeking when the time is right.

Seek and you will find. Wisdom is the reward of patient seekers.

3. Strain: The third and final dynamic I want to warn you about is the strain deconstruction will put on your life. Especially on your relationships. Especially on your marriage. I saw it in my own life and I see it all the time in the lives of others.

No matter how young or old you are, it's like a mid-life crisis happens. Indeed, I claim that deconstruction looks very much like a mid-life crisis. It is a crisis. And it drops right in the middle of your life.

Just as I'm writing this I realize that this deserves far more attention than I can give it here. So I'm thinking about writing next week's pastoral letter just on this issue. But for now let me say this: the worst time to make big life decisions and changes is in the middle of a crisis. Endure the strain and wait.

I remember the overwhelming feeling I had at the end of my time in the church. I felt trapped. Then one evening it became clear that my escape was laid out before me and I should take it. I did, and the freedom I felt was amazing. But this feeling of being trapped infiltrated everything else in my life, including my religion, my home, my marriage, my family and friends. I wanted to run away from everything.

Including nakedpastor. Lisa's always been great. There was nothing wrong there, but my attitude betrayed that I didn't want the feeling of being trapped, that I didn't want any more commitments, and that I wanted to run free and alone for the rest of my days. I just wanted out of everything! But I imagined myself a grumpy old man alone in a one-bedroom apartment, standing over a stove and cooking Kraft Dinner with a cigarette hanging out of his mouth, a tumbler of scotch in one hand and a stirring spoon in the other. A nightmare. But at the time, it felt better than being trapped.

I'm so glad I didn't act on this. Whew! So glad! But I confess to you that I dragged Lisa and my kids through my own personal hell and made them share it for a while. Rather than taking some advice from people like, "Do what will make you happy right now!", I took what ended up being saner and wiser advice like, "Wait until the crisis is over and decide then. You're not in a healthy enough space to make a wise choice." I did wait. I'm happy I did.

What worse devastation I could have caused!

This is not to say that your marriage or relationships won't suffer, or that they don't deserve to end or change. That's not what I'm saying. The strain will either expose the faults that are in your relationship, or it might create new ones, or it will attempt to. I just want to warn you that during your deconstruction the strain on your relationships and your marriage will be real and threatening. So go in with your eyes open. Or open your eyes now.

If you hang on, your marriage will be better. Stronger. Happier.

Depression. Confusion. Strain. Not happy words, but real ones that describe a reality. My promise is that if you endure these unhappy realities, happier ones will result.

Some of the ugliest seeds produce the most beautiful flowers.

DECONSTRUCTION AND LONELINESS

In last Sunday's weekly letter I issued a gentle warning about how deconstruction can affect your relationships.

So I want to develop this topic a little further to talk about how, even though you might be in relationships with family, friends or partners, you may experience an inexplicable kind of loneliness that feels existential in scope.

One of our members in our Facebook group wrote about this loneliness. So, here it is (used with permission):

"I am curious. How many people reading this post feel like they are practically completely alone regarding their spiritual "aloneness."? I have to say that I love my family and many friends, but there may be one or two (apart from some of my Facebook friends) who can truly identify with my plight."

This perfectly articulates a dilemma many of us face during the deconstruction of our faith and beliefs: we can be in relationship yet at the same time we can feel very lonely.

This is normal.

I'll use my relationship with my wife Lisa as an example. We have a good relationship. We are friends and talk a lot. I've been through many deconstructions, but the most intense one that began four years ago put the most strain on us. We did tons of talking, as we've always done. Lisa was a good friend through the whole ordeal. But one of the issues that contributed to the strain was that she couldn't understand me. And what contributed to her not being able to understand me was that I couldn't understand myself. Lisa and I therefore came to conclude that it is not compatibility of beliefs that held us together, but a mutual respect for each other's journeys, no matter where they led us. This is the glue. Not agreement.

Even the person who loves me most couldn't understand me or what I was going through. I had to walk this path, in a sense, alone. Lisa was with me physically and in many ways emotionally and spiritually, but she was almost like a silent partner. Even though she loves me, she was just as perplexed as I was about what was happening, and this had a way of making me feel isolated and alone.

I believe loneliness is an existential human reality. It is something we all must deal with, and we all deal with it in different, unique and individual ways.

Someone once said that the cure for loneliness is solitude. Which means we can better deal with loneliness when we are at peace with ourselves. It takes some work, but if you can get to the place where you can say, *"I'm in a place of real confusion right now, but I'm okay with that. I know that if I just remain calm and wait, clarity will come."* The result of this will be your own sense of inner peace, but it will also help those around you to relax.

If you desire to go deeper and become more authentic, you must embrace the accompanying reality that you will experience this loneliness. That even in the middle of a crowd, even among friends, you will experience the feeling of not quite being understood or fully known.

But then, something else I've discovered is that when I came to perceive that all is love, that compassion of and for all things is the ultimate truth, then I knew that somehow I am fully seen, fully understood, fully known and fully loved.

This transformed my loneliness into an intentional solitude, and I've learned to live with it, but with gratitude.

DECONSTRUCTION AND MORAL CONFUSION

One of the things I experienced when I left the church was moral confusion.
I think this is something to be expected during the deconstruction of our religion, beliefs, or faith.

Like I've said before, for the first year after leaving the ministry and the church, I was numb. Frozen. I thought I was doing great, but looking back I obviously wasn't.

Then, as I thawed over the next two years, this became a time of very intense moral confusion. I drank more than usual, wanted to smoke and sometimes did, thought about trying pot but didn't, increased my swearing vocabulary and frequency of use, dared to get really angry at people and tell them exactly what I thought, and outright avoided people in the grocery store or whatever.

Ya! I know. Small potatoes. These things are meaningless to me now. They weren't at the time, though.

So here are some big potatoes. I'm going to be as candid as I dare. I also got very confused about my marriage, my family, my home, and even myself. I felt trapped, and I wanted to cast off all restraint. All of it! I'm not joking—this was one of the most traumatic times in my life, in our marriage, for my family (because my kids knew what was going on), and for the few friends we had left. I couldn't understand this strange and unfamiliar powerful drive within me that just wanted to run away from everything! I wanted out! Out of every responsibility. Every commitment. Every union. Every expectation. Even my own personality. Everything! I didn't care. Even when Lisa was crying, I felt nothing. Even when she left those few times, I felt nothing. When I think back to the pain I was in and the pain I caused, I still get very emotional about it.

You know what this sounds like, right? Adolescence. In many ways, many of us are unprepared for the real world. It's not our fault. We just haven't been given the proper tools to grow up yet.

There are stages of moral development. I haven't looked these up. These are mine:
infantile: fear of punishment
childish: fear of rejection
adolescent: fear of limitations
adult: fear of betraying our conscience
mature adult: fear of harming humanity

"Fear" isn't the best word, especially as we mature, but you get the point. Also, at some point the law, which is external to us as infants and children, endeavors to become internal as we mature so that it becomes a part of our own moral fiber. We develop moral integrity and a mature conscience. We aren't good because we must but because we desire it.

I think the church is excellent at fostering infantile and childish stages of moral development. But, and I speak generally, it sucks at helping us break free of the external law to learn how to internalize what is right and good and integrate this with our consciences.

Now, some people mosey along with no spikes in aberrant behavior. They just gently develop like the unfolding of a rose in the morning dew of a sunrise.

Not me. And not like some of you. I've always had to test my boundaries.

Like an emotionally adolescent kid going off to college, I employed the good old pendulum swing. You too? We act out. We experiment. We go overboard. We break all the rules that restricted us before. We alarm not only those around us but even ourselves. We can actually become reckless and careless and hurt others. And if you're anything like me, there's something about all this that makes you just not care.

Lisa and I talked about this quite a bit because she experienced this phenomenon in her own way as well. We concluded that this happens because:

We were never taught to be independent.
We left the policing church community.
No one was watching.
There were no ramifications to our actions.
Basically, when we left the church and that whole culture, there was no one watching how we lived, and there would be no serious consequences to our actions, such as shaming, shunning, excommunication, or me losing my job as a pastor. That was all behind us. It was a strange and scary feeling, realizing that I could leave Lisa and no one in my new world would even bat an eye.

It took a couple of years, but finally that which was morally important to me percolated down into my deepest self. What I valued most became internalized and eventually integrated itself with my inner life. And just in the nick of time.

There were plenty of people telling me to "follow your heart" or "do what you want to do right now" or "just do what makes you happy"! I'm not sure why, but I didn't follow their advice. I can't say it was because I was strong. Maybe I was afraid. Or maybe something kept me back. I just don't know. I salute Lisa's grace, patience, courage, and candor with me. That is the first ingredient. I also thank my counselor who dragged me through brutal sessions of painful honesty. That's the second ingredient. But why I didn't trash everything I now value more than ever, I'm not entirely sure.

That's the secret recipe I haven't figured out yet. I'm grateful though.

Also, you may come out the other side with a different morality than when you went in. It is quite amazing what the lack of community policing, monitoring, and control can do to the liberated individual.

Maybe I'm giving you the heads up that this might happen to you.
Or maybe I've explained what has happened to you.
Or maybe this is a promise that if you somehow find it in you to hold on, what you value most will integrate with who you truly are.

LEARNING HOW TO LOVE YOURSELF

Here's a simple exercise to practice love. Specifically…
How to love others.
How to love your loved ones.
How to love yourself.

So in a way, this is about kids. An upcoming weekly letter is going to be about what we do with our kids while we deconstruct. But for today I want to talk about another issue. One of the most challenging things in my life has been raising children. Lisa and I have three. They are adults now, but it was hard work. I used to think that once they reached 18 or so and left home that parenting would be over. I was wrong! In fact, the parenting gets harder because their problems are larger. We worry more about them now than when they were teens. And believe me, parenting them through their teens was no piece of cake!

1. Loving Others: I was educated and trained as a pastor. I took tons of counseling courses and had years of counseling experience. I think I'm a good counselor. I'm empathic. I'm very nonjudgmental. I believe I have some wisdom. I'm a great listener. I'm gracious. I know how to validate and encourage people. Also, as you can notice, I'm not ashamed to own these qualities. In fact, I think counselors are people trained in being a good, healthy, functional human being. It is natural to be a good listener, gracious and encouraging. It shouldn't require special skills. This is how I endeavor to love others: I relinquish control.

2. Loving Our Loved Ones: However, when it comes to parenting our children through difficult times, my empathic and gracious qualities can fly out the window pretty quickly! For some reason, when it comes to our kids, I lose perspective. Things become urgent! I see the dangers of their possible choices and the array of possible consequences to those choices. In a word, with my kids, I tend to freak out. I can hear them saying, as they often have, "Dad! Calm down! Everything's going to be okay. Geeeeeeez!" I relinquish control.

So I now have a strategy. When I'm dealing with my children, I imagine them as just normal young adults who are my clients. I treat them as if they aren't my children, but just regular adults I'm counseling. Suddenly, when one of my kids is going through a crisis, all my great counseling skills come into play. I listen. I let them talk. I don't judge. I don't try to instruct or give advice. In a word, I don't freak out. I'll admit, there is the parent-part of me that is deep down inside screaming to be unleashed, but I keep it locked in the basement of my heart. Maybe Lisa and I at another time will get down and dirty honest and share our freak-outs with each other. But with our kids, no! It's making us better parents. We relinquish control.

3. Loving Yourself: Now, I've taken this strategy even further. How? By applying it to myself! When I'm going through a crisis of my own, or when I look back over my life at the choices I've made and the directions I've taken, I used to be quite hard on myself. I am my own worse critic!

I can be very judgmental with myself. Some of you who know me well enough know this about me. Even last week a friend of mine said to me about the changes I am implementing on The Lasting Supper: "Don't look at the changes as mistakes. Consider them learning moments! They are developments in the right direction." He was right. I needed to hear that nonjudgmental word about myself. I sometimes forget to be my own best counselor and apply my good counseling and coaching skills to myself. I am where I am today because of everywhere I've been before. Sure I've made mistakes. Sure I've had terrible experiences. Sure I've taken wrong turns. But here I am exactly where I'm supposed to be right now! I relinquish control.

When I read your stories on The Lasting Supper, I am amazed at your ability to listen graciously to one another. You are all such good listeners. You all seem like good counselors. You are people I feel safe sharing my story with. So I just want to encourage you to apply those same skills to yourself. They call these "soft skills" because they require you to be soft with yourself.

Try it with others.
Try it with your loved ones.
Try it with yourself.

HOW TO DECONSTRUCT IN FRONT OF YOUR KIDS

I'd been looking forward to working on this letter and sending it to you this morning. Many people have been asking me to write about this issue. Obviously it is an important one that occupies many of our minds and evokes concern in our hearts.

It's about our children. How do we deconstruct in front of our kids?

NOTE: This doesn't just apply to our kids. You can apply these principles to any loved one… a partner, a family member or a friend. One thing I've learned: The way you do one thing is the way you do everything.

The way you treat anybody is the way you potentially treat everybody.

I'm going to talk about how to deconstruct with your children. As parents we like to appear that we are in control of our lives and by inference the lives of our kids. We like to be responsible. So when we experience the death-throes of the deconstruction of our faith and beliefs and experience confusion, how do we take care of the spiritual lives of our own children? How do we oversee the spiritual development of our kids when we can't even oversee our own?

Here are a few suggestions that are more about themes than advice.

1. Relinquish Control but Not Responsibility: When I look back to when I was growing up, it seems to me that my spirituality and life were assigned. So, when I became a father I wanted to help my children find their own selves and their own paths. Lisa and I relinquished control. At the same time, we saw ourselves as gentle guides... like spiritual Sherpas... showing our kids where the possible pitfalls and the safest pathways were, what foods were good and what weren't, and who and what to trust or not.

When Lisa and I left the church, our children were in their older teens, so they were already on their way. We could hold adult conversations with mature themes. When Lisa and I were talking about this topic the other day, she said our kids were deconstructing before we were because we allowed them to question from an early age. They had the ability, minus our baggage, to be honest about what was real, authentic and true, and the strength to reject what didn't pass that test. They were far more sensitive to control and lies than we were because they were raised differently than we were. So when we started deconstructing, they were already well prepped for it.

We had obviously raised our kids in the Christian faith. We still have a collection of children's Bible story books that we used to read from every night. They grew up in the church so they knew the stories, the traditions and what church means. But we never required them to believe this or that. Like the sower with the seeds, we cast the seeds everywhere, knowing that what was good would stick and what wasn't wouldn't because it depended on what kind of soil their own hearts were. They'd develop their own spirituality and therefore find the special food that needed to feed it.

In 2002 Lisa's father had come to live with us because he was dying of cancer. This was when we were in New Hampshire planting a church for an international ministry. The day before Christmas, Lisa's father died. Our approach to it was to try to understand it theologically, and we had our long-held world-views and the ministry people to bolster this attempt. Not our kids! They loved their papa, and when they watched him die in our house despite all the prayers and promises, they immediately felt they saw all those prayers and promises for what they were. So they not only questioned that, but the source: God! This isn't to say they became atheists, but it is to say they realized that the idea of God everyone talked about and what actually is are completely different things.

On top of this, the ministry fired me the next day and the church I planted and all the ministry staff ignored us. We never saw them again. This, for my kids, was inexcusable. So they saw the church for what they felt it was: just another collection of idiots. Not to say that they don't think people and our groups can't be good, but that the church has no divine right to claim that it is good by default. If you say you're good, you must walk the talk.

So we continued relinquishing control but kept our responsibility by allowing them to process this trauma in their own way. If our kids cried "I don't believe in God anymore!", we didn't try to correct or balance or even affirm their developing belief. We just let them say it and deal with it in their own way. They now, years later, have their own spirituality that is uniquely theirs. It isn't the same as ours. And this is as it ought to be. We saw that they required a spirituality free of smoke and mirrors, magical thinking, and horse-and-pony shows.

2. Acknowledge Their Intellectual Curiosity and Honesty Without Surrendering Yours: When our children asked hard questions we found it very tempting to give easy answers. Sometimes we're just too exhausted to explain everything. Sometimes we're just too confused. Sometimes we're afraid and just want them to believe the magical thinking that religion is so good at nurturing. Sometimes we just couldn't care.

Lisa and I sometimes fought. We decided when our kids were young that we wouldn't pretend that our marriage was straight out of Disney, but the struggling union of two real flesh and blood people. Lisa and I have been married going on 35 years. So our kids have seen us fight. Our strategy was to let them see us argue, but also let them see us resolve it. If I offended Lisa and the kids saw it, we would also let them watch me apologize and see us reconcile Yes, it was usually my fault.

So when we went through our own deconstruction, we let our kids watch. When our kids questioned the existence of the rescuing God that our Christianity at that time promoted, this affected us. We didn't interpret it as a rebellion, backsliding, or foolishness. We recognized the fear that their questions invoked with in us. It's terrible to think your children are forsaking your path and taking their own instead. But we had to believe that they, like us, would find their way. We would continue to point out dangers and make suggestions, but primarily we trusted that if their intelligence had integrity, they would make it.

I always recommend the book *Passionate Marriage*. Relationships are formed and transformed in a crucible. When one person changes, it forces the other to change. Otherwise the relationship will fail. It's the same with our relationship with our kids. If they change, it forces us to change. If we change, it forces them to change. It's a perpetual dance. So when our kids changed direction theologically, we had to in some ways go their way while at the same time not forsaking our own. When we changed, if they wanted to remain in relationship with us, they had to adjust their steps as well without forsaking their integrity. Unlike the homes many people grow up in, it wasn't "My way or the highway!" It was an intersection of our own highways weaving in and out of each other. As a result, we hopefully fostered a respect for their journeys and in them a respect for ours. That still holds.

3. Respect Their Discoveries and Conclusions but Allow For Cross-Pollination: Our children formed opinions that differed from ours. So in our house there was the fascinating interplay of five different opinions. This isn't to say that the five world-views blended together to become one syncretistic stew called Haywardism. Instead, our different beliefs were uniquely our own in a home that fostered a mutual respect for each other. And when I say different, this could even mean contradictory… like a United Nations of Spirituality. But Lisa and I learned early in our relationship that it wasn't compatibility of beliefs that held us together. It was a love that respected the other no matter where they were. Lisa and I believe very differently, but we love each other. That's the glue that binds us. Not ideological agreement.

There have been difficult times when our differences created sparks that could have possibly ignited a raging fire that might have incinerated us. But I guess we learned how to negotiate those heated moments in ways that enabled us to put the fire out, divert it, or let it burn off the dross and change us.

Without a doubt, our kids learned from us. Without a doubt, we learned from them. Perhaps our kids learned from us how to be persistent, steadfast and faithful through difficult times. Perhaps we learned from our kids how to be honest, independent, and outspoken through times of pressure to conform. While we taught our kids to think for themselves and believe what they believe with integrity, they also forced us to do the same. We told them our version. They've told us theirs. We've told them our stories. They've told us theirs. We pollinated them. They pollinated us. Like a hardy apple that has developed over the years through cross-pollination, we have nourished each other and developed traits that hopefully help us to survive even in the harshest of conditions.

Conclusion: I don't want to give the impression that we are a perfect family. We are not perfect! In fact, this kind of way of life is rather chaotic. Which is why I think most families opt for a more controlled environment for their kids. We have our issues and problems as individuals and collectively. But we are perfect in that there is a love and mutual respect that keeps us together. There have been moments and seasons of unbelievable stress and confusion. There have been terrors and tensions. But so far we have survived them.

I was tempted at first to give maybe a 10 point list of advice for parents going through deconstruction in front of their kids, things like let them see the books you read and answer their curiosities about them; teach your kids how to think, not how to believe; tell them everything you're going through and let them deal with what it means for them; ask them what they believe and listen objectively and engage in conversation about it; openly share your struggles with what you're going through with the church and let them process it themselves, and so on. Rather, I thought I would give the three points above as sturdy blocks that help build an authentic, honest and thoughtful life.

WHY I LOVE YOUR LOVE FOR TRUTH

I'm going to mention some scripture here. Hold on. It won't last long.

One of the most influential passages for me for my teaching career is the one where Jesus sees the people wandering like sheep without a shepherd. He has compassion on them. What did he do? He began to teach them! Jesus is also quoted as saying that the truth sets you free. What this means to me is that truth is the way to our freedom and contentment. In other words, it is what we most need.

Mazlow's hierarchy of needs puts self-actualization at the top. It is the pinnacle of human experience. In our deconstruction, I believe it is the truth that draws and drives us toward our own spiritualities.

Even though our private group and main site is largely the exchange of stories and experiences more than ideas, I think what is behind them all is your hunger for truth. You want to know what is true. All the stories and experiences and news that we share are measured against this incessant hunger to know.

Your critiques of the church and Christianity and the Bible and everyone's interpretation, articulation, or experience of these things are not primarily the manifestation of bitterness, hurt, disappointment, anger, resentment or revenge. Rather, I think our criticisms and even our sarcasms are secondary but inevitable symptoms of our love of truth and our disdain for deceit.

When people criticize you for being too critical about what you believe is deceitful, abusive, manipulative or superstitious, they really are wishing you would keep in line, not stir the pot, and not tip over the apple cart. Most people seem to embrace the notion and lifestyle that as long as it's working, then leave it alone.

I have a story that directly illustrates this. In 1995, when I left the Presbyterian Church, Lisa and I were looking where to go next. I'd had a dream that inspired me to quit and start all over again. It was one of the most adventurous times of our lives! We wondered if it meant we should go back into the Pentecostal Church from whence we came many years before. So we applied to the denomination and were given the opportunity to meet with the district board. We got cleaned up and entered the boardroom at their headquarters to sit before a council of 18 large men in dark suits. It was a grueling and intimidating experience.

Everything was going along fine until they came to the question of alcohol. They wanted me to say that I believed drinking was a sin. I would not. We debated over scripture. One pastor brought up Paul's verse where he instructs Timothy to drink a little wine for his stomach's sake, meaning that we shouldn't drink wine, but maybe use a little for medicinal purposes. I said I felt the verse was saying, "Timothy, try to cut down on your drinking. Just try having a LITTLE wine instead of a LOT!" They laughed along with me because I did mean it as a joke. But all the men there insisted that I would need to teach that drinking was a sin. They agreed there were no verses explicitly calling drinking a sin, but the social benefits of not drinking justified the preaching that it was. In other words, and one pastor said this explicitly, it was worth preaching it was a sin to prevent people from doing it. It was an intentional strategy to mislead the people but for their own good!

As a result, we were not admitted back in to that denomination. I laugh at that now, and I'm thankful. But it made me realize that this is not an isolated incident. It is a rampantly utilized technique in the church to deceive people to achieve a desired goal.

It is our right and responsibility to defy these commonly used techniques. We must fight against lies! You are right to resist and reject deception. Even if it means not being admitted into the group.

So I admire you for it! As I watch you post and engage with each other, I am daily impressed by your tenacious hunger for truth and your consistent persistence to find and live by it.

Please don't give up! Why? Because not only will you live more and more into the truth you discover, you will also continue to inspire others to do the same.

I don't know how many times I receive messages from people thanking me for stubbornly exposing lies and seeking truth. It inspires them to do the same despite all the opposition they experience. They love the reward it brings!

So when Jesus taught because he felt compassion for lost and wandering people, and when he said the truth sets us free, we must conclude that when we find what is true, we will experience freedom and contentment within it.

Seek and you will find!

YOUR ROOTS AND YOUR FRUITS

Right from the start I want to say that I am only sharing my perspective from my experience and study. This is my journey I'm sharing. Not yours.

However, I am not only a survivor of deconstruction, but a thriver.

97

I've made it! I have travelled the treacherous path. It has taken me many years, lots of study and contemplation. This is not to say I have arrived, but that I have mastered it. I am, like many of you, an expert in deconstruction. I have a wealth of experience and insight. So I feel it is my responsibility, as well as my pleasure, to help others along similar paths. If any of what I write is helpful for you, then I'm satisfied.

One of the most important moments in our personal spiritual development is when we embrace our independence and become responsible, independent, and autonomous adults. In other words, a crucial turning point in our spirituality occurs when we claim and assume authority over our own lives. This includes our theology.

But what do we do with what we knew? What do we do with our previous religious experience? What do we do with the Christianity we adopted? I would like to examine this as though we were examining our roots.

1. Appreciate My Roots for What They Are: I appreciate my roots. I decided some time ago that it was unnecessary and even unhealthy for me to reject my roots outright. There was a lot I didn't agree with. But there was also a lot of good that contributed to who I am. I am who I am in part because of my religious roots. Like it would be foolish for me to see a beautiful rose bush and figure its roots were ugly, dirty, unnecessary and dispensable, neither do I do that with my own life. I learned a lot of good things that are still meaningful to me. I experienced a lot of good things in Christianity and the church that I treasure. Even though my religious roots are tangled, dirty, messy, and spread all over the place, there are a lot of them that have been helpful, nourished me, and perhaps even kept me alive.

So in many ways I keep my roots. Like Jesus' proverbial tree, though, I dig around them, fertilize them and trim away that which is dead. This means I appreciate the bible, the faith and the church. I value them. I have even needed them. They have nourished me and made me what I am today, which is me, David Hayward. I don't accept all of it, but I keep them and appreciate them for what they are. I am familiar with the God of Abraham, the God of Moses, the God of David, the God of Jesus, the God of Paul. I'm grateful for it.

2. Appreciate My Roots for What They Are Not: My roots are not my fruits! One of the biggest problems with Christianity today, as with all religions, is their absolute and unquestioning allegiance to the past. There is undue focus on the roots as the whole deal! Oh what wonderful roots! In fact, Christianity made a point of cementing their roots in perpetual preservation forever to be worshipped, adored and obeyed without question for all infinity. It's like Christianity concluded that all that could be revealed or believed had been established, and so it locked in its account settings for life. And it did this vicariously for you and every Christian in its wake. As a result, all we have is a splendid root preservation. Like a museum. Abraham's had his revolutionary revelation of God. Moses had his revolutionary revelation of God. David had his revolutionary revelation of God. Jesus had his revolutionary revelation of God. Paul had his revolutionary revelation of God. Period! Done forever and ever. Amen!

No! All of these are fruits that have withered and died and fallen to the ground, split open and spilled into the earth to nourish the roots but also to plant new seeds for further growth and more varieties of fruit. I believe it's my responsibility, and yours, to have our own revolutionary revelation of That-Which-We-Call-God, even if it means the withering, dying, falling and spilling of all the beliefs we've inherited. This is called deconstruction. Without this unsettling process we wouldn't experience the necessary development of our own spirituality. Our own fruit.

We are living in a very fertile age. The ground is rich for nourishing our roots and for creating new fruit. But we have to be willing. This takes courage. I recognize in all of you an essential bravery and integrity to break up the ground around your roots, to fertilize them, and to give them the space to grow into something profound... your own distinctive and independent spirituality.

Your roots are good. Therefore, your fruits are too! What a garden!

WHAT DO YOU DO AFTER THE SPIRITUAL TSUNAMI HITS?

What do we do after a tsunami hits? What do we do after the devastation of deconstruction of your faith, your beliefs, and your religion?

I was inspired by a video series I watched on YouTube about the famous tsunami of 2004. I want to talk about after the tsunami, not our anticipation leading up to it or our experience during it. So I'm not talking about the denial, the shock of it, the extent of our pain or anything like that. This is about what we do after the destruction has already hit us.

1. Assess the Damage: You've seen the movies where people are walking through the devastation following a tsunami. They are dumbfounded as they look around the flattened landscape where their homes, villages and people used to be. Pretty much everything is gone! As painful as it is following our own deconstructions, we have to see it honestly, with eyes wide open, and look the wreckage straight in the face. We have to be honest with what happened and what it has caused.

There's no point in saying that nothing or little happened, that it's not that bad, or that this is manageable. It's none of those. Like nature's tsunami's, spiritual ones are just as overwhelming and destructive. They level, destroy, and take things. They change our landscape forever. Let's be honest about it. When I went through my deconstruction, the damage was unbelievable. I still have a hard time remembering and accepting it. It did take me a while to wake up and finally assess it all. Everything had been touched: my church, my faith, my beliefs, my religion, my career, my family, my friends, me. Everything!

2. Toss and Save: Even though it looks like a complete waste, there are things in the mess that can be saved. Underneath the rubble are things that can be salvaged. It means poking through all the mess to find a little good. When we realize everything and anything can be taken from us in an instant, every little thing takes on enormous value. It might be small, like a photograph, but how precious such a little thing becomes. There was a lot I had to throw out. There was the church I had to let go. There were people I had to say goodbye to. My relationship with Lisa changed dramatically. We had to say farewell to our naive kind of love and welcome a changed and more mature one. I had to immerse myself into a much deeper and honest kind of thinking about what I believed and what I knew to be true. I had to let my career go as well as my sense of destiny. There were a lot of beliefs I allowed to go. There were a lot of things I thought which needed work. There were some things that survived but needed repair or upgrading. As brutal as tossing things might feel, saving things feels hopeful and somehow redeems the process.

3. Rebuild: This is the necessary and costly but fun part. Unfortunately, what happens in some tsunami devastated areas is that the villagers are encouraged to move to what are considered safer places, and then expensive resorts move in and take over the beachfront property. We see this sometimes too with some people after deconstruction: they totally reject everything and move away to start a brand new life all over again in a totally different way. Although I'm not saying this shouldn't be done, I am saying it doesn't have to be. You can rebuild where you are. You don't have to leave your church, you don't have to leave your faith, beliefs, or religion, and you don't have to leave your partners and friends. Even though with some of these we might not have a choice, often we do and can renegotiate our relationships to them. I can say that I'm happier now than I've ever been. I'm also more sober. What I mean is I'm more serious, as in mature or wise. Lisa and I were talking about this just yesterday. I posted a picture of Lisa and I leaving on our honeymoon. We were talking about how innocent and wide our smiles were. We wondered if we ever smile like that now. Lisa suggested that we do smile large now, but there is experience behind it. Lots of history. We also agreed that we want to continue moving on in our rebuilding project, that our home is not yet totally completed. We want to get to the place where the devastation is behind us and we approach life with joy again. We're almost there because we intend to finish this well.

I know we are all in different place on our journeys. Some of us are watching the tsunami coming, some of us are in the middle of it, some of us are just realizing it has happened, and some of us are past it. So take this letter for a way to prepare, a way to survive or a way to rebuild.

THE THREE PARADOXICAL THINGS I LOVE ABOUT YOU

As you probably already know, I think about TLS and TLSers a lot. It's not a burden. I enjoy it because I enjoy you guys. We've gone through some rough times. That's only natural. But we're survivors and thrivers, and I think we're doing really well.

But as I was saying, I enjoy you guys so much. Here are the 3 things I like most about you:

1. You're weak but strong: What I mean by this is that you are no weaker than anybody else, but you are not afraid to expose your weaknesses to the rest of us. It amazes me how vulnerable, open and honest you guys are. You ring authenticity, and that is a remarkably rare thing. What I've discovered, though, is that this kind of person is actually the stronger kind. Those who are not afraid to show their weaknesses are a rarer and tougher breed of person. I watch you allow your afflictions to instill empathy and compassion in yourselves so that when another TLSer struggles with an affliction, you listen, understand, and console in non-coercive and supportive ways. You're so non-judgmental. As far as I can see, you show amazing respect for the dignity of each and every individual in their struggle. That's because you're empathic. You're in touch with your weaknesses and are therefore not disgusted with the weaknesses of others. I love this!

2. You're honest but smart: The level of honesty on TLS is astounding. Don't you think so? I think honesty is a rare commodity these days. Unfortunately, the church doesn't encourage it. But you guys dare to ask the tough questions. You take the risk of saying "I don't know!" or even "We can't know!" This takes a courageous kind of honesty that I admire and covet. You are quick to confess your confusions. You don't mind professing your perplexities. Usually, these are seen in a negative light. I don't see it that way. I think this kind of honesty is a manifestation of a deeper kind of intelligence. To say that we are enveloped in unknowable mystery is a sure sign of wisdom. You guys are reading books many would consider heretical. Why? Because you want to understand! Well, actually, before you want to understand you want to tear down untruths that you inherited or adopted and grow wise in what is really true. You don't want to be told what is true. You want to discover! To me, this is smart. I love hanging out with all you brainy folk.

3. You're humble but assertive: I think one of the reasons so many of us experience trauma when struggling with the church is because in our desire to be humble we mistake this for allowing others to determine our lives for us. In fact, for some of us, it meant letting people run over us because it was the Christian thing to do. At least this is a part of my story. Your humility is quite remarkable, and I feel very comfortable among you. Even though there are strong personalities, they are tempered with humility. That's what I mean to say. Even though I see humility in you, I also see that you are very assertive. I remember someone saying that humility is simply being true to yourself... neither acting above nor beneath who you are. Being you, definitely and only you, is humility. So being you, definitely and only you, is also assertiveness. Many of us have learned or are learning how to not be taken advantage of anymore. You know what abuse and manipulation and control look like from a mile away, and you stand your ground and deflect it. Like Gandalf: "YOU SHALL NOT PASS!" To me this is the picture of humility and assertiveness. This is you!

Guys! I hope you don't think I'm just blowing sunshine here. I'm not! I'm serious. You guys are an incredible and surprising mix of amazing individuals. I hope you realize that.

Actually, the above things I like about you are what makes, in my opinion, a mature person. The remarkable journeys you've been on and the remarkable ways in which you share them with the rest of us is simply amazing.

WHAT DO YOU DO IF SOMEONE WON'T FORGIVE YOU?

I genuinely hurt a good friend many years ago. I regretted it as soon as I did it. He hasn't really forgiven me. I've made every attempt to repent and repair, but it changed our relationship. We rarely, if ever, see each other anymore.

There have been many people I've offended. In fact, I offend people every day. When we went through a church split in 1997, one pastor visited me to tell me I needed to go to every person I've offended and ask their forgiveness, including people who read my blog. I laughed that ridiculous suggestion off. I feel no responsibility for people who get offended by me. If they can't forgive me, that's their problem.

That's the way I look at it. Could you imagine if I went around apologizing to every single person I ever offended? That would have been a full time job.

But it's totally different, isn't it, when you really love someone, you really do hurt them, and they won't forgive you. How do you get over that? How do you move on?

I don't claim to have mastered this one. I'm just going to share what I've done. Let's be clear: my heart still hurts over it, but there are things I can do to ease the pain that might help you ease yours.

I repented: I asked for forgiveness. I explained what I did wrong to make it clear to him that I was aware of how I hurt him. It wasn't a fake apology, like, "I'm sorry if what I did hurt you." It was genuine: "I'm sorry I hurt you! This is what I said, it was wrong and stupid and I regret it. I wish I could take it back. What can I do to make this better?" I even went out of my way to try to meet him as much as I could and talk through it. So my repentance and attempts to repair our relationship were clear. I really do think I did everything I could.

I forgave myself: I learned an important lesson. I have to forgive myself even if others won't forgive me. This is my right, my privilege, and my responsibility. I have to forgive myself. So I did. But I have to admit that it is much harder to do when the offended won't forgive. Right? I mean, when you do something and everyone forgives you, it paves the way for you to easily forgive yourself. But if they withhold forgiveness, then you have to forgive yourself in spite of their withholding it. That's very hard to do. But it must be done. Especially when you have done the other steps… you know what you did, you've repented, you've asked for forgiveness, and you've made every attempt to repair. Now it's up to you to forgive yourself even if no one else will. This is the core of compassion.

I resisted resentment: You are aware of the famous Hatfield-McCoy feud in the USA in the late 1800's. Feuds start with an offense, followed by an unwillingness to forgive, followed by a resentment because of it, followed by… well… you get the point. This is the cycle of violence that manifests in division and disunity. I have to admit that there are moments I get sad that my friend won't forgive me. I notice how this can easily morph into resentment and ultimately hatred for him, followed by some kind of retaliation such as a series of attacks against him. I have to remember that this is his problem, not mine. I could make it my problem, but what good would that do? I am powerless to change him and his mind and heart. That's his job. All I can do is keep my heart clean and then wait.

I concluded I am forgiven: I embraced the fact that in this universe I am forgiven and nothing is held against me. Nothing holds anything against me except my friend. I did all I could. I am released. In fact, I've come to the conclusion that there was nothing to be forgiven. True forgiveness isn't even aware that it forgives. Compassion is continuous, thorough, and timeless. Forgiveness is not an event but an environment. It's a reality. Like air. It just is. Some parents understand this with their children. You learn what it means when you can say, "You were forgiven before you did it." When I discovered this new reality, I determined to live in its realm. Even if my friend doesn't forgive me, I am still forgiven. I hope you understand this.

DEEP THOUGHTS A HONEYBEE EVOKED

Do you ever get the feeling your life is like the movie *The Matrix*?

If you haven't seen *The Matrix*, it is about the true, real world versus the false, controlled world. The red or the blue pill. The scary or the secure. You either live in one or the other. You can't live in both.

What prompted this line of thinking was that I tried an experiment. Let me tell you about it.

Even though I love the internet and our online community, I really miss meeting with live people in a room. There's a different kind of energy. So, I've organized some local TLS events. I rented a very nice meeting room at the local library and announced the events online. The turnout has been meagre.

At this point I'm not sure what to do about it. Should I continue trying? Or should I take this as a sign?

Yesterday while I was sitting outside a honeybee visited me and hovered in front of my face for about fifteen minutes. It was during this very surreal and contemplative moment I realized that I've been trying to live in both worlds… the Christian world and the post-Christian one. I've been trying to hover, suspended between the past and the future but not in the present. There's a hesitation to moving on.

This isn't to demean Christianity or the church. There are some of you who are still in it. I applaud you. I still love it. So, this is to try to explain that I somehow no longer seem to fit in it. I am in a kind of no-man's-land… in between the church and the complete lack of it. Very few people live here. I know many of you do.

Hovering like a bee.

Here's what I've come to conclude: you can't live in both. The bee did hover for a long time. But it can't stay there. It either has to come or go.

There's work to be done.

But I have to tell you that it takes a lot of effort to let go of the old world. *The Matrix*. It's hard to let it go! It's so much more comfortable, familiar, and secure.

On the one hand, it was so meaningful. It makes up a huge part of who I am. It's like it is sewn into my DNA. One of our members posted this:

"I am realizing today how much of my spiritual journey has shaped who I am and how important it all has been in my life, even if much of it is now an unpleasant memory... I never thought it would end up being that important, but I am discovering that my story runs both broad and deep."

Then again, I recognize that even though it is an important part of who I am, it no longer determines who I am or can be. Even though it shaped me, it doesn't handle me anymore. It was a launching pad, not an anchor.

On an episode of *West Wing* that I watched recently, a therapist tells Josh that the sign that you are cured of PTSD is that you can remember the event without reliving it. Yes! Can I remember and even embrace my past without having to relive it over and over again in everything I think, say, and do?

Can I live free, a brand new creation, each and every day, with a brand new bright horizon ahead of me, without living under the shadow of what I came out of?

Isn't this our question?

So, back to my local TLS events. Am I trying to revive my church experience or resurrect my pastoral vocation? Am I trying to repeat the previous? Am I still somewhat caught in the mental church/pastor paradigm mentality and still haven't learned how to live and be completely free of its determining power? And am I not communicating some kind of confusion to those I'm trying to help because I'm confused myself in where I stand?

I insist this doesn't reflect a hatred for Christianity or the church. I love it. But I feel like a young adult who has realized it is time to leave his family and house and perhaps even his country of origin and move on into his own destiny. I really do think the Church and Christianity are morphing into something that looks nothing like what they came from. Just like a cornstalk looks nothing like a kernel of corn!

I still choose the red pill. I wish I could forget the blue one quicker.

All that from a bee.

THREE BATTLE GROUNDS YOU MUST NOT SURRENDER

I want to write to you today about the three battlegrounds of deconstruction that you cannot surrender.

(This reminds me of a totally unrelated story. Many years ago after we went through a horrendous church split, my wife went to see Francis Frangipane who authored the book The Three Battlegrounds. This was back in the day when we were totally immersed in that prophetic culture. At the time I liked the book. But I wasn't ready to expose myself to more religious crap so fresh after a church split that killed my spirit. Lisa has a softer heart and wanted to hear him. That evening when she came home she said I just had to go hear him the next day. He'd approached her and told her he wanted to meet her husband because he had a word from the Lord for me. So I reluctantly went. After I heard him speak I went up to meet him. He said something like this: "I just wanted to say that you went through this church split because God wanted to show you the pain of division. From now on will be planted forever in your heart a deep disdain for division, but also an undying passion for the unity of all God's people." As weird and out of character for me as this may sound, I still cherish the essence of that message to this day.)

But the battlegrounds I want to talk about today are specific to deconstruction. They may or may not match your battlegrounds. These are ones that are mine that I've had to fight for and win, but also keep!

1. The Mind: The most heated battle for me was the mind, the intellect. This to me was the most important ground to win. If I won this one I was convinced that all other battles would eventually fall to my rule. It wasn't enough for me, when I left the ministry and the church, to say, "What the heck was that?" and reject it all as foolishness. I had invested too much serious thought and time and energy in trying to understand myself and my universe and all mysteries to toss out all my investigations, studies and contemplations I had engaged in. I agree with the mystics who discover that their miraculous discovery, their revelation, their samadhi, ends up being completely different than what they were searching for. This doesn't mean it negates the search. Rather, it simply distinguishes them from each other. The revelation I received that night was the dream of the waterfall that started my development of what I call the z-theory. That was the key that opened everything for me. It was my revelation, my samadhi, my nirvana. My peace of mind. And it has never left. I believe we need a way to try to understand ourselves, our universe, and all mystery, in order for our minds to enjoy a peaceful poise. Even if it is chaos theory, we must trust that our true mind, not the ego mind but our true mind, can come to a place where it is at peace with itself and rests in the wisdom that all things are one, including our past journeys, thoughts, and endeavors. You haven't wasted your time or your thoughts! I claim that if you keep pressing in you will win the ground and suddenly all the strange-shaped pieces will click into place and create a complete picture for you that will bring an everlasting peace to your mind.

2. The Heart: This was the second battle for me. This has to do with my emotions, and specifically my relationships. I knew when I left the ministry and the church that the nature of my relationships would change. Granted, I had no idea the extent to which this was true. But I knew when I left the church the relationships with my friends, with people in the church, and with my family, would change. I experienced a drastic drop in friends, I bewildered members of my family, and the loneliness I'd only heard about for those outside church fellowship became a stark reality for me. Like I said before, it's one thing to gain ground, but it's another thing to keep it! This is a battle I still wage. Keeping this ground and not surrendering it takes due diligence! As soon as I left the church the shallow superficiality that I suspected in many of my existing relationships became grossly evident. Many people I thought were friends were suddenly gone. I understand that relationships change and don't need to stay at the same level of intensity. I also understand that I left them, not them me, and I brought much of this upon myself. But I also know that I am looking for significant relationships that are meaningful and substantial. The temptation to go back into superficiality is sometimes strong because loneliness is a terribly toxic feeling. Filling it with disappointing relationships though might only feel good for a moment but doesn't last and just makes things worse! There is also the temptation to enter into inappropriate relationships that almost everyone experiences at some time or another. Deconstruction can create the unhealthy opportunity to betray the good relationships we already have. But I've learned that staying the course is the best strategy when fighting for this battleground. I'm certain that healthy relationships will come into my life. In fact, Lisa and I have some friends now who are satisfying. There's more work to be done, but I think we're on our way to victory here.

3. The Body: By the body, I mean my whole self, including my spirit. It's like when we go to a good doctor with an ailment, he or she will ask not only questions to do with our actual bodies but with things like stress. It's all connected. I will confess to you that during the most intense period of deconstruction, I was probably also at the unhealthiest. I adopted a heck-with-it attitude and let restraint fly out the window. I smoked, ate, and drank too much. I lost all discipline because, I suspect, at the root of it was a kind of self-destructive impulse. Life was so overwhelming, disappointing, and incredibly sad that I think there was an "I just don't care anymore" mentality at work. My relationship with Lisa suffered the most and poisoned every aspect of our life together, including our sex life. After months of enduring this piece-by-piece deconstruction of all I'd held dear, a severe hopelessness set in and I truly wondered if I would ever make it or if it was even worth the effort.

I wanted to run away from everything I knew. I felt like Frodo trying to get the ring to Mordor and the further he got the more hopeless and lethargic he became until Sam had to practically drag him. The truth is, Frodo was getting closer, and the fight is always the most intense nearest its completion. I know because I completed it. It was darkest before the light!

I want to encourage you to keep moving on. I do not for a second promise that the battle will soon be over. But it will change. It will change from exterminating the enemy to simply keeping it at bay. I found that it is important to dig down and gather every bit of energy you have to invest in what you have already... your body, any family or friends or partners you have, and your spiritual life. Because, as attacked and beleaguered though these may be, there is reward in investing in these and breathing life into them again if they are worth it. Do like the flight attendant advises: put the oxygen mask on yourself first! As soon as you are breathing again, life will return to you and you can turn to those around you.

So, take care of your body. I try to watch my diet, practice moderation with alcohol, not smoke, and run. Develop new spiritual disciplines. I meditate, read philosophy, practice awareness and being here now, write in my journal, paint. Work on being a good friend to someone. Lisa and I are restoring good old friendships, we are making new friends, and we are learning how to be alone without being lonely.

I want to recognize how repugnant what I'm saying could be to some of you. I know when I was going through it the best advice was the most annoying. Looking back now, I wish I'd listened to it. At the time, though, it sounded like platitudinous clichés. If you want to call this that, you are welcome to. I just want to say this: I've gotten to the point now where I think I can safely say that my borders are fairly secure and its mostly a matter of keeping my ground. I know many of you are here. But if you aren't here yet, fight the good fight and you will be here eventually.

HOW TO FIND AND USE YOUR OWN VOICE

I know I'm probably preaching to the choir. You guys are amazing at speaking your mind. The level of honesty, vulnerability, openness, and skill at articulating complicated, intense, deep thoughts and emotions amaze me every day.

Almost every day I get notes from people in the form of an email or a direct message or a private message thanking me for saying something that has inspired them.

They don't want their family or friends to know this because they will suffer for it. They ask me how I found the courage to be so open and say the things I say or ask the questions I ask.

So today I will talk about how to find your own voice and how to use it.

1. Test: It takes some time to find out what your voice actually is and what it sounds like. I know for me it started with finding out what my voice wasn't. So the first real expressions of my voice were in the form of questions. I'm still not sure exactly what I believe sometimes. But often it's very, very clear what I do not believe. It's like you have to keep testing to hear if the voice you're using rings true to you and that it is the truest expression of yourself. It is my belief that the quality of a question reveals the wisdom of the questioner. Ask yourself: *"What have I been believing that I actually seriously question now?"* You might be surprised.

2. Write: Write in your journal. I don't know about you, but for me, writing things down actually clarifies what I'm thinking. It helps to shape my airy thoughts into a more solid form. Write down the questions you come up with. I have stacks of journals that show the development of my own personal wisdom. And it's my wisdom! It's not someone else's. It's mine. Sure, there are elements of the wisdom of others there, but they come together and mix into a unique concoction that is particularly mine! Write things out. It could be in a journal. Or it could even be in an anonymous blog. I know some people who started this way. Under a pseudonym, they had the courage to speak openly without edit. They plan on maybe one day ripping off the mask and going public. Or maybe not. In any case, they practice using their voice.

3. Wait: I know many people who like my stuff but are afraid to publicly let their friends and family know they do. So they'll message me privately to thank me for something I've said that they appreciate. The ramifications they would suffer for being found out or coming out with something they don't believe or do are so great that they can't find the nerve to express it. So I tell them to take their time. In time the courage to speak your mind will gather. In fact, I sometimes think our truth waits within us like a pressure cooker and that it is just a matter of time until it cooks to the boiling point and blows the lid off. The gospel stories suggest that Jesus waited until he was about thirty before he came out. In fact, he apparently even resisted this when Mary tried to get him to take care of the wine shortage at the wedding. He said, "My time is not yet!" But the lid blew off. His cover was finally blown. And, as pressure cookers that blow their lids do, the mess created was beyond repair. There is no getting everything back into the pot.

4. Practice: Find a good friend or a partner or a safe group (like The Lasting Supper) to practice using your voice. Or your cat, dog, canary, or goldfish! Start with just small bits, like sound bites, little phrases, shares, or likes. You don't have to start with your Magnum Opus, a symphony or opera or constitution. Just a sentence will do. You, as well as I, know the power that one tiny little sentence can hold. In fact, I bet many of you can remember the one sentence, that one little question, which betrayed your inner thoughts and exposed you, forced you to come out, and invited the assault that you're under right now. I know I remember. Many years ago, I said something like this to someone important: "I don't know if I believe that anymore." Simple as that! It exposed me. Like I said, it opened the can of worms. After that it was impossible to get them back in again. Just start with a good friend, your partner, one of your children, a parent, an uncle, a closed group, anyone! Just say it. I promise: once you say it the rest takes care of itself.

5. Risk: What I mean by this is that you must count the cost. Unfortunately, most people don't want you to speak your truth. I do, and many of us here do, but most people don't. And there are some very mean people out there who aren't afraid to use their voices to seriously hurt others. So be careful. Even today, someone commented on one of my cartoons, "And you call yourself a 'pastor'! Go f#*% yourself!" Thanks for that! It was in response to me using my voice to question someone telling parents to shun their homosexual children and turn them over to Satan. Now, some time ago this would have really hurt me, made me question my pastoral gifts, and made me feel like I'd been thrown a curse. Now, words like these fly by and no longer stick to me. I'm used to it. We all know what it means to lose friends and even family members because we've come out in some way or another. It hurts. It sticks. But we realize that using our own truthful voice is more important than carrying the weight of others' expectations.

6. Encourage: If you are a parent or a friend or a family member, encourage others to use their own voice as well. Lisa and I encouraged our children from a very early age to find their own voice and use them. They do! In fact, I'll humbly admit, I get embarrassed by some of the things they come out with publicly. We may not agree with everything they express. But what delights us more than agreement is their freedom! It is wonderful to watch people find and use their own voices, especially when they are your children or friends or loved ones. Hanging out with free people is a great way to enjoy our own freedom. I think it actually teaches us how to think, speak, and live more freely. I also believe that trusting people with their own freedom helps them discover their own integrity and autonomy.

7. Enjoy: Have fun using your voice. Like a singer, just enjoy singing your thoughts. It's not all terrible and costly. I just finished watching a documentary that won several awards, *Twenty Feet From Stardom*, about backup singers and how amazing they are, how close they are to the limelight, but mostly how they just enjoy the music. In the same way, we might not be center stage with tons of likes and shares and traffic. We just enjoy the music! We enjoy the sound of truth on our own lips. We love the wonder or shock that our voices bring to the expressions on peoples' faces. We come to a place where we actually enjoy upsetting the *status quo*, tipping the apple cart, and causing a deep or even heated conversation. When I use my voice, sometimes I get silence. But mostly I get boos or applause. All these are good because I'm more passionate about the freedom of expression rather than the editing of it. My edit button's broken by now. I forget how to use it anyway.

I hope this helps you wild and crazy singers out there! Your voices are amazing. Each one is so unique. The world would suffer without the expression of your own voice. No one else has it. It's yours!

Now, turn to your cat, dog, canary or goldfish, and say something amazing that you've been waiting to say for a long time! Then go from there.

DO NOT CAST YOUR PEARLS BEFORE SWINE

You've heard the saying of Jesus, "Do not cast your pearls before swine."

The basic meaning of that is don't share yourself, your truth, your life, anything of yourself that is of value to you, important to you, with those who won't appreciate it. They'll trample it underfoot. Not necessarily out of anger. Pigs just trample pearls underfoot because pearls mean nothing to them.

You have the right to not share what is valuable about yourself with others who won't get it, won't understand it, and won't appreciate it. You do not need to give yourself away to those for whom it means nothing. You don't have to reveal all of the real you, the true you, to people who won't care, or will care but in the wrong way, or who will hurt you for it.

Jesus was an expert at this. It infuriated the religious leaders because they always wanted to trap him. That was the main motivation of their questions, not curiosity or a desire to know.

Now, I cast my pearls out into the world every day. Some people are sweet and some are swine. But that's how I roll.

However, when it comes to more immediate relationships, I apply this principle: When you train your mind, heart and ear to discern, you can tell when someone's asking you out of a malicious desire to catch you *or* out of a sincere desire to know. *Withhold* your pearls from the first. No explanation needed. That's just another pearl that means nothing to them. *Give* your pearls to the second. They will appreciate their value and treasure them as gifts.

One of our members asked: How can we tell the difference between a swine and a sweetie? Good question! Sometimes we don't know until it's too late. I have no test-proven method of telling the difference. In fact, sometimes people can be both and switch from sweetie to swine in a flash! But, when it comes to sharing yourself with others, here are a few pointers to apply to keep from being trodden underfoot.

1. Never share publicly online or anywhere! Unless you're into that game like I am. Just don't! There are too many swine out there just waiting to trample over anything and everything good. They're called trolls. It seems one of my roles in life is to expose myself. Hence the name "nakedpastor". But I'm doing it for a reason. And I have built up a pretty good immunity to stomping swine. It still hurts but I'm on a mission. Just don't do it unless you must.

2. Don't trust swine. This could be family or friends or acquaintances or whomever. If you know someone that you just know would not appreciate your pearls, then don't fantasize that they will. Face facts! Reach an agreement with reality. If you share your pearl with this someone and they stomp on it, it doesn't do any good to say, "I was hoping you would care!" No… you were hoping your fantasy of who you wish they were would care. Don't go there until people prove themselves trustworthy with your pearls.

3. Test trust levels. If people ask about your pearls or you're feeling like you'd like to share them with someone, start with the least valuable of all your pearls. Don't start with the most precious. Here's an example: if your beliefs are changing and you wonder if you should reveal this to a person, you could say something like this: "If a friend confessed to me that their beliefs were changing, I wouldn't judge them but would do everything to help that person feel accepted, appreciated, and loved!" Notice their reaction. If it is positive, perhaps they've passed the test. Share a pearl. If they react negatively to your feeler, don't share your truth with them that you yourself are gay. Not yet.

4. Trust the trustworthy. If someone over the course of time proves trustworthy to you, if they are a good listener and don't judge you, then venture into this territory. Go as far as you feel safe to go. Don't dive right into the deep end. Wade in. I emphasize *over the course of time* because too many people trust too many people too soon too many times. Suddenly, something goes wrong and all the trust and safeguards are disposed of and your pearls spill out everywhere and end up on the black market. Take your time. Please, for your own sake, take your time. It is wise to treasure your pearls. Which means it is wise to love yourself and take care of yourself. Just like you would any other person you love and care for, do the same for you. This isn't selfish, but compassionate.

We all have pearls and it's nice to share them. I hope you find someone or more than one that you can share them with, because you guys are all so amazing! In fact, sharing your pearls with us in our group is a great way to begin! I really do consider it safe to share your precious self with others here.

I promise I won't trample on you. I'm certain everyone there would promise the same.

THREE PROGRESSIONS TO SPEAKING YOUR OWN LANGUAGE

Good morning my friends. It's been an exhausting week, but I finally saw the completion of my book, *The Liberation of Sophia*. I started drawing Sophia right after I left the church and completed 59 drawings and meditations 4 years later.

There was an overwhelming sense of grief as I closed that chapter of my life. I can safely say my deconstruction process is pretty much complete. I still have tons to learn, but I feel I'm in a very good space.

I'm being very productive, and I have a ton of books to make… mostly collections of my cartoons. But the big project ahead of me is writing my z-theory in a very clear and simple way. I hope is that it is going to be very helpful for people like us who are trying to figure out a way to intellectually understand our spiritual journeys.

Sophia's journey articulated my passage from feeling trapped to experiencing spiritual independence. It is the chronicle of how I learned to speak my own language.

I wanted to share those 3 stages of progression with you today:

Thought language: Think your own language. It starts in the mind. You and I both know that our so-called rebellion began with our thoughts. We started to think differently. We saw we were expected to believe a certain way, and even though we complied for a long time, the time finally came where we had to admit we were thinking for ourselves.

It began simply for me. I remember someone reading me a story about a man being swallowed alive by a shark and surviving after several days and that this was proof of the story of Jonah and the whale. I remember my young mind thinking, "Mmm… nah!" The same when my family took a trip through the States and visited the Grand Canyon and being told that sea fossils near the rim was proof of the great Flood and Noah's ark. I remember my youthful mind thinking, "Mmm… nah!" This continued on up through my college days, seminary days, and throughout my ministry, and even to this day. When someone says something they expect me to believe, I catch my mind thinking, "Mmm… nah!"

My own language started in my own mind.

Verbal Language: Speak your own language! It took a long time for me to get to this stage. In fact, I was a married adult, really, before I allowed that nagging thought, "Mmm… nah!" to become a verbal expression. I recall the exact moment when someone important said something to me that I didn't agree with. My mind said, "Mmm… nah!" But it was like a volcano, and those words erupted all over the room. I simply said, "Mmm… I don't think I think that way anymore, actually!" It was like I stabbed that person in the chest with a switchblade. Their eyes widened and their face turned red. Very dramatic. But I said it. A heated argument ensued, but it was too late. I couldn't retract my words. They were out there. They pushed me away from the dock.

I know many of you are finding your own voice. It's something we always talk about. You're trying it at home with your partner, your family, your friends. We are trying on TLS. Others are writing in their blogs or other venues. Some of you are exercising your voices and finding the best way to communicate your dissent and disagreement. But more than that, you're finding a way to stand your ground, protect your borders, and establish your own official language.

Your own language starts in the mind, but eventually it has to come out of your mouth.

Body Language: Live your own language! Finally, it comes to body language. Towards the end of my time as a pastor, I clearly remember my thoughts needing to be articulated verbally. It started on my blog.

But I remember the tension this caused in my church.

Eventually, the tension became so great that I had to walk. We all agreed that we were no longer compatible: for me to continue growing and for them to remain the same, I had to move on. So, even though it started in my mind and was expressed through my speech, it eventually was manifested in my feet. I had to walk the talk. I had to practice what I preached. It was painful and difficult, but it was necessary.

The fact is, this is how we eventually discover how to live a life of integrity. Jung talks about individuation: when we learn to reconcile all the parts of ourselves into one undivided individual. We come to a place where we have true integrity. It always takes time to get there. It takes a lot of courage as well. Our social environments work hard to prevent it, so it's like paddling upstream.

But we have to do it if we want our words to match our thoughts and our lives to match our words.

I am thrilled to watch you guys striving to become and remain people of true integrity. I see what it is costing you. But you're willing to lay it down because, as we all know, there's nothing more satisfying than feeling the unity of our own lives. Like all the tumblers in a lock just click into place.

Or like inserting the final piece of a puzzle.

I encourage you to speak your own language: in your thoughts, in your words, and in your lives.

We are here to listen.

HEAR MY CONFESSION

I know. That's a really dramatic title. But I seriously would like to make my confession. Will you hear it?

We had an incident in our Facebook group this weekend. Some conflict. What was really frustrating for me was we were in the middle of the post-tropical storm Arthur and lost power. All I had was my iPhone that loses its charge quickly if I'm online and requires quick thumbs to type with, which I hate. I was getting messages from some concerned people wishing that I could intervene. With the weather storm and the aftermath, plus the TLS storm and aftermath, I became very anxious and stressed out. I had been writing with several of the members trying to help resolve the misunderstanding and conflict one on one. When I finally got power, I quickly wrote a post that I hoped would alleviate it all and calm the waters.

Since then I've heard from TLS members and read responses and got caught up more comprehensively. Plus, I've evaluated how my performance was. I realize now that my response was not perfect. I could have moderated so much better.

So here are my confessions:

1. I'm very uncomfortable with conflict. You might be surprised by that, considering that I'm the nakedpastor. Ever since I was a small child I did everything I could to avoid conflict and end it quickly if it erupted. I don't like fighting, arguing, disagreements, tension... all that stuff. So I just know that there are times I will try to make it stop before it should. This is weird for me to understand about myself because rationally I know conflict is natural. We are humans, not robots, so disagreements are going to happen, as well as misunderstanding and miscommunication and even division. I also know conflict can be very fruitful.

Creative chaos! Often the best developments come out of a conflict. I know this. I've seen it. I've experienced it. So it is strange to me that I still find conflict very unsettling and that my knee-jerk reaction is to stop it prematurely. Like on TLS this weekend. For that I'm sorry. Forgive me.

2. I'm always wiser 20/20. I've done a lot of work with this, and with the help of therapists, counselors, mentors and spiritual directors, I've come to the conclusion that while I'm in the middle of conflict, my coping mechanism is to go numb and wait until it passes. Something about intense conflict blinds me, deafens me, and paralyzes me. I remember in 1997 on a Sunday morning while my church was splitting right down the middle, and rather violently, I was standing there in a stupor. One of my leaders came up to me and whispered in my ear, "Dave! You're the pastor! Act like it!" That startled me awake and I became more aware of what was happening around me. Looking back on what happened at TLS this weekend I can now see that I was not

121

fully aware and that I did not respond with all of my faculties firing at 100%. For that I'm sorry. Forgive me.

3. Sometimes I resort to old pastoral habits. I was a pastor for 30 years. I had decades to learn methods of how to manage or moderate or mediate conflict. I'm sorry to say this, but my observation is that most church people want a king for a pastor… or queen. They want you to rule them, manage them and regulate them. I honestly found that sometimes the fastest way to fix something was just to do it myself. I found the same dynamic this weekend. In fact, one of our members wondered why we were all waiting for the pastor to get back online before we could do anything. Valid observation! But I do want to confess, even though I am a very empowering person who despises manipulating or controlling people, that I still know how to do it and sometimes do. For that I'm sorry. Forgive me.

4. I occasionally forget that you know how to resolve things. Another member mentioned that you are all adults and know how to communicate well and that if we let the conversation run its course, there was a good chance that it would have resolved itself well. It was also suggested that rather than the "leader" coming in and effectively silencing everyone, if it was allowed to proceed organically, it would have concluded organically. The way I responded reminded some of the church they ran away from or the pastors they'd sat under. I totally understand that. In fact, after I posted my comments and took the time to read back over what had happened, it did look like it was going to resolve itself well and would have proceeded naturally and democratically. I should have involved myself with the conversation itself instead of making a proclamation from above that had the effect of silencing people. For that I'm sorry. Forgive me.

Those are my confessions. These are where I feel I fell short.

I just want to say, in conclusion, that I want to be a good moderator. I think I'm pretty good, but not perfect. And, yes, I aim for perfection. Our site does require a moderator. I've seen other sites and communities blow up from poor or absent moderation. I don't want that to happen to us because I value TLS and each one of you so much. It's working! I want it to continue to work. I'm thankful for you guys for your patience, not only with each other and with TLS, but also with me. We are all learning here. So continue speaking your mind to me and to each other, and I will do the same. I trust you guys to do community well. You've proven it so far.

So, let's play ball!

LET'S TALK ABOUT TRUST

I still feel like I'm in vacation mode. We had people drop by and stay for a couple of days, so the party continues! Plus, my websites were down for a couple of days. That was freaking me out. But all is well now.

I've been thinking about trust. There's a lot of pressure on us to trust people.

We get it from our teachers: We are taught that we should always trust people. You know the verse we hear at every wedding from 1 Corinthians 13, the "love chapter", that "Love always trusts." If we don't trust a certain person, then that means we don't love them. And if we don't love them, then God doesn't love us. I've dealt with a lot of guilt because I haven't trusted people in the way I felt a Christian should.

We get it from others: People want our trust. I don't know how many times someone has expressed disappointment and dismay because I couldn't or wouldn't trust them or someone they recommended the way they felt I ought to. I'm an easy person to guilt!

We get it from ourselves: Because of the teaching we've received, because of the expectations of others, and because we want to be good, don't want to displease God, and don't want to offend anybody, enormous pressure builds up inside our hearts to trust people even when our guts are shouting, "CAUTION!"

But it doesn't have to be this way!

I've learned that it is wise to trust people at the level they can be trusted. This is not only good for me, but respectful of them.

Let me explain:

I used to have a motorcycle… a '79 Suzuki GS850. I loved it. I took my daughter Casile for a ride on the back of it one day. She asked if she'd be able to try driving it. I said no, of course, because it takes a lot of training, testing and experience before someone can be trusted to drive a motorcycle.

I'll say it again. She had no training, testing, or experience.

To trust her to drive my motorcycle would have been foolish and dangerous. She would have hurt herself and others and likely brought grief to many. I said no to protect her, to protect others, and to protect myself. Never mind the bike!

When it comes to personal relationships issues, though, I often feel my Christian sensibilities rising up when I'm asked to trust someone more than they are capable of handling. Guilt raises its ugly head and says that I'm unloving, petty, and not spiritual if I refuse to trust them.

But now I know how to handle it. I just tell myself, "It would be unfair to them and unfair to me to trust them with more than they can handle. People will get hurt if I do, including them. So no, I will not entrust them with this."

"This". What is "this"? I'm not talking about motorcycles or other possessions, although that is included. I'm talking about information.

It's almost always information. It's almost always personal information about ourselves.

I don't know how many times I've entrusted someone with information about myself that they couldn't handle. That is, they couldn't deal with the information about me that offended them, shocked them, or disappointed them. Or they found it so juicy that they just had to tell other people about it.

Of course, I'm not even talking about dealing with our own trust issues at this point. That's a whole other topic. What I'm talking about here is YOUR RIGHT and YOUR RESPONSIBILITY to discern and decide at what level to trust a person, no matter where you are at on the trust issue scale!

So here's my advice:

Don't let a teacher tell you who to trust and how much to trust them with.
Don't let a person demand your trust, even if they are in your life.
Don't let guilt force you into trusting more than you are comfortable with.

Just trust yourself to know. TRUST YOUR GUT! Let's start with that.

THREE LIES YOUR EX WANTS YOU TO BELIEVE

I'm not talking about your romantic or marital ex. I'm talking about your ex-church.

Now, before I begin, I want to clarify a couple of things:
These can apply even in existing relationships *(your partner or church now)*.
These are not all the lies, but a few of them *(there are lots of lies available)*.
Not all exes are like this, but enough are *(enough to warrant making this list)*.

1. "You can't live without me!" Another version of this is, "You need me!" The truth is you don't. Unhealthy relationships are often based on codependence, which is basically a fixation on meeting the needs of the other person for your own sense of self-worth. Unhealthy relationships might sound really romantic and loving when they say, "I can't live without you!" But in truth this is not healthy. It is a lie!

Lisa and I had to come to the painful but liberating realization of this in our relationship. The truth is she can live without me. The truth is I can live without her. But we choose not to. It is not an unhealthy drive out of a desperate neediness to be loved. It is a choice. We choose to want each other and to make life meaningful with each other. I suppose I could even say we choose to need each other. But that's different that neediness. Understanding this has actually made our relationship richer and more meaningful. It puts the power in our own hands rather than in the fickle arms of romance or passion.

Many churches teach that you cannot live without it. They can be very possessive. The old maxim, "No salvation outside the church" is beat into our brains to the point where we believe it. We are convinced we absolutely need the church and will perish without it. We are terrified of life without the church. But it's not true. It is a lie. Like leaving a bad relationship, sometimes it takes years to realize you are even better without it. You are healthier, happier, and more alive than ever before. And if you are still in a church, your relationship with it will be healthier if you realize that you don't need it, but choose to be in relationship with it. I hope your church feels the same way. That would be a happy relationship.

2. "You will never love again!" In other words, your ex would like you to believe that he or she is the one and only person who can satisfy your wants and needs. They want you to believe in the magical idea that you were made for each other, that you are soul mates, and that no one else in the entire world can give you the love you need.

Now, I have to admit, the idea of soul mate and made for each other and destiny all sound very appealing to me. Lisa and I fell in love as teenagers and have been together ever since. It sometimes feels like magic. But I'm not sure this is true. Lisa and I have talked about this a lot... like when we consider what she would do if I should die before her, and vice-versa. I tend to think I would never find another love like her. She says the same about me. But we both know, deep down, that we are clinging to an idea that may not be true. We agree that it is entirely possible that we could fall in love again. It wouldn't be the same. It would be different. But it would still be love. It would still be meaningful.

It's the same with many churches. They can be very jealous. Many churches like to believe and insist that they are the only ones, special, and that all others are superficial, fake, impostors, and mismatched. After many years in the church, I just came to realize that this wasn't true. It was a lie! I wanted to be a Christian, a church-goer and even a pastor because I chose to be. I chose this and its entire package above all others. To me, this was more honest and healthy.

Now, I realize that it is possible to love others and be loved by others outside of the church in different but just as meaningful ways.

3. "It's all your fault!" This is another lie your ex would like you to believe. Your falling out of love with each other and separating is all your fault! You have problems. You've got issues. You need help. This shouldn't have happened. But you made it happen. I'm totally fine, but you're definitely not. You wrecked this, and now you're going to suffer for it.

One of the issues I've been thinking a lot about lately is victimhood. I think many churches nurture a victim mentality in their members. In fact, as a pastor I harbored a victim mentality because I thought it was biblical and Christ-like. So I taught it! The *suffering servant* idea was deeply embedded into my psyche to the point where I think it became a part of my cellular makeup. The church attracts victims and nourishes a victim mentality. Please don't get me wrong... there are lots of real victims. I have been one and so have many of you. But I'm talking about a victim mentality that needs and welcomes being a victim. It's taken me years to break free of this unhealthy and unnecessary mentality. In fact, I'm still in progress.

I'm going to mention an awesome book. The most powerful

autobiography I've ever read or ever will read—*Life and Death in Shanghai*, by Nien Cheng. She was imprisoned in China for 6 years during the Cultural Revolution. If anyone was a victim, she was. If anyone didn't have a victim mentality, she didn't. You must read it. You will get a kick out of her feistiness that alarmed the prison guards. It was reading this book years ago that alerted me to the fact that I had a victim mentality and didn't have to. It's making more sense even now. Please read it!

So, no, you are not to blame! And if you are, so what? Who cares? If you broke up with your church, maybe it was because you did it as a bold act of self-care! Finally! This is good. I just want to encourage you that you are the captain of your life. You are the master of your destiny. Whether it is your fault or not, this is not the point. The point is: are you taking steps to take care of yourself? That's the point. No other. Something I've been telling myself lately: "Live your life. Don't let it live you."

I hope that you found this helpful. Because that's what I want to be: helpful. I'm sorry I've dropped the ball a few times. But after 2 years of running TLS, I think I'm finally learning how to do this.

We've made huge decisions with huger ramifications. I want to be here as a helper. I want to provide practical advice and support so that you can get through this successfully. I also appreciate the help you've given me. What goes around comes around. Thanks!

Remember: Life is full of richness. Love is everywhere. Take care of yourself.

HOW TO TALK TO A RELIGIOUS PERSON IF YOU MUST

This first thing to realize when talking with anyone is that it requires cross-cultural communication skills.

Let me tell you a story about something that happened to me yesterday:

I was taking my dog Abby for a walk. An old friend I hadn't seen in a while (let's call her Sue) was driving by and I waved. She stopped her car and rolled down her window and we talked for a minute. It was 10am Sunday morning. She was all dressed up and made up. So I said, "Heading to church?" "Yes" Sue said. I asked, "Where do you go?" She said, "So-and-so's church. Do you know him?" I said, "No, I haven't heard of him." More talk about his amazing church. There was a car approaching from behind, so she said, "Well, I gotta go." I said, "See you!" Sue replied, "Praise God!"

I thought about that conversation for the rest of my walk. I'm still thinking about it now. That was an exercise in cross-cultural communication.

Her language is very familiar to me. I have never spoken that way, but I have used some of the words, like "God" and "praise". But not so prolifically.

The thing is, not too long ago I would have been repulsed by this kind of speech. Maybe even repulsed by that kind of person. A few years ago I might not have even waved.

It's very strange to me that even though most people know about my serious theological, religious and ecclesiastical shift, they still talk to me as if nothing's changed. But everything's changed! My mind. My language. My life! It's like they refuse to admit that I am a different culture.

I've learned a lot. And one of the most important and practical things I've learned is that we all live in our own little micro-cultures with their own paradigms and languages.

Let me give you simple examples of how I do it:

"God" for me means the source of all that is. All that is. Reality as such. Sue might mean a benevolent, wise old man in the sky. But I understand when she says, "Praise God!" that there is reason for me to somehow trust that all is well, that even though I do not understand the mystery of all that is, I can rest in knowing it is for me and not against me. I can even trust that though I may not know what it is, there is meaning and purpose in life. There is no arguing with reality. There is no denying what is. In fact, the truth is what is. There's nothing truer than that. And nothing greater. It is the Great I Am.

What is important for me to remember when talking with Sue is that her language is an expression of her paradigm. Just like mine is. I'm not saying hers is wrong. I'm not saying mine is right. I'm just saying they are different. And it is so important for me to remember this when communicating with her. We are different cultures trying to talk.

Now, I do happen to think my paradigm and language is more helpful. But everybody thinks this way. We all believe what we believe because we believe it's true. That's why when you talk with your religious parents, they totally believe in their paradigm and assume you still do too because it is right, and, if you don't, then you are living in blindness and error. Simple as that.

So I will go ahead and say that I feel the way I think about it is healthier and more helpful because I think Sue's paradigm and language is narrow, exclusive, out of touch with reality, and less equipped to deal with it. On the other hand, I've me people with her worldview who are very kind, gentle, gracious and compassionate. Like Sue. But I do think at many points in reality her belief-system would fail.

These days I'm endeavoring to articulate a unifying theory that is open, all-inclusive, in touch with reality and fully equipped to deal with it. Even though I "see" it in my mind's eye and enjoy its benefits personally, I still need to write it down for the benefit of others.

So far, this is what I've got in a nutshell:

"God" is the infinite source of all that is; "Jesus" is materially all that is; and "spirit" is that which connects all that is.

For me, all religions, philosophies and world views can find their place in this trinitarian theory.

So when family, friends or acquaintances say things like, "Papa God, or Abba Father, or Daddy, or Higher Power, or brother Jesus, or Lord and Savior, or the Messiah, or Holy Ghost or Spirit", or whatever, I let the words fly past and keep the gist of what they're trying to communicate so that I can respond in a way that respects their culture while respecting mine.

And I do my best to communicate to them from my perspective without arrogance or fear, because that's what communication is.

WE MUST DISCARD THE CHURCH'S VICTIM MENTALITY

Today's letter is about a very sensitive topic: victim-mentality.

(*** So right from the beginning I want to assert that I know there are real victims in this world and even among our membership. I know what it is like to be victimized. I and my family! There have been times when we've been treated very unjustly, unfairly, with crass disregard and even cruelty. We have been victimized by the ill intent of others. Many of you know what I'm talking about.)

But what I want to talk about is when we take on a victim-mentality.

So, yes, I was victimized. And I had the right to be sad about it. To complain. To lament. I even had the right to feel sorry for myself. But at what point does this become not only pointless but unhealthy? Some might say right from the beginning. Others might say it's okay for a short season. Others might say never.

To make sure I'm not misunderstood, I'm going to share my story.

I think the church did a poor job of preparing me to be independent. The church often nurtures a victim-mentality. How?

The suffering servant motif: The symbol of the cross—the suffering servant idea and being like a lamb to the slaughter—was something I latched onto really early in my Christian life. And this idea stuck with me all through my ministry. It still lingers to this day. This idea is rather fatalistic in nature, accepting affliction as inevitable, desirable, and even deserved. Its logical end is that you should turn the other cheek always and never stand for yourself or fight back. In fact, any effort to change your situation is dishonorable.

Humiliation: The whole idea that many of us were raised on is that we are broken, sinners and always in need of a savior. We are always weak and in need of serious help and constant rescue. That we should become completely dependent on God so that we have no will, power or voice is taught by many spiritual leaders to be the most perfect way. We are just a tool in God's shed for him to use when he wills. In fact, independence is considered rebellious. So the "poor me" attitude is actually an effective way for the church to keep you humiliated before God, the pastor and the church.

Helplessness: Because suffering, servitude and submission carry such currency in the church, the church feels no need to, and in fact feels prohibited from, providing tools for us to become spiritually independent and strong. The whole "more than conquerors" idea is solely for the purpose of controlling our sinful nature, not for the purpose of us living confidently in all areas of our lives. But the church not only doesn't provide us with tools, but in my observation it doesn't have any. It could, but it doesn't. Not all, but I dare say most. We are to be and remain helpless. The church assists us in this regard.

Let me be more personal and specific. For me, this applies to my attitude towards money, marketing, business and success. I don't mind when others succeed and make money, but for me it is a complex moral issue.

I've never been good at making money and I've always struggled. For the many years I served as a pastor, I never saw any raise in my income. I was a victim of church miserliness, but I let it sink into my own damaged feelings about myself to the point where I actually felt I never deserved more. I was a suffering servant, and proud of it, though resentfully so.

My dependence on God never ever panned out. Forsaking all methods of making more money as a compromise of godliness, I consigned myself to a victim-mentality that actually translated itself into a poverty-mentality. I never asked for more and the church was always happy to comply with my servitude attitude. My sense of helplessness and the church's appreciation of it was a perfect working relationship that kept me victimized and the church unchallenged. The end result was me leaving the ministry filing for personal bankruptcy, the ramifications of which I still experience.

When I left the ministry I felt a personal challenge to cast off this victim- and poverty-mentality and to learn business, marketing, as well as develop a healthy respect and appreciation for money. It's been the hardest school I've ever been to because it's not just about learning skills, but about overcoming deep-seated, unhealthy attitudes about myself that are so embedded that they're taking me years to discover, expose and extricate.

So now I'm determined to stop saying inside my head, "Poor me!"
I've also decided that I am responsible for my life. I say, "I am independent! I can take care of this!"
I also say, "I am not helpless. I can help myself. I can change my life. And I will help others by providing them with tools that will help them develop skills to realize their own independence."

As Nelson Mandela's Invictus says, "I am the master of my fate and the captain of my destiny." This is not necessarily a rejection of God. For me it is a bold declaration to fully participate in one's life rather than surrender it to fate, to circumstances, or to the will of another.

You have the power!
You have the right to change your life!
You can be independent!

THE PROBLEM'S NOT RELIGION

I think this letter is going to be short and to the point. I'm writing this for me. I hope it helps you too, if you need it. I've been thinking about this a lot.

If I could summarize why I left the ministry and the church as I did in just one word, what would it be?

Exclusivity!

That's why I left all that behind. Because it was exclusive.

In what ways?

Exclusivity of thought: I like thinking outside of the box. Not just for the heck of it but because I want to understand. I want to be wise. When God told Solomon he would give him the one thing in all the world that he wanted, he said, "wisdom". Because God was so pleased, he granted him everything else as well. So from a very early age I wanted to be wise. Unfortunately, the church I experienced was exclusive in its thinking, very narrow, constricted, and confining. Limited. As a result, when I did cross intellectual or theological boundaries, I was disciplined and punished for it. Corrected. Rebuked. My experience of this exclusivity of thought was not only local but global. I noticed that generally speaking, the church teaches its blend of orthodoxy and demands that you believe likewise.

Exclusivity of lifestyle: I love diversity and I always have. My experience and observations of Christianity have lead me to conclude that it has a very certain idea of what our lives should look like, and if our lives differ in any way from that norm, then we are trespassing. Sinning. It used to be things like drinking, smoking dancing, movies, and things like that. And it was also things like dirty jokes, swearing, pot, and things like that. And it was also things like sexual orientation, church attendance, premarital sex, and things like that. It seemed to me that no matter what kind of differences emerged in the lives of its membership, it was always moving the goal post to make it more and more difficult to belong. U2 calls Christians who are included the "squeaky cleans". I wasn't one of them. I was excluded.

Exclusivity of membership: The result of all this is that in order to belong you have to be a very certain type of person. You have to fit the mold. I never fit the mold. Never. I always had a hard time belonging. People always had difficulty figuring out where to slot me. Where to put me. I was always an enigma wrapped up in an anomaly. I was absolutely terrified on the eve of my ordination. I couldn't understand why then, but now I think I intuited that I was walking into a trap that I would not come out of until 25 years later. My whole ministry in the church was tumultuous. In an effort to be free and free others, I was what many people considered a "shit disturber". In fact, just this weekend a friend told me that's what I have always been. Finally realizing that my struggle with the church's exclusivity of membership was futile, I left. Now that I've left, I want to be very careful not to enter into those very same attitudes again. Why would I want to leave the exclusivity of the church to enter another brand of exclusivity elsewhere? Why would I just jump from one exclusive tribe into another exclusive one?

Therefore…
I am careful not to feel I know better than anyone else.
I am careful not to feel I am better than anyone else.
I am careful not to feel I am in a better tribe than anyone else.

In other words, it's not Christianity or the church that is the problem. It's not atheism or agnosticism. It's not Islam or Buddhism or Hinduism or New Age. Rather, it's the attitude that these systems foster. The system of Christianity and the church, like all systems, encourages exclusivity.

Exclusivity is the problem. That we're special.

Thinking that we are the right. The best. The preferable. I refuse to embrace that value. I always have. I always will.

HOW BELIEF CAN PREVENT CHANGE

Today I want to talk about belief. Specifically, I want to talk about how belief can be the biggest barrier to change.

I realize that many of us are still believers or agnostic or atheists. So I want to be sensitive to that.

Therefore, I'm going to share my own story. I want to talk about this through the prism of my own experience and personal insight.

To me: I've come to the conclusion that belief actually prevents change! I suggest this is true for many others as well.

Let me explain:
For the most part, I always seemed to find myself mentored by strong, bible-believing mentors and churches. So I suppose it was no accident that I went into the study of the bible, theology, and eventually the ministry. I made sure I studied under one of the most highly respected Old and New Testament scholars like Stuart, Kaiser, Scholer and Fee. I studied years of Greek, Hebrew, and Aramaic and dived into the deep end of Reformed Theology with the likes of Calvin and Barth. Even to this day I am fascinated with theology. I just recently ordered a book about Hurs Von Balthasar and Karl Barth. The Bible, theology and belief... these have been unbelievably strong forces in my life, especially in my intellectual and spiritual life.

But I also began noticing early on that there was another mind competing with this theological mind. Within me, I had struggling against each other a believing mind and an inquisitive mind. Conveniently, the church taught me that this struggle was between the carnal mind and the spiritual mind, the mind of the flesh and the mind of the spirit. It taught me that my temptation would always be to lean on my own understanding rather than to trust in God. It lectured me in how to listen to the Lord who is the Light rather than to Satan who disguises himself as an angel of light... something that sounds true but is actually counterfeit.

I noticed this alternative thinking bouncing against the walls of my belief system. Because, as we all know, it is belief that not only provides the foundation of our thought, but the walls and roof as well. My alternative thinking, my curiosity, my inquisitiveness, even sometimes my common sense, was bouncing, bouncing, bouncing off the hard solid walls of belief and continually falling back on itself in its padded room.

How I was taught to deal with it was by confessing, repenting, and seeking forgiveness, and making my belief stronger.

But what was actually happening was that the continuous assault of my alternative thinking against the walls of belief was slowly but surely expanding the walls of my belief.

They were stretching. Like elastic. They were getting pushed out. My belief was growing as much as it could to accommodate my alternative thinking until it sometimes felt like it was going to snap.

Once in a while, though, an alternative thought was too strong for the walls of belief to resist, and it would break out and separate itself from my intellectual house of belief. What was I supposed to do with that? Nothing. I called it an anomaly. A mystery. I tried to comfort myself by saying that even though I didn't understand then, one day I would, and it would get integrated back into my belief system. These thoughts were like prodigal sons, rebellious and careless, but one day would come to their senses and return to the father's house of belief.

This is the only way I could let this process happen and keep a clear conscience.

The very peace it promised eluded me.

Is it possible, I asked myself, that belief is keeping in fear and keeping out peace?

Then something traumatic happened. In 2010, I had a dream one night that exposed my intellectual house of belief for what it was: an illusion. It was completely false. A fabrication. A facade. This isn't to say that everything about it was false, but the system, the structure, the ideology as a whole, was limiting, oppressive, an expression of fear, and a block to my mind's renewal. It was preventing me from changing!

Belief was actually dividing my mind rather than unifying it. It was causing a fissure in my thinking that was causing a fissure in my perception of what is. It was causing strife in my mind, my heart, and my world.

When I woke up that morning from my dream, the need for belief was gone. Its life line was severed and it bled out before my feet hit the floor.

Now there is an awareness. Just an awareness. An awareness of what is. A love for what is. There is no belief and then also knowledge. Now there is just a knowing. A knowing that is more like a loving. A loving of all that is.

And the peace I sought is there. It just is.

Try it!
If you are an *atheist* then do you have anything to fear?
If you are an *agnostic* then isn't the risk is worth it?
If you are a *believer* then wouldn't God desire this for you?

Especially if it means meeting the most holy in the what is?

THE ONE THING THAT WILL KILL A MARRIAGE

One of the areas of our life most affected when we go through major spiritual change is our relationships.

Fellow workers, employers, family, friends and even enemies, significant others, and partners or spouses.

So today's letter is about our romantic relationships or marriages.

I've shared this with you before, but one of the most precious things I nearly lost during my time of deconstruction, changing my theology, leaving the ministry and the church, was my marriage to Lisa. We have made it and are better now than ever. But if we didn't have some marriage knowledge and tools, we might not have survived the traumatic shifts we were experiencing.

(*** *disclaimer:* This isn't to say that I believe all marriages should stick together. Sometimes separation and divorce is the healthiest thing for one or both of the partners. I just wanted to put that out there that I don't assume because you are married that you should always be or that if you have experienced divorce that somehow you failed.)

One of the books I've always fallen back on and always recommend for marriages is David Schnark's, *Passionate Marriage*. I'm glad I have that book and had read it.

But there's more!

Some years ago, after reading about it in Malcolm Gladwell's book Blink, I read John Gottman's book *The Seven Principals for Making Marriage Work*. Even though he gives seven principals, he says there is one major one that makes or breaks a relationship. Gottman can listen to a couple for five minutes and determine with 91% accuracy whether the couple will divorce or not.

Do you want to know what the key ingredient is?

First, let me tell you about Gottman's "Four Horsemen" that will split up a marriage. They are:

Criticism: where you attack the person, not just their behavior.
Contempt: name-calling, eye-rolling, sneering, mockery and hostile humor.
Defensiveness: blaming the other for all the problems.

Stonewalling: where you disengage, stall, deny, or ignore problems.

But the one thing that will split up a marriage faster than anything is #2, contempt. If Gottman detects this in the first five minutes of a session with a married couple, that helps him determine if they're going to make it or not. If one of the partners conveys disgust about their spouse, it is virtually impossible to resolve any problems. This, he claims, is the deadliest poison to a marriage.

I believe he's right. I've seen it myself after years of giving marriage counseling!

The fact is, this is the deadliest poison to any relationship. I see it online all the time. Many times every day. If someone expresses disdain, disgust or contempt for another person, it is absolutely impossible to have a mature and fruitful conversation. It's just not going to happen. The truth is, it pollutes the whole thread and turns everybody off until everyone eventually leaves. I witness this far too often.

One of the most difficult things to do in a marriage relationship is to allow the other to grow at his or her own pace while they let you grow at yours. When Lisa and I were in the ministry and in the church, we were pretty much on the same page. In 2010, after I had my waterfalls dream and started developing what I temporarily call "The Z-Theory", plus started experiencing difficulties staying in the ministry, we could feel the bonds between us starting to stretch.

It got to the point where we sometimes felt we were not only no longer on the same page, but no longer in the same book. But time… four or five years in fact… has taught us that indeed we were in the same story. Ours! Our different spiritual journeys have shown us that we can grow together not only in depth but in breadth as well. We have widened the skirts of our tent and assumed even more under our roof.

Our relationship, our marriage, is richer for it.

Fortunately, we avoided the biggest pitfall... contempt. Somehow we maintained our mutual respect for one another, even though we may have been completely mystified by and irritated with one another at times.

I entrusted her to her own journey. She entrusted me to mine. We trusted that we would eventually feel like we were sharing the same story.

It worked.

So I guess you need to ask yourself:

"Do I have contempt for my spouse?"
"Does he or she have contempt for me?"
"What am I going to do about it?"

Anyway, I sure hope this helps guys! I know it would have helped me when I needed it most.

MOVING ON BY MOVING THROUGH

I have difficulty with these two extremes:

1. wallowing in misery
2. floating in fantasy

That is... we can get stuck in our own suffering and even become attached to it. The world becomes a very dark and nasty place, and we become its helpless victims from which there is no escape. I've seen this in myself. I now recognize it. I don't like it. I don't want to get stuck in that again.

Or we can adopt some of the popular ideas that float around that there really isn't any suffering, that it is all an illusion in our minds, and that if we just think right, that there's nothing wrong, then we can be eternally and blissfully happy if we can just tap into this secret, positive energy.

I don't believe either. One is just as bad as the other.
One is fatalistic
The other is denial.

They are both an escape from reality and responsibility.

In the first case, there is good and life can be trusted and maybe enjoyed.

In the second case, there is evil and we may make life better.

One of the things I did while I was a pastor in the last church was to see if, when we are given space to move through our pain and suffering, we can successfully move on.

That was my experiment. And it worked. I watched many people process their pain to move on to their gain. They moved on by moving through. Some took days. Some took weeks. Some took months. Some took years. Different inflictions and afflictions. Different intensities of pain.

Different pain thresholds. All in their own speed, at their own pace, in their own time. It worked.

I watched lots of people move on from pain through process to peace. What made it really interesting and even life-giving and fun was that we had a mixture of all three in the community:

Those in pain, those processing, and those who'd come to a place of peace. And, of course, no one stays in any one place all the time. Not if they're growing. And also, of course, we can learn to work through these stages quicker. We learn from ourselves and others. That's what made it so rich.

This is what I've modeled The Lasting Supper after. You'd think everybody would've loved this. But no, most didn't.

Let me clarify: those who were trying to process their pain appreciated the space. Those looking on criticized it.

Most people, I've discovered, don't like being with people in pain.
Most people, I've discovered, are afraid of sitting with people who are processing confusion and pain.
Most people, I've discovered, are annoyed or intimidated by those who've arrived at a place of peace.

I guess not only misery loves company. So I just want to encourage us all to embrace our journeys.

Embrace the pain.
Embrace the process.
Embrace the peace when it presents itself to you.

That's what we're here for.

I WOULDN'T BE WHO I AM IF I WASN'T WHO I WAS

Good morning my friends. At least it is morning to me.

I was just outside to watch a flock of geese fly overhead. It was beautiful and melancholic at the same time. Winter's coming.

I've been thinking all week about what I'm going to write about today. That is...

I wouldn't be who I am if I wasn't who I was.

What do I mean by that?

I grew up in a religious home. Spiritually aware. Christian. We didn't go to church regularly when I was younger. But in my teens we became regulars who became very involved in the church. I was a keener. I read a lot. Helped a lot. Lead a lot. I went to Bible College, seminary, and another seminary. Got ordained. Pastored for about 30 years. I was in deep.

I'm very different than I was, though. My thinking has changed. My life has changed. So when I look back on my life, I feel a mixture of emotions and have a variety of thoughts.

Like these:

Seeing the weeds: There have been a lot of things in my life that I look back on with embarrassment and dismay. I can't believe I believed or did those things. Some of the weeds I planted. Some of them were by others who snuck in at night and planted them. In either case, they are just weeds that I notice, uproot if I can, or ignore if I want. No big deal. I just don't let them take over.

Loving the wheat: There have also been a lot of things in my life that I look back on with pride and pleasure. I actually thought and did some things really well. There are really valuable things in my life that have been there from the beginning. My truest self. My core. My essential being. I'm going to appreciate that. I'm going to love that.

Embracing the field: I've come to the conclusion that it is neither the wheat nor the weeds that I should focus on but the field. I mean the totality of my life. My life is the field. It's gone through a lot of transformations. But it is a good field, rich with its history of ownership, invasions, care, plantings and harvests, removal of stones and stumps, with tons of manure folded in. It's a very good field.

I guess what I'm trying to say is that I don't throw out my earlier self. I don't mistreat him. I don't hate him. I don't reject him. What I see is a boy who wanted to know, understand, and be spiritually wise and helpful. Helpful not only to the church but to all people. All the weeds and wheat are just a part of my history. My story.

It took me my entire life up until now to make this field, me, a good field, where many could enjoy the harvest. I know there are still weeds in my life. I also know there is wheat.

But I'm confident that it will only get better and better for me and for others. Ten years from now I will look back on now and embrace it just like I do my earlier life and self.

In a word, it's all good. All good.

So are you! Your life. Your field! It's all good.

WHY YOU FEEL LIKE YOU LEFT A CULT

I'm becoming increasingly aware that even though I wasn't in a cult, I feel like I'm learning how live beyond leaving one.
Do you know what I mean?

Most of us know the signs of a cult:

one charismatic leader
very strong herd mentality
uses of guilt and shame to pressure you to conform
insists that this community is the right or best one
claims of special knowledge
independent thought is discouraged
elevates the community and its leader above relationships
demands to invest time and money in order to reach the next goal
it is or feels impossible to leave

So, even though I could say that all those signs could apply to some degree or another in my Christian journey, I still say I was never a part of a cult.

But is that really true? This is a question I'm asking myself lately.

Because if all the signs are there, then why wasn't it a cult?
Pile on top of the signs of a cult the advice given on how to leave a cult, and it only makes me question even more.

Here are the steps suggested for leaving a cult:

recognize that you're in an abusive religious group
list the reasons why you want to leave the group
plan your departure
have a place to stay in advance
leave
be prepared for judgment and attempts to get you back
remain strong in your convictions
seek support from other people
continue journeying

Well now! These also apply to my life! What does this mean?

If the signs that I was in a cult and the ways to leave a cult both apply, then was I in a cult or not?

For me, it means admitting that the Christianity I found myself in embraced cult-like values with its members.

Here's a clue: a lot of the sites devoted to listing the signs of a cult share the same characteristics as the cults they are warning us against!

I conclude that my desire and willingness to submit found a perfect home in the church. I did it because I wanted to be mentored into a wise and holy human being. Instead, I became its slave to meet its own ends.

Any religion, any group, any relationship, any job… anything… can possess cult-like qualities! That's my claim. Remember the movie The Firm? It clearly had cult-like qualities, and Abby began getting clues that it was when she was told, "The Firm encourages children", even exercising dominion over her reproductive rights.

I suppose I'm telling you this because sometimes one of you will remark on how long it is taking to get over changing your beliefs, leaving the church, or even rejecting your inherited beliefs. You're finding it more difficult than you imagined it would be. It's taking longer than you thought. You are feeling afraid of the unpredictable and unpleasant emotions you're feeling as you try to move on.

Now maybe we know why: leaving a cult can take a long time to process. But you're doing it! Be patient with yourself. One day you will not only know you are free, but you will feel it!
Oh, the memories and the wounds will still linger, but as a fading badge from an ancient war. I know this because I'm seeing this happen with so many of you.

And it's wonderful to watch.

YOU, YOUR RELIGION, AND RELEASING THE MUTUAL GRIP

I want to talk today about how to let the mutual grip you and the church, or religion, have on one another.

Your Grip on Religion: It's one thing to let go of the grip you have on religion. Many of you have done it and have done it well. You've released some beliefs and some practices. I'm not saying this should be done and that these beliefs or practices are wrong. I'm just talking about how we may loosen our grip on them.

Some of the beliefs that you've released your grip on could be things like the belief in hell, the atonement, the divinity of Jesus, miraculous healing, the infallibility of scripture, the necessity of the church, the existence of God, etcetera.
Some of the practices you've released your grip on are things like reading your bible every day, going to church, paying offerings or tithes, being accountable to a pastor, prayer, special services, serving in some voluntary capacity, restricting your reading and the arts to the religious genre, etcetera.

Even though this can be difficult, it can be done. Sometimes it's just a matter of time. Sometimes it happens through concentration and courageous thinking. But it's not all that difficult a process if we want to do it.

Religion's Grip on You: Now, this is the hard part. It's easy to let go of something. It's another thing to get that something to let go of you. Many of you are struggling with this. It is so difficult to get free of religion's grip on you. Perhaps, specifically, it seems impossible to get free from the church's grip on you. I'm talking about things like fear, guilt and shame.
So, even though you've let go of the concept of hell, why do you still fear going there? If you've given up on going to church, why do you still feel guilty for not attending? If you've failed in a relationship, why do you still feel shame for being single? These are just examples.

I've thought about this a lot, because I'm fascinated by the fact that even though we can, for example, leave the church, we can still allow it to have control over our lives. Even though you've said, "No more!" to the church you left, you still feel its terrifying grip on your heart and mind.

It's like a friend who dropped too much acid and sometimes slips into a trip.
Or the vet who still crumbles at the sound of a gun.
Or a child who cringes when an adult moves his hand swiftly.

I've found there are ways to get free from this death grip:

Talk about it with someone, hopefully a pro, and process it.
Dissect and empty the fear, shame and guilt of its guts until it no longer lives.

Hang out with other survivors to let the healing rub off on one another.
Be patient until a different and better reality dominates.
Trust yourself and trust what is. This is good. Trust this.

I'll share a personal example:

My theology and practice has radically changed from five years ago. I am very much at peace with where I am. In fact, I've never felt this much theological peace my entire life. I relish it. However, every once in a while, usually at night, a silent, dark tide of fear rises over me and attempts to drown me. It used to take a little while to loose its hoary fingers from my mind. But now when it happens I recognize it for what it is...

an irrational fear...
an ancient residue...
a delicate scar...
a distant memory...
a phantom echo...

... and this helps to let it go just as quickly as it came.

I can't tell you guys how much I admire your courage, your determination, and your success in achieving a healthy spiritual independence. Look how far you've come in just a week, a month, a year, two years!

Bravo! Keep going. We've just scratched the surface.

THREE OBSERVATIONS FROM SPEAKING AT A CHURCH

I spoke at a very liberal church today.

I made a few observations this morning that I want to share with you.

We're all human: I'm always a little nervous going into a context where you are going to speak to people who may be on totally different pages.

A couple of weeks ago I spoke in a university's philosophy class. I was told there were going to be believers there, including Baptist missionaries on furlough, atheists, agnostics, devout Catholics, and others. How do you talk about spirituality in a way that engages all of them without alienating any of them?

Same with today. This church is very liberal in its theology. They encourage each member to pursue their own spirituality. They are a very diverse group. How was I going to speak about what I'm passionate about?

But in both cases, the philosophy class and the church, I had them laughing, tearing up, asking questions, and following along with what I was talking about. It made me relax and realize that basically people want to laugh, want to be curious, and want to be heard. Our commonality is simply being human.

Certain believers are evangelists: I say certain with double entendre, meaning "some" as well as "those who are certain". Not all believers are like this.

After I spoke sweet, older woman came up to Lisa and me and thanked us for coming. She said she would be praying for us. She continued saying something like, "I say 'prayers' because I don't know how else to say it. I don't even know what I'm praying or to whom I'm praying if anyone at all. I just want you to know that... well... I'm... you know..." Lisa and I knew exactly what she meant and warmly thanked her.

I found this very interesting because another man was there, a very nice man, who was obviously a believer. I say obviously because he let everyone know it as often as he could. He made it clear he believed in God and in Jesus. He kept saying, "You better hope you're right and I'm wrong, because the consequences will be severe if you aren't!" in a kind of ribbing way. I just laughed because I'd heard it all before. The others in the room would just chuckle or ignore what he was saying. He was obviously out of sync with most of us there, but they somehow had patience for him.

Uncertainty often stimulates a humble silence and respect, whereas certainty often stimulates the opposite.

No community is immune: Once in a while someone will comment on my cartoons or posts by saying that this kind of abuse, this kind of idiocy, this kind of silliness, this kind of error, or this kind of whatever, only takes place in more conservative churches, or evangelical ones, or protestant ones, or charismatic ones, or Catholic ones, etcetera. I try to help them realize that it doesn't matter what kind of community it is, none of them are immune to abuse or idiocy or silliness or error.

I believe the gravitational pull of all organizations or communities is towards the dehumanization of people. If we are not diligent at every moment, manipulation, coercion and even abuse will slip into our relationships. We have to be constantly careful. Because where there are people, there will be forces at work to dehumanize them. I'm not being a pessimist but a realist. In fact, we can be optimistically diligent in resisting these dehumanizing powers, believing that we will indeed overcome!

The same happened at this very liberal and progressive congregation. Mistakes were made, misunderstandings developed, conflicts arose, and divisions occurred. Because there are people there.

This is why I am so diligently involved with TLS. I thoroughly believe that if left unattended, TLS could derail into an unhealthy community. This isn't to criticize any certain person. It's not about a person or people but the collectivity. It has more to do with powers that systems generate. This is what Paul meant when he said that we don't wrestle against flesh and blood but against principalities and powers. This is something that prophetic people like Walter Brueggemann, Walter Wink, and William Stringfellow have written about. Good people can gather with the greatest of intentions, but as soon as a system develops, systemic evil will constantly try to find a way to slither in and destroy the fellowship and the human spirit.

On my way out, someone said, "Thanks again. We really enjoyed it!"

And I responded, mistake or not, with, "Any time! I did too!"

We'll see.

REFRAMING YOUR STORY SO YOU CAN HEAL

I am so thankful for all of you. I'm feeling especially thankful today because I am seeing how much you guys care for each other. You affirm, encourage and support one another in amazing ways. I feel appreciative because I'm the recipient of your care as well. It feels good. Very good.

I've been doing some studying on PTSD. They are making incredible advances in that field. One of the things that they are trying to do is help those who suffer from PTSD to reframe their stories so they are no longer a victim but a hero.

Let me explain.

Our bodies react in different ways to trauma.

If our body shuts down in the face of trauma, it can leave us wondering why we didn't do something more to protect ourselves. Even our loved ones might ask why we didn't fight back.

This can lead to feelings of helplessness, failure and even shame.

As a result, this can get in the way of healing.

I watched a video where a therapist talks about how important it is to reframe the story in a way that affirms you rather than shames you. He encourages sufferers to reclaim what happened to them and to reinterpret their response as the only adequate response they had at the time. It was a mechanism their body used to keep them alive. So rather than being a weak response that they need to be ashamed of, it's a strong response they can embrace.

MY DOG DIED: REFLECTIONS

On Friday Abby died. I was out when Lisa called me on my cell and said Abby was actively dying. I rushed home. Abby was lying on a pillow on the floor. Lisa and Casile were with her there. I got down too. Eventually Jesse came home and joined us. Joshua was in another city at the time. She had stopped blinking her eyes and was breathing irregularly. We just lay with her and stroked her and spoke softly and lovingly to her. After about an hour she breathed her last little breath. Lisa got her stethoscope and put it to Abby's chest. Nothing. She was gone. We cried. We are still crying.

I'm surprised by my reaction. I really underestimated the impact her leaving us would have. The grief I am feeling is enormous. She was like our child. I had obviously taken this for granted. There was no expectation that her death would devastate me so much.

So I've been thinking about it a lot. I would like to share a few reflections:

Creation: There is a hollowness in my life after Abby died. There is a vacancy, an empty space, a loneliness. I considered how in the Christian religious story God desired companionship and so created man. Then man desired companionship so God created woman. Then Adam and Eve desired companionship so they created children. When faced with and experiencing death, I saw how we could be tempted to interpret history to make sense of our emptiness and loneliness. Of course if there were a God he would want to make us in order not to be lonely! Space abhors a vacuum. So do we. So must God.

Soul: What a strange feeling when I picked up Abby after she died. Whenever I picked her up before, she was always full of life and energy. There was personality plus! But when I picked her up to take her away, there was absolutely no life. Completely limp. This is the most graphic memory I take from that sad day. Whatever was there before was now gone. There was something here, but now not here. I can see how we would come to this conclusion. I could feel it in my arms. I can see how we would like to call it soul or spirit.

Eternal Life: Where did Abby go? Where did her "Abby-ness" go? What happened to her energy, her life? How can this little ball of endless energy, joy and unconditional love suddenly end? Is it really possible for anything to really end? Doesn't that create a black hole? I can see how fear, the fear of the unchallengeable power of death, might motivate me to say there has to be life after this. Or perhaps curiosity would lead me to ask if it's all just biology. Energy doesn't just stop, does it? It transforms or spreads or creates something, doesn't it? Or perhaps magical thinking might want me to conclude that there must be another place… let's call it heaven. I cannot prove anything. I can only surmise.

I have no problem considering that our religion is our own complete, delicate, and sometimes majestically beautiful construction.

I also have no problem considering that our religion is not an end in itself, but behaves like a sign pointing to the irreducible mystery that we find ourselves in.

You guys are amazing, and I love you and thank you for the support you've shown me through my own struggles.

THREE STEPS TO CHANGING YOUR BELIEFS

We are changing our beliefs!

What I have always tried to do is provide a safe space to do that in. And, if possible, gather people together in order to support one another while going through this experience. I think this is what The Lasting Supper is mostly about. We are a hotbed, a petri dish, an experiment, of theological transitioning and belief-changing. It's a place where we achieve spiritual independence.

It's difficult to change our beliefs. But on the other hand, it's easy. If we just follow these three basic steps, it will happen. In fact, I believe that if we apply the right effort, we will come to a place where our minds are finally at rest. That's a promise!

Here are the three steps to changing our beliefs:

Question Its Credulity: Unfortunately, for many people this first step isn't even allowed and therefore never contemplated. To even question a deeply embedded idea is anathema, rebellious, heretical, and therefore punishable. But this is always the first step. This isn't the end, but it certainly is the beginning. You have to be able to get to a place where you can ask yourself, "Is this really true?" This first step starts the unstoppable process.

Consider Other Possibilities: In other words, what will replace the unhealthy, unnecessary and erroneous belief that was there before? This doesn't mean that we replace, say, resurrection with reincarnation. Rather, we replace resurrection with questions such as, "What could this have meant?" "Why was this important?" "Does this point to a deeper truth?" "Why would someone or something want me to believe this?" "What would it mean to me if I let this belief go?"

Wait for Truth: This is the hardest part. This is exactly where many people either give up to retreat back into comfortable beliefs or leap over into other ones that are just as unhealthy, unnecessary or erroneous. Waiting for truth to come with its attending peace is sometimes a long and arduous test of patience. But I assure you that if you wait long enough and trust in love to reveal itself, a deep and abiding truth will slip in and overthrow your fears. And the truth is not just another informational fact. Rather, it's love and peace that transcends intellectual formulations. It's the mind finally at rest. It does come!

Many things I used to believe have drifted away.

On the one hand, intellectually there is a deep and abiding peace. On the other hand, there is, I'll admit, the emotional residue of fear that I'm wrong and will pay for it eternally. This takes a while to depart. It's like the echo that resounds long after the originating sound is gone. But when I remember that perfect love casts out fear, that residue eventually loses its power over me, no longer crippling me in my own growth.

HOW POETRY CAN HELP YOU SURVIVE

I've been thinking a lot about poetry lately.

Why poetry? One writer has said poetry is important because we can "say what needs to be said in a direct, powerful and beautiful way".

Which is how I really want my life to be right now: direct, powerful, and beautiful.

I no longer want to waste time skirting issues or shrinking back from a just cause.

I no longer want to invest in fear, cowardliness and playing the victim.

I no longer want to invest in what is ugly, inhumane and deadly. Direct. Powerful. Beautiful.

Poetry, for me, as do good song lyrics, these have a way of pulling me down into a deeper and more honest connection with myself and with mystery and wonder. Words that are direct, powerful, and beautiful liberate me from silly, cruel and false attempts to control me, my mind, my heart.

My thoughts have been turning to one of my favorite writers, poets and speakers, David Whyte. I read his book *Crossing the Unknown Sea: Work as a Pilgrimage of Identity* during a pivotal point in my life. Years ago he decided to leave the corporate world to risk living as a full-time poet. He's doing it. His words helped me muster the courage it took to make bold moves for my personal health and happiness.

I used to read and write poetry. Then I stopped. I'm picking it up again. Because it takes me deeper.

One of my paintings was used for a cover of a book of poetry, *Frozen Latitudes*, by Thérése Halscheid. They paid me properly, but they also sent me 5 copies of the book.

Here's one of the reviews from the back of the book:

"In *Frozen Latitudes*, Thérése Halscheid welcomes the lucky reader into a world of deep love, familial illness, and the dual human urges to speak and be heard. The narrator takes a look at 'how it really looked long ago' and how 'lips, bright as scars, are parting open with words so the great air can take them.' The settings of these exquisite poems range from a childhood home colored by a father's dementia to the northern interior of Alaska with its stories from The Real People in which each word is 'a language of light.' These are moving, masterful poems in a brilliantly cohesive collection."

I found myself in tears as I read her beautiful poetry.

Direct. Powerful. Beautiful.

I will share a poem I wrote in 1986 to God when I began noticing God's absence and silence:

I Have a Room

I have a room
full of obsolete dictionaries
about you
I used to delight
in reading
… but…
you evade periods
duck behind question marks
jump from parenthesis
and applaud continuations.
You're the greatest satirist of all time
breaking pens
hugging fat pencils
caressing erasers
wasting paper.
I picture you laughing

at my picture of you
laughing.
How dare you dare me
to 'etcetera' and 'so on',
to erase 'in conclusion'
and burn my head.

IT'S YOUR LIFE AND YOU ARE THE BUILDER OF IT

In 2002, in New Hampshire, I was fired from an international ministry for insubordination. I refused to participate in an enforced repentance that the leader demanded in order to cleanse the "sin in the house" that was adversely affecting book sales.

That suddenly left me illegally living in the USA, being unemployed. I received no severance. We had no money. Lisa and the children piled into our van and fled back to Canada to the church community and friends we'd just left six months earlier. I stayed in New Hampshire to dump our newly acquired house, van and belongings as quickly as I could. Within a couple of months, I accomplished the cleanup and returned to Canada.

Fortunately, we had some funds we'd earned from the sale of the house. With that money I made a down-payment on our home here where we now live. That also gave me enough capital and collateral to buy a dump of a house just down the road. Since I was still unemployed, I thought I would buy this downtrodden house, fix it up, and flip it. I did, and it sold about a year later.

Why am I telling you this story?

Because the dump of a house I bought was unbelievable. I bought it for $50,000. It sat on a huge piece of land. I got a surveyor in and had it measured and discovered it was legally large enough to split into two lots. I did that and sold the other lot for about $25,000. With that and a line of credit, I fixed up the house. Little did I realize the extent of work had to be done. I didn't lose money, but I didn't make any profit either. It did provide income for that year though.

I ended up selling a lovely home to a single woman.

When I started renovating the house, I thought I would mainly have to do cosmetic repair. No. When I took the paneling off the walls, I discovered the insides full of rat, squirrel, and mouse nests. The roof leaked. The basement was full of rot. The plumbing was rusted out. The wiring would not pass code. I emptied the house of all the previous owners' junk and began stripping the house down. And down. And down. And down. Eventually, all I had left was the bare skeleton. I was filthy, sore, and exhausted.

I had an ethical choice to make:

I could do the cosmetic work and flip it quickly. For some reason, I just couldn't. The house has a great view of the river, and I imagined a beautiful open concept home with hardwood floors, cathedral ceilings, and contemporary accents with large windows and sliding doors spanning the front of the house out onto a wrap-around deck.

I couldn't betray my imagination!

So I spent an entire year building the physical manifestation of what I imagined. And I created exactly what I pictured. Beautiful!

This is exactly the same with creating our own spiritual life:

The deconstruction will be overwhelming, time-consuming, painful and exhausting. The reconstruction will be costly, time-consuming and hard work.
The results can be glorious!

I encourage you to imagine what you want!

Who are you?
What inner life suits you best?

What kind of life do you want to live in?

What do you imagine a good, wholesome and fulfilling life looks like?

These are fair questions that maybe you haven't been allowed to ask before. Or maybe you haven't even allowed yourself to ask yourself these questions yet. But they are yours to ask because it is your life and you are the builder of it.

YOU MAKE ME WANT TO BE A BETTER MAN

I want to talk with you about my friends for a moment. I want to tell you about them.

My friends let me be me. They love me. Me as I am, not as I should be or not how they think I ought to be. They love me just as I am. I am free to be me without fear of censor or censure from them. I don't always have to be second-guessing around them. I can live unedited. How I love this!

My friends actually care for me without a hidden agenda. They do not carry ulterior motives behind their words and actions. They relate to me simply. Openly. Without any shadow. They are simply them. What I see is what I get. There's no wondering if there's an iron fist inside their velvet glove.

My friends inspire me to be a better person. Just being around them makes me realize that it is possible to live freely and to encourage others to be free around me as well. They feel things, think things, say things, and do things that amaze me for their openness, generosity, honesty, authenticity, rawness, and loveliness.

Would you like to meet my friends?

Well, I'm talking about you guys at The Lasting Supper. Every day I delight in the amazing capacity of you guys to expand my mind, my heart, and my world. You make me feel more positive and trusting and hopeful.

You also, and this is key, bring a great deal of joy and laughter into my life.

You make me feel!

Remember how most of us came from a church culture that encouraged us to be followers?

I can boldly claim that you guys are incredible leaders! You are anything but followers! You are leading me into a greater revelation of myself, others, the universe, and profound mysteries.

I'm sorry for sounding mushy or cheesy, but I love you.

You make me want to be a better man.

I AFFIRM YOUR PAIN

I've been thinking a lot about the pain of transformation.

Like growing pains. I sprouted up very fast as a teenager. It actually physically hurt. Especially in my legs.

They say that the greatest stressors in life are things like illness, death of a loved one, divorce, finances, and moving. Essentially, these are all about change varying in degrees of intensity.

I claim that spiritual change is traumatic. It can actually be painful.

Stress manifests itself in my life physically. In the past, a doctor thought I had MS. An MRI proved that wrong. Then I got shingles the same week. A doctor said, "Stress is a bitch!" This happened to me during a very stressful spiritual time in my life. I was going through a traumatic spiritual transition and it showed up in my physical self.

161

Actually, it confirms my conviction that there is no separation between the physical and spiritual self. We cannot separate spirit from flesh, soul from body, energy from matter.

I am One. We are One. All is One.

Having read a lot of lives of saints, spiritual leaders, and mystics, I've noticed that many of these people share their own struggles through spiritual transition.

In Eastern mystics, such as one of my personal favorites, Krishnamurti, he went through an excruciatingly painful change that boosted him to the next level spiritually. Those who wrote about it from an Eastern perspective talked about his Chakras and the Kundalini process.

I read the biography of Byron Katie. Her husband at the time desperately tried to buy up all the copies because it showed her in less than a complimentary light. What a fascinating read! It talks about her painful transition from a depressed, mean, and miserable woman into the mystic I believe she is today.

Some aboriginal peoples have vision quests where you go into the wilderness and under harsh conditions ignite your challenging spiritual transformation.

The story of Jesus talks about him going into the desert for 40 days to fast, be tempted by the devil, and be tormented by wild beasts. From here he launched his ministry.

So I wonder if different cultures in different times take these painful transitions and call them something, label them, name them, and package them into a desired, expected, or even elicited formative process.

Some call it Kundalini, or vision quest, or desert experience, or dark night of the soul, or dying to self.

(**NOTE:** During these times it's important not to lose it! It helps to have guides. But if they aren't available, it helps to have read up and understood that you are about to go through a very intense transformation that will tax you spiritually, physically, emotionally, socially… in so many ways. It's during these times some people lose their moral footing and wreck their lives. Stories of this abound!)

Maybe we could call this painful spiritual transformation deconstruction.

Yes, this is my attempt to encourage you that the pain you're experiencing is the dawn of personal transformation. As painful as it is, as impossible as it seems, as undesirable as it presents itself, it is necessary for our growth.

For me, it is important to keep this in mind while I'm going through this painful transition. This way I don't despair that it will never end. This way I realize this is a part of my growth process. This way I don't get careless and resort to unhealthy behaviors to escape the changes I'm experiencing.

When I read your updates, I get very encouraged. I admire the bravery you display. You are amazing human beings going through amazing changes to become even more amazing human beings.

I'm glad to be journeying with you. It decreases the intensity of my pain.

I WANT TO TELL YOU A LITTLE SECRET

I'm looking out over the river I live on. It's called the Kennebacasis. It comes from the aboriginal Mi'kmaq word meaning "little long bay place". It's a ninety-five kilometers long tidal river, beautiful and wide and running deep. It is full of living beings… anything from harbor seals to salmon, trout and even sturgeon at the deepest parts. Birds of all kinds like waterfowl, seagulls, hawks, osprey and eagles fly continually by. It is teeming with life. Not only the life it supports, but the life of its own.

It speaks to me every day, communicating at deep levels. Sometimes it's as calm as a glass surface. Sometimes it's a raging and dangerous beast. This morning it's dark, brown and brooding with a halo of fog suspended overhead.

Today it is speaking to me about the unity in diversity we experience at The Lasting Supper.

We do occasionally experience conflict on TLS. Sometimes there are misunderstandings. Sometimes there are inappropriate words. Sometimes there is anger, bitterness, resentment, and sharp retorts. But most of the time there is love, support, care, and a deep connection with one another's sufferings and joys.

Some of you have called me father, some uncle, some brother, some friend, some facilitator. Whatever my role in TLS is, I just want to do it well. I want to do whatever I can to help TLS be the kind of place we've tasted more than once that is beautiful, inviting, full of nutrition, and satisfying. I apologize for those times I've failed. I promise, and I'm committed to this, that I only want to learn and get better at this.

But listen...

Our brave attempts to eat and share together are beyond any predictions I could have made.

I couldn't have guessed the love and support I feel or the joy I experience when I come to this table.

No one could have foreseen the awkward moments we have when someone brings food we've never seen before or don't like.

We couldn't have known that sometimes the food we bring to the table is neglected or rejected.

Sometimes the food we make together doesn't turn out as well as we'd planned.

It doesn't look anything like the pictures. But then many times it's far better than anyone could have dreamed!

I'm going to let you in on a little secret: I don't have a plan!

That's right! I have no agenda. I don't have a goal I'm pushing TLS towards. Sure, I want more members because I want us to provide what we are enjoying for more people. But I have no idea how we're going to become better than we already are or how we're going to get others to feel invited.

We've been cooking for over two years now. If someone told me before I started that this is what TLS would look like, I wouldn't have believed them. I wouldn't have thought it was possible. Not even remotely!

This is what got me into trouble at my last church: I refused to organize the spontaneous beauty of our community. I wouldn't relegate it into a vision, goal or agenda. I kept my hands off the wheel and let the community develop and define itself. Whatever was its recipe, much of it was secret and mysterious. But I saw its death in the controlling and packaging of it. And that's exactly what happened. I just found out last week that the church there is officially dead and closing its doors forever.

I know some of us experience frustration because I will not control what happens on TLS. Sometimes it doesn't go your way or mine. It often reminds me of Hell's Kitchen. It frequently feels willy-nilly and chaotic and messy. It sometimes even gets out of control. There's swearing and laughter and irreverence and defensiveness and hurt and anger and frustration and pain.

But the meals we make!

Am I naïve, or are we not the best tasting community we've ever had?

You cannot plan that.

WHAT DO YOU DO WITH SO MANY OPINIONS ABOUT YOU?

This letter contains an important message about being yourself.

I'm eating Lisa's homemade granola and listening to the "Deep Dark Indie" playlist. I'm rejoicing that all my kids are going to be home this Christmas starting late tonight… the first time in years. We've also bought some wine and other concoctions that I'm looking forward to imbibing. When I hit a block in writing this letter, I sneak a peek at our TLS Facebook group to see what's happening! Even though we sometimes share some hard stuff there, I find it very life-giving. It reminds me that I am not alone in my struggles and joys, but that I'm traveling this road with formidable comrades.

Recently I sent out a letter to as many people as I could think of who may have been affected, alerting them to my closing comment on the now infamous Tony Jones post. It was my attempt to offer a conciliatory gesture to those who were voicing concern over it.

The variety of responses I received astounded me. Some loved it and others hated it. Some saw it as I intended: as my attempt to reach out with care to those who were concerned about that post and its comments. Some saw it as completely other than what I intended: as my attempt to protect my reputation or to repair it and excuse myself from all responsibility, even believing I closed the comments not to prevent a flood of more opinions but to display my own power and control over the conversation. On the one hand, there were some who appreciated it and expressed their appreciation for me. On the other hand, there were others for whom it only stoked their fires of disdain for me and what I do.

I don't know why this continues to surprise me. Nakedpastor has always had a polarizing effect on people. I always get both encouraging and discouraging emails and messages every day. This is nothing new. Approval on one hand. Disapproval on the other.

It's the same with my most challenging posts. There are a large number of people who see that post as a historic and rare and beautiful event where silenced victims were able to share their stories without censure or censor. There are a smaller number of people who see that post as a shameful display of damaging meanness towards respected Christian leaders.

What do I do?

You know the feeling! There are some people in your life who have a low opinion of you, while there are others who have a high one. Who are you to believe? What do you do?

Many members, before they joined TLS, suffered under the conviction that they were completely crazy, backslidden and hopelessly lost. However, once they joined TLS, they suddenly realized that they weren't crazy but wise, not backslidden but free, not hopelessly lost but confidently searching.

But this is the problem: Who do you believe?

My world is full of people who either hate me, don't understand me, are confused by me, are angered by me, and then there are others who love me, who get me, who identify with me and cheer me on.

Here's what I do. It's very simple.

My wife: This can also be a very close friend or a loving relative. Someone who does love you but is also honest with you. Lisa loves me and is honest with me. I can ask her what she honestly thinks about me or something I'm involved in, and I know she will give me her truth. If I'm making a mistake she'll let me know. If I'm doing right in her eyes she'll encourage me to continue. I listen to her.

My counselor: I have a counselor/ spiritual director that I can call who doesn't dice words. This person doesn't take my bullshit and cuts through my defenses and blind spots and tells it like it is to me. This person is once removed from my wife and is not as enmeshed with me as Lisa is, so this person may feel even more free and released to tell me as it is.

Friends: I have a few friends I can talk with about things who don't blow sunshine up my ass all the time. They're genuine friends. I know when they are suggesting I might be wrong or whatever, that they're doing it in love. They're not trying to hurt me, rein me in, or control me. They genuinely are concerned for me. They'll tell me if I'm being stupid or smart, self-destructive or heroic, mean or kind.

Enemies: I do listen to my enemies. I try to listen between their vindictive or hateful lines to hear what they're really concerned about. Sometimes I have heard in the voice of my enemies the voice of wisdom. Sure, there's a lot of weeding that has to happen to get to the wheat, but sometimes there is wheat there. This can be hard to do, but if you're mature enough and confident enough in yourself, you can do it.

Finally, Me: That's right. This is the most important one. Of course, this can't happen without the support of the other four. But we have to get to a place where we are finally confident in ourselves. No matter what we do, it is going to be interpreted and misinterpreted. We can't count on any one group for our identity… a defining of it or an endorsement of it. These other voices assist my own journey of self-discovery. They don't steer it.

I remember when Jesus asked, "Who do people say that I am?" Everyone got it wrong. Even his closest friends had no idea who he was or what he was about. But it gave him an idea of what opinions of him were out there. He necessarily had to discover who he was and what his mission was in this world. I think he learned about himself through others. But these could only confirm and augment what he already knew and was

168

learning about himself with himself.

I think this is one of the greatest benefits of The Lasting Supper. It can be a place where you can expose yourself and get opinions. We're not yes-people. We will be honest. But we will also, hopefully, be kind and supportive to one another as we find our way to being who we are and doing what we feel we would like to do.

Each one of you is amazing. You really are. I'm not flattering. You are all unique individuals that make up the community called The Lasting Supper. Together we will discover more about ourselves and more about how we then live in this world.

I know you do that for me.

HERE'S TO BEING OURSELVES

I'm going to try to keep this letter a short one. I'm still recovering from the holidays.

I've experienced a kind of recommitment to what I feel my purpose is in this world. It didn't come easy. It didn't come in the form of a burning bush or a billowy cloud or a beautiful angel or a gentle dream. It came in the form of intense conflict and criticism.

I've drawn many cartoons and written posts lately advocating for survivors and challenging the tendency to silence them. It came as a surprise to me that there are many people who don't like advocates for survivors and resent survivors when they share their story. I've also found that it is especially fierce when I provide a place for women to share their stories.

The result of this is that I've received tons of encouraging communications from people who were so grateful to finally see a place where people could hold their own truths and share their own stories without being edited or shut down. However, there were others who were alarmed by this frankness of speech and naming of names. And some of those named felt slandered and betrayed. I've heard from many of them too.

As it stands, I have become an advocate for more people who feel victimized and silenced by Christianity, the church, and its leaders. On the other hand, I have lost friendship, respect, and credibility with many others. It has been a constant source of pain for me because it was totally clear that I had a choice to make: continue doing what I do or tame myself.

To be honest, it felt like it really came down to choosing who to be loved by.

Actually, this isn't true. The core truth is I had to choose who I would be true to: the expectations of others or to myself.

So for 2015, I've rekindled my determination to be true to myself.

I want to encourage you too. I know how difficult and costly it is to be true to yourself. But how else can we live, if not with integrity and a clear conscience? And in the end, I think this is how we will truly help others, in spite of the losses we experience.

So here's to me being me and you being you in 2015! I'm with you. Are you with me?

WE ARE LIKE PENPALS FOR LIFE!

Today I spoke at the Unitarian Universalist Church in town. There was a small group there... about 20 people. I gave a slide show presentation on "Questions are the Answer: Questions as Tools for Personal Growth". It's the topic of my book that I'm working on for a publisher. It was well received, and I had a great time connecting with real flesh and blood people.

But I must say I find the community very special. Let me explain why.

1. Some insist that the internet only provides superficial relationships.
I've heard it over and over again. You have too! We hear it all the time
that the relationships we have online aren't really real, but superficial
and possibly even fake. We're told that we aren't our true selves online,
and that the people we apparently relate with aren't themselves either.
This, we are taught, makes for a very artificial relationship supported
by artificial intelligence… or technology. We're presented with such
horrifying movies such as Catfish (which you should see if you haven't),
where a romantic relationship that develops online is totally fabricated.
We hear sorry stories of people leaving their spouses for someone
they met in an online game room and ruining their families and even
their own lives. We hear about all kinds of phony interactions, fraud,
deception, and broken dreams. I'm frequently reminded by "helpful"
people that the people I think I know and even come to love online aren't
really who they say they are. Just the other day I read someone's rant
against online communities, that they simply cannot replace church
and that they are a counterfeit to the real flesh-and-blood church that
we should be attending locally. We are chastised for our online spiritual
interactions as though they are a poor and cheap trade for real live
human beings, that we are cowardly copping out of true face-to-face
interactions with the human race, avoiding people because we can't
handle it or don't want to. Some theologians even suggest that we're the
new Gnostics who like the idea of a person more than the person him
or herself. In a word, we are told that we've settled for second best and
are losing out of the richness of real relationships with real people.

**2. My experience is that the internet is a convenient means that
provides real relationships.** Yes, today's experience at a real live
church was nice. I shook hands. Met some new and interesting people.
Smelled body odor. Ate real food and drank real bad coffee. We sang
together. We laughed together. Yes, it was nice. But it wasn't as deep or
meaningful as my relationship with you guys at The Lasting Supper.
I disagree that online relationships must be superficial. They can be,
but they don't have to be! In fact, I can strongly testify that I have
made some very significant friendships through this community. This
community really IS my tribe. It's not a superficial one, a phony one,
or a fantasy one. It really is real. Even though we may not see eye to eye

(in more ways than one!), we still enjoy the benefits as if we were. I'm being encouraged, challenged, supported, cared for, caring for others, listening, sharing, arguing, mediating, doing some conflict resolution, giving space, laughing, crying… you name it… all the things we would be doing if we were in the same room together. I would also argue that our community makes reasonable relational demands on me, pulling me in to a conversation when I'd sometimes rather not, involving me in issues that are conflictual, placing me in relationships that are sometimes challenging, and evoking a wonderful variety of emotions that are only aroused by other people. Call me crazy, but I really do believe I have developed life-long friendships with many of you. I would even dare, if asked "Do you love them?" say, "Yes!"

That being said, I think it would be like the cherry on top if we could meet some day. Whenever any TLSers get together, I always hope they take a photograph so we can all see it. I do have a dream of one day as many of us as can meeting up somewhere for a weekend. That would be one of the most delicious experiences of all time. For me. I think for you too, because I'm fun to be around.

So… here's to our online community! It rocks. It is a tribe of relationships. Let's ignore the naysayers who say it ain't so!

I COME BY CANOE

I compare our journeys of leaving the church, or changing our minds, or deconstructing our faith, to taking a canoe down a river.

Sometimes there are very smooth periods when you hardly even have to paddle. All you have to do is keep your paddle in the water and make sure you don't hit the shore or rocks. These are very easy and even relaxing times where you can enjoy the ride. You feel yourself moving at a comfortable and peaceful pace, and you can even enjoy the scenery. I would characterize these times as potentially happy.

Sometimes there are rapids where, again, you don't have to paddle. You still have to keep your paddle in the water to avoid damaging your vessel or yourself. This is a time when things happen very fast and furious. There doesn't seem to be any time to take in the scenery. It's all about survival. I would characterize these times as a mixture of excitement and fear.

Sometimes there are doldrums when nothing at all is happening on its own but requires you to put in all the effort to get anywhere. Everything feels dead. You'd love to enjoy the scenery but you can't because you're working so friggin' hard. Oh, you know you could do nothing and just sit there forever. And sometimes you do. But realizing you could die here, you put your paddle in the water, engage your muscles, and push yourself forward. I would characterize these times as boring.

Sometimes there are places you have to portage. This is just plain old hard work where you have to drag your canoe out of the water and carry it with all your gear usually through very rugged terrain. These are the times when you wonder what the heck you're doing out of your environment, sweating bullets and exposing yourself to the wild beasts. I would characterize these times as meaningless and frustrating.

Sometimes you fall in. Either you do something foolish like try to stand up or you hit a rock or a log or water-log the canoe and you're done. It's always an accident. When I took canoe training, one of the things I had to learn was how to right a canoe in water over my head in depth. It's hard work. Then drying everything out. I would characterize these times as dangerous.

Sometimes you are canoeing all alone. No one else is with you and you have no idea if you're doing it right or not. There's no one to talk to. No one to encourage you. No one to listen to your woes or joys. No one who even cares. I would characterize these times as very lonely.

Sometimes you're canoeing with another person or two in the same canoe. At times there is fun or deep and meaningful conversation. Other times there are confusing, irritating and annoying exchanges. At times you're glad for the company, and other times you'd like to throw them overboard. I would characterize these times as either delightful or aggravating.

I'll tell you how I like to do canoe trips.

I like to have my own canoe, but I like to meet up with other canoeists with their own canoes when I want. This is how I integrate my introverted and extroverted self. Of course, I am aware that sometimes I have no choice in the matter. Sometimes I just find myself very alone. At other times I suddenly find myself surrounded with other canoes.

This is why I like TLS. This is how it feels to me. I feel like we are all in our own canoes making our own trips but that we have the privilege of meeting up with others who are on the same kind of river. Before TLS, I often felt like I was the only living soul on the whole river. Since I started TLS and we gained almost 400 members, I now know there are many others on the same river and they are my companions. When we collect, and maybe even when we stop and sit around the campfire, we can share our stories and feel reinvigorated for the next day.

What's cool to know, though, is that I'm not going nowhere. The river is taking me somewhere. While for me the river is the destination, it is also a way. I'm taking in every minute of it now, but I also feel, deep down, that I'm being taken to a more wonderful place somehow and that I'm going to be a better person for it.

I'm glad you're on the same river with me, guys. See you at the next campfire!

Happy paddling!

WHY I CALL THE LASTING SUPPER A SAFE PLACE

Almost all of the time, The Lasting Supper goes along just great. Not just goes along, but thrives with awesome interactions. I'm almost always impressed with the quality of people and conversations in our private Facebook group. Pretty much all the time, I'm very thankful that I launched TLS back in the fall of 2012.

But then once in a while I'm not. Well... that's not really true. I'm always thankful. It's just that sometimes it is very difficult to facilitate the community discussion on TLS. It is very time consuming, exhausting, and often discouraging. I do not claim to be an excellent facilitator, but I want to be, and so I experience some frustration with myself as I stumble along trying to make it work and trying to get us to an amiable and agreeable place.

So last week we had some issues. Some pretty strong disagreements arose and some very real conflicts. As a result, some people have said that it is a lie to say that TLS is "safe".

I still stand by that claim, and I want to explain why. I'm going to use an analogy that I've used before, and that is the traffic analogy.

Here in New Brunswick, Canada, we can claim that we have "safe roads". What does that mean? Does that mean that there are never any accidents? That no one ever gets hurt?

No, it doesn't.

I think it means three things:

The roads themselves are in safe shape. That is, they are planned, paved (well... most!), and maintained. That is, if there is ever an accident or someone gets hurt, they should never be able to blame the condition of the road itself.

There are rules, laws and etiquettes in place to drive on them. That is, everyone who drives on them must be licensed and know the rules and laws that govern the road they're driving on, such as speed limits, signaling, braking, spacing, passing, etcetera. This is probably the most crucial aspect of making sure a road is safe.

These laws are enforced. That is, there are people... police... who punish people who break the rules and endanger their lives and wellbeing as well as the lives and wellbeing of others. There are warnings, fines and other measures used to make sure people obey the rules and keep the roads safe.

There could be more I'm not thinking of now. But these three things are the essentials for safe roads. Even though there are accidents here, and even though I've been in some of them, I would still claim that the roads here are safe.

I compare this to the TLS community. I claim that it is a safe community because the same three essentials exist:

The platform itself is in safe shape. That is, the incredible planning, creating, and maintaining that goes into The Lasting Supper is all to make it a safe space for healthy conversations to happen.

There are rules. We have rights and responsibilities as well as values and principles in place to ensure that we use TLS in healthy ways. If you weren't aware of this, it might help to check out those links. This, like driving, is crucial to know. If we would observe these then we would avoid most conflicts or at least handle them in a healthy manner.

These are enforced. Well... I don't like to use the word "enforce". I prefer to call myself a facilitator or a reminder of who we really are and what we really are about. If someone breaks their responsibility, or conflicts with our values, or interferes with our principles, then it is my job or anyone else's job who cares to facilitate or remind, to step up to facilitate and remind them.

Does this mean no one gets hurt? No. Does this mean we will always feel safe? No.

There are so many factors that can come to play. Weather. Inebriation. Moods. Blind spots. Road rage. Language. Cultures. Assumptions. Animals. The internet. Lack of certain social skills. Passion. You name it. There are all kinds of factors.

But as long as the platform is built for safety, as long as there are rules to remind us, and as long as there are people willing to facilitate, remind, and enforce if need be, then I would dare call TLS a safe space for community and conversation to happen. Even though at moments we may feel unsafe, I hope we can say that generally TLS is safe.

The analogy can be pushed further. For example, we could say that some people have to have their license to drive on this road because they keep causing accidents. That's only happened a few times in over two years. Thankfully. Most times we issue gentle warning that their patterns of driving are potentially dangerous and could hurt someone else. Other times it is clear that whenever they get on the road they are going to hurt others. We revoke their license to drive.

Then there are other things that defy explanation. I've driven with many people. Some drivers frustrate me. They aren't doing anything illegal, but I just can't stand their driving. It makes me nervous. Then there are some drivers who just make others angry and bring out the worst in us. For example, someone driving way below the speed limit. My dad used to be a cop and he said they caused more accidents but they never knew about it because they never looked in their rear view mirror. Then there are drivers who think they own the road and you're in their way. There are other drivers who are so nervous that they make everyone around them nervous.

Something interesting happened to me the other day. Well… it started a couple years ago when Lisa and I were driving on the highway on a rainy day and we hydroplaned. We spun out of control and ended up on a guard-rail. Ever since that day Lisa prefers to drive slower and wants me to drive slower. So, the other day I was out with Jesse, our son, in his big 2500 Dodge Ram Diesel, and we hit a little patch of ice and his truck slipped just ever so slightly. I could barely feel it. But my heart dropped into my gut.

Triggering! There are certain things about TLS that make me nervous.

I've been through horrible church experiences. I can't stand conflicts even though I've learned to work within them. But sometimes when someone says something, I immediately get triggered and wait for an accident to happen and for someone to get hurt. But that's my issue, not yours. I'm just sharing this because we all may have triggers that make our driving on TLS a little bit of a challenge sometimes.

I want to say that TLS isn't perfect. Neither am I. I have failed in the past. I have relied on my poor judgment, taken bad advice, and made mistakes in decisions. I myself have caused accidents to happen and got people hurt! I truly regret these times and promise to make TLS a safer place with clearer values and me a better facilitator.

Stay safe. And thanks for helping TLS to be safe too. I mean, as safe as possible.

HOW TO HANDLE YOUR SECRET IDENTITY

I've noticed lately in our private Facebook group that many of us are dealing with the fear of coming out to our families, friends, and acquaintances. When we change our beliefs, our faith, our religion, or lose them altogether, many of us feel the pressure to keep it inside for as long as possible.

I know I did.

I just wanted to share some ideas about this today. It's cold out, and we are buried in snow with more coming. We are expecting to lose our power, so we are ready for it. In the meantime, I'm writing you this letter. I want to talk about our secret identities.

Rather than considering our secret identities as shameful, why not consider them our secret strengths? From my observations of TLSers, every one of you is amazing. I'm not just saying this to make you feel better. I mean it! I brag about you guys all the time because you really are incredibly strong and independent... forces to be reckoned with in the universe. You do realize, don't you, that "out there" you often edit, control, modify, and abridge who you really are? But at The Lasting Supper, you don't have to. So inside TLS we see a more accurate presentation of who you are. When you enter into the TLS space, you can let down your guard, rip off your civilian clothes, and be the superhero that you really are without fear of being ridiculed or rejected.

I'll have to admit that when I first became aware of my secret superpower I really didn't know how to handle it. I knew that if I showed it, that it would embarrass me and freak people out.

So the first thing I had to do was get over my shame and embarrassment for being different, unique, and even special. After a while, this shame morphed into actually embracing who I was, owning it, and realizing that I, with my special superpower, was the best contribution I could give to the world. I'd always been warned in the religious circles I kept that one shouldn't stick his head above the rest because it would get chopped off. This was the community's way of maintaining control and the status quo. After a while, though, it dawned on me that this was its way of controlling me and separating me from myself. I had to get to the point where I could reject the threat and take that chance.

As a result, I never lost my head but instead became more of myself in this world, and now feel as though I am free to grow into my own expanding container. I feel more useful now than ever before. I feel like I can actually contribute who I am to the world. I no longer feel confined but free. Free as a bird with wings. As free as a superhero can be. So when someone ridicules me or rejects me, it doesn't hurt as much because I know I am far better off now than if I submitted to their expectations of me. I'm happier, freer, and more in my skin and fulfilled than ever before. Ridicule and reject away! I can take it. In fact, that's another one of my superpowers!

Remember those scenes in the movies when people are in trouble and they need the superhero to rip off their clothes and reveal their true identities? The superhero knows the risks involved, but then motivated by a deep desire to be true to themselves as well as the matching deep desire to help, they come through and amaze everyone around them.

This is why superheroes hold such a fascination for us. I believe they are calling us to come out and be who we really are so we can make a difference. The other day someone suggested that my spirit animal is the honey badger, who "wouldn't think twice about starting some shit and are actually totally fearless". Maybe that's my secret identity and superpower.

Who are you? What's your superpower?

You guys amaze me. I know. I know it takes time to show more and more people. It's one thing to reveal yourself to people you trust. Then to people who you hope you trust. Then to people you're not sure you trust. Then to people you know you can't trust.

But what's the alternative? To live in a confined world of small-minded, helpless drones.

We need you.

CAN I SHARE MY GRIEF WITH YOU?

Sometimes things seem so surreal.

The last church I pastored, a Vineyard church, just closed its doors and sold all assets, including the building. All the people have dispersed, and the pastor I'd left in charge moved away.

Gone. All of it. Gone!

Lisa and I moved here in 1995. I became the pastor of the Vineyard church in 1996. We went through a devastating church split in 1997. Basically, aside from that disastrous stint in New Hampshire, I was pastor there until I left the church and the ministry in 2010. During this time, we managed to burn the mortgage. Just before I left, I handed the church, the amazing leadership team, and the congregation over to the new pastor. We were good friends at the time. I really did it in hopes that he would help move the church on where I no longer could.

But as soon as I gave him the church, the church began to distance itself from me. Then, slowly over the years, it started to dwindle away until by the end of 2014 there were just a half dozen people left. It came to the point where it was no longer viable. So they closed it down, sold it off, and he moved away.

I heard that there were attempts to have a reconciliation of sorts between all the pastors in the history of the church when it was looking like it was going to fail. I heard a rumor that none of the other ones wanted to meet because they saw me as the problem. They never bothered to contact me for this reason. They say it was my fault the church split in 1997. Therefore, it is my fault that I allowed myself to deteriorate to the point where I lost my faith, turned my back on God, and left the ministry and like a hireling ran away from the church. Then, it is my fault the church never succeeded after I passed it on because, basically, I gave the new pastor a dying baby that he nursed to its death.

You can't win.

I'm used to being accused of stuff. They can blame me if they want to. I don't care. Really. I mean it does affect me, but not in a serious or debilitating way.

What I'm really feeling is a sadness. I'm grieving the death of that church.

It was a wonderful community when it was working well. It eventually came to the place where we were no longer compatible. But the potential for us to continue to grow together was there. It's just that certain strong people took over the morale of the place and eventually made it oppressive and impossible for me. But when it was good it was amazing. Actually, The Lasting Supper reminds me very much of that place when it was at its best. The skills I learned in that church I apply in TLS.

I've learned a lot about community. I've still got a lot to learn and a long way to go. But it's made me very grateful for what we have. Look! I even feel free to share my grief with you guys. So thanks. I enjoy you guys and appreciate the community we have.

I hope you do too.

ME AND MY FOUR FS

After I left the ministry and the church, it became very clear to me very quickly the areas of my life that needed immediate attention and improvement.

I call them the 4 F's: Family. Fun. Finances. Friends.

Of course, first and foremost, I had to take care of myself. That's a given. My personal health and hygiene, inside and out, needed to be attended to.

But the four areas of my life which seemed to suffer most where these four F's. While I was in the church, and especially as a pastor, these things were taken care of in their own churchy way.

I had my biological family, but the church also provided a surrogate one.
I had fun, but it was mostly activities in and around the church.
I had finance, but it was an unhealthy attitude about money that kept me poor.
I had friends, but they were all church people that left when I left the church.

So I had to fix these four areas myself.

Family: We no longer had the spiritual family, the church. It was instantly gone. Now, I felt attention to my biological family became necessary. Things were strained with some. I learned a huge lesson, though: I was holding my family, especially my parents, to a fantasy about who they should be that they simply could not and would not live up to. I had to learn to let them be and relate to them on their terms, just as I was trying to help them learn to relate to me on mine. I knew that as soon as I let my father-fantasies go, then I could perhaps see my dad as he actually is and relate to the real person he is in front of me rather than the false image I have of him in my head. It was a couple of years into this that I started The Lasting Supper that provides a surrogate family as well, for which I'm truly thankful.

Fun: All the fun we used to have centered around the church. As pastors of the church we were very busy. We were always doing things. Busy church equals busy schedule. It was rare to have a quiet night at home. Then, after we left the church, suddenly free time was all we had. We had to start actually planning things to do. Some of them simple, like going for walks, going to the shore, going out in the canoe, or just going out for a coffee. Some of them more complex, like planning a road trip or vacation or going to a concert or something. It's so easy for us to fall into the trap of waiting for good times to come that we forget to make ourselves go to them. Lisa and I have to make fun happen now. We don't want to be pulled down by the gravity of life. We want to be happy, so we'll make it happen because no one else will!

Finances: I had a very unhealthy attitude about money during my many years in the ministry. As a result, when we left the ministry, we also filed for personal bankruptcy. Even though I enjoyed a steady salary from the church, it had never seen an increase but in fact decreases over the years I had been there. I was such a sacrificial servant. After leaving the ministry and the church, I knew one of my number one tasks was going to be to heal myself of this poverty mentality I had acquired over the years. It's been five years now, and I'm far better about money then I used to be, but I still have a long way to go. One of the most significant components to this healing was valuing myself and the things I make and do. My art, my books, my blog, my online community, are things of value and deserve to be appreciated as things of value. I am no longer easily shamed by people who insist I should give myself away and wait to be rewarded for it. I tried that. It doesn't work. I do still give myself away in many ways, but I also sell my goods and services that deserve remuneration. Things are getting better.

Friends: One of the greatest values the church has to offer is instant fellowship, friends in an instant, community ripe for the picking. When I left the church, I left a whole intricate network of friends. One could question how genuine the friends were if that's all it took. But that's another issue. Lisa and I suddenly were faced with an overwhelming loneliness. It used to be we felt peopled out. Now we felt lonelied out. We realized pretty quickly that friends were not going to magically appear. It was going to take effort. We were going to have to initiate by making calls and extending invitations and contacting people and testing ourselves with new people. I've come to realize, actually, that this is pretty normal for most people. Unless they have friends from high school or college or their business, most people find it difficult to find friends. For us, it meant making contact with people we already knew and trusted. We have a handful of couples now that we can call and meet at a movie or a restaurant or have over. It means nurturing these relationships. Again that's normal. But it is a necessary skill we had to learn if we didn't want to end up lonely forever.

It took me some time to finally realize and admit and embrace: I am the master of my destiny. I am at the steering wheel of my own life. It is magical thinking to think that my relationship to my family is going to fix itself, that fun is just going to show up, that finances are going to appear, and that friends are going to be knocking down our door to get in.

If I wanted to see these things happen, I was going to have to do it myself. I did.

YOUR ABILITY TO DISAPPOINT PEOPLE

One of the strongest messages I received growing up in the church is that it is my job to not upset people.

I mean, it's okay to upset sinful people who are doing wrong, like Jesus overturning the tables of the money-changers in the temple. Hurting sinful peoples' feelings is okay.

Just don't upset your brothers and sisters. That's a no-no.

I'm the oldest of five kids. I grew up super responsible. My goal was to never disappoint my parents. As a good church-goer, my goal to never disappoint my parents transferred onto every other Christian. I never disappointed anybody.

Disappoint: "to fail to fulfill the hopes or expectations of someone".

My parents had hopes for me. All my brothers and sisters in the faith had hopes for me.

And I never disappointed them. Until I did.

I started thinking I was going to have to disappoint people when I was around twenty-seven years old. I'd experienced a kind of spiritual crisis and realized I needed a spiritual director. Yes!

It was then I knew that I was going to have to start disappointing people, letting them down, and not fulfilling their hopes for me.

For me, it wasn't a sudden rebellious outbreak: "I'M GOING TO BE ME!" It wasn't like me suddenly turning from the lovely Jekyll to the evil Hyde in one fell swoop. It was more of a slight turn in direction.

This was the turn of direction: It was a subtle decision that I was going to stop disappointing myself rather than others. I was going to commit myself to personal transformation, no matter what the social cost.

You have to decide to disappoint people. Now, it doesn't have to be active. It is usually passive. That means, you don't set out to disappoint people. You set out to be true to yourself. You commit yourself to change, interiorly and exteriorly. This is going to disappoint people.

So the primary decision is to commit to authenticity and the change this requires. The secondary decision is to acknowledge, accept and bear that this will disappoint people.

When someone says (and I get this frequently): "You're a disappointment to me." I respond, "I didn't mean to disappoint you. I want to live with integrity. I can't help if this disappoints you."

I disappointed people when I was 27. I disappoint people now. I am changing. I am faithful to my transformation. I am respectful to myself, no matter what the cost.

The disappointing of their false hopes is all an illusion anyway. Their expectations on you are their expectations, their hopes, their fantasies. These fantasies really have nothing to do with you anyway, but with the fantasizer's desires.

Commit to change. You may disappoint others, but in the long run you will not disappoint yourself.

HOW GOD LET ME GO

Lisa and I went on a much-needed vacation last week. We haven't been on vacation since Lisa went back to university seven years ago. We left in a snow storm. I had to use the snow-blower to get ourselves out of our driveway to get to the airport. We went to Mexico. Stunning! I was sad coming back to winter. We're already talking about our next vacation.

I thought of you guys every day. Not because I felt obligated to, but because you are my friends, and I always wonder how my friends are doing.

Today I want to write about an aspect of my own personal spiritual or theological journey. I want to explain how I've come to a place where I'm reluctant to use the word "God", or even express "belief" in this "God". I prefer to say, "That Which We Call God" to speak about what people call the Divine. I want to describe the process of how I've come to a place where many people assume I'm an atheist, even though I wouldn't use that label to describe myself. I couldn't go from firm believer to where I am now overnight. It took several stages and years. It took my idea of "God" gradually allowing me to go until I got to where I am today.

I want to sketch with words my journey to where I am now, where I am in complete theological peace devoid of the anguish I experienced for decades.

Please understand that this is my journey. This is my story. I do not expect anyone to believe it or apply it or adopt it. This is my personal journey that I'm sharing, hoping that maybe someone might benefit from it, get clarity from it, or even find comfort from it.

These are the stages of belief in "God" I went through:

God as Jealous: This was my first presentation of God. He was jealous and would have no other gods before him. He demanded my complete and undying loyalty. I had to think about him 24/7, and if I didn't, I would be a disappointment to him. He required my all, everything of me and about me and anything that was mine… it was his. I could not think outside the parameters that had been set by him and his Bible because it meant certain spiritual death. I was to read only the Bible and tested theology and nothing else. It was complete 100% domination and slavery. At times it was pleasant, but at other times it was miserable. My life wasn't mine, but his.

God as Open: Then I came to a stage where God was open to other ideas. He admitted that he revealed himself to others, to people of other cultures and even religions. He invited me to read about similarities to him, to Jesus, and to the bible in other religions, spiritualities and philosophies. Oh, God was still jealous because it was him he wanted me to see in all these other religious and spiritual expressions, not someone else or another god. This was God inviting me to recognize traces of him and his work throughout the world and down through time. This was a season of intense exposure and learning and integrating of other expressions and ideas.

God as Gracious: This was a period when, now influenced by recognizing God throughout the world and throughout time, I started to realize that God was gracious. God was a god of love, not malice. It was through my reading of Paul and Pauline theologians. The letters of Romans and Galatians, etc., were incredibly influential during this period. Barth's famous commentary on Romans rocked my world. I started to wonder if I was a universalist. Barth was and still is accused of that, but he tried to avoid using that word to express his belief that God really does love the whole world, and that somehow through the work of Christ the whole world was reconciled to God. I came to understand that God was so gracious that he would even allow me to question, doubt, and change my beliefs.

God as Releasing: There is a cheesy saying I saw on a poster of a butterfly being released from someone's hand: "If you love someone, set them free. If they come back they're yours; if they don't they never were." I started to believe this about God. If God would allow me to question my beliefs, then he must be willing to allow me to question my beliefs about him as well. I somehow absolutely knew this to be true. I no longer believed God was an insecure lover, but one very secure in himself and could handle my questions, even me questioning him! I came to understand that the ideas in my mind about God were not actually God, and I knew God already knew that. So I was allowed to question the ideas I had in my mind and even reject them as not God, fully confident that God not only permitted it but encouraged it. He knew that when I finally hit rock bottom, whatever remained of him that was true, I would be faithful to this. God was so gracious he let me go.

God as Not-God or All: On a night in May, 2009, I had a dream of a waterfall. The dream was a picture of reality, including "God" and All-That-Is. I understood that above the rim of the falls I cannot see. This compares to God. God is invisible. An infinite source. Never-ending supply. But we cannot see it. We can only guess what God is from what comes over the falls. This is the Incarnation, or the manifestation of the Mystery. Christians would call this Christ. It is a picture of what may be over the rim of the falls. Then when the water hits the ground and spreads, this is the Spirit, the application of the Mystery, the assimilation of the Mystery, into the affairs of the world and humanity. The Spirit is about love, justice, joy, and peace. When I awoke from this dream I suddenly knew that the All really is All. I saw that we are all one, connected at a deep level, unified and not separate. Separation and division is only an illusion that impresses our eyes and minds. I suddenly realized that the only thing that seems to separate us is language.

Thoughts. Words. Ideas. Beliefs. That's all. We all feel the rain as it falls on us, but we all have different experiences of this rain, thoughts about it, words for it. Same with reality, the universe, the mystery, or God. It's just words. Believer or atheist or anyone else. We are the same. God as Not-God or as All. It is the same. I saw this as clearly as anything I've ever seen, although it is the hardest thing I've ever tried to articulate. But this has given me a peace that passes understanding.

If I were pressed to make a statement, I would probably still consider myself a Christian, but an unusual one. My new theological framework is strangely trinitarian (above the rim, the falls, the spreading water). But it is so open to be all-inclusive, all-consuming, like a unifying theory that applies to everyone from atheist to believer in any religious or spiritual tradition, that most Christians wouldn't accept me as a part of the club. You see, most believers in most religions are exclusive. This theory is universally inclusive. That creates political problems for most believers. Not for me, but for them.

It was the God in my mind that eventually and gradually let me go. It took, as I said, so many stages and so many decades for my idea of "God" to get to a place where I rest in Reality, what is True. I went from believing in a jealous God to a completely open idea of What-Is that is joyfully all-inclusive.

All-inclusive! Just like the resort we went to in Mexico!

ARE YOU BORED TO DEATH?

Every Easter I'm reminded of a Keith Green song I used to love that I would sing this time of year. One of the lines are, "Jesus Christ rose from the dead, and you can't even get out of bed!" Yes! I just loved that attitude, although I didn't think it was judgmental at the time, just honest preaching.

What if I really can't get out of bed? If not physically, then emotionally? Or spiritually?

Do you ever get bored? I don't mean like a temporary boredom because you can't think of anything to do today. I'm talking about a boredom that seeps right down into the core of your being and makes life feel meaningless and empty for you.

Did you know that this boredom, this sense of lethargy, sloth, laziness, depression, or this feeling that you just can't or don't care about anything, is a normal feature of the spiritual life?

It's called "acedia" or "ennui". Literally, it translates as "a lack of care".

This term's origins are found with the earliest desert monks in the first few centuries A.D. They would pray, sleep, eat, study, and weave reed baskets, then do it all over again… day after day, year after year, for their entire lives. They would often be struck with this overwhelming feeling of acedia… boredom, ennui, and caring for no one and nothing.

It's an ancient malady.

In Kathleen Norris' book, *"Acedia & Me"*, she says:

"… I think it likely that much of the restless boredom, frantic escapism, commitment phobia, and enervating despair that plagues us today is the ancient demon of acedia in modern dress. The boundaries between depression and acedia are notoriously fluid; at the risk of oversimplifying, I would suggest that while depression is an illness treatable by counseling and medication, acedia is a vice that is best countered by spiritual practice and the discipline of prayer."

For many people today, "spiritual practice" and "prayer" may not do. Instead, I would've preferred she dialed down the Christian lingo to benefit people in other religious traditions or with non-religious mindsets.

For me, it could be running out to take a photograph of the full moon setting over the river early on a cold winter morning, like I did today. Or it could mean taking a long walk in nature, like I did today. Or it could mean drawing a picture, like I will later. Or meditating. Or stretching. Or yoga. Or reading a book. Or watching a movie. Or making love. Or anything that helps ground me in my own body and maybe even get my body moving.

So, based on Norris' book, here's what I would suggest:

1. Determine if it is acedia or real depression.
2. If it is depression, get help.
3. If it is acedia, continue your practices, things you know help you, and gently nudge yourself to be creative, physical, or whatever.

I want to be careful here. I'm becoming increasingly aware that we live in an "-ist" culture: racist, sexist, misogynist, ageist, and this one… ableist. Ableism is when you look down on people who aren't able to do certain things. You think you're better than they are because of your physical supremacy. For example, consider the Nike ads that implicitly belittle people who are physically ill, disabled or in less than perfect physical condition with their slogan "Just do it!" What if I can't just do it? An ableist attitude says things like, "If you exercised harder your migraines would go away", or "If you worked out with weights your back pain would disappear", or "If you did power training you wouldn't be depressed anymore." I don't want to suggest that if you just followed some disciplines or exercises, then your acedia would go away. No! But I am suggesting that we can perhaps manage our acedia better if we do or if we can do these things. Anything we can do for self-care may alleviate or even erase our acedia.

I've gone through periods of acedia. Sometimes it can last a short time. Other times it can last a long time. But they come and they do go. Hopefully.

But it should help you to know that you are not alone in your boredom or lack of being able or willing to care. This is normal. And it is treatable. It can be managed.

Acedia and me. Acedia and you.

APPRECIATING THE SEASONS OF YOUR LIFE

I live in a geography with four dramatically distinct seasons: fall, winter, spring, and summer.

And I'll have to admit to you that this last winter was the hardest winter I've ever endured. It was brutal. In fact, almost every day I was asking myself why the hell I live here.

There were some days when I was trying to remove snow that I thought I was literally going crazy. Many days we were housebound. We hardly saw anybody. I was spending hours a day just managing the weather's effects on my property. There were extended days of boredom, extended days of frustration, extended days of anxiety, extended days of confusion. There were many days when I wondered if spring would ever, ever come. I was so tempted to talk Lisa into moving somewhere warm.

Then something broke. Grass appeared. It's last year's. But it is still grass. Which means less snow! Spring is on its way.

Each season means something different for me:

Fall means introspection. It means slowing down. It means a kind of dying. It means reflection and thoughtfulness, solitude and contemplation.

Winter means barrenness. It means stopping. It means a kind of death. It means having no choice but to stop and do nothing because we literally are not able. It means learning how to hibernate and be dormant.

Spring means promise. It means waking up. It means coming to life. It means finding hope again. It means starting to see the possibility that our labors bear fruit.

Summer means life. It means living. It means sunshine and happiness. It means partying. It means seeing, appreciating, and participating in everything that lives and gives life. It means enjoyment.

Now, these seasons might mean something different to you. But this is what they mean to me.

And I've noticed that my life has all of these seasons.

Unfortunately, or fortunately, they do not follow a rhythm like nature does. There's no predictability. There's no timetable. Any season can come and stay for a short or long while, and go just as suddenly or slowly as it came.

For me, the key is remembering that it is just a season. It is not the totality of my life.

It's important for me to remember that the weather is not the climate. The climate is steadfast. Seasons are, well, seasonal. They come and they go.

I know from my experience this winter that I can forget that this is only temporary. I really did despair at how long this was taking. But then one day I awakened to the warmth of the sun and to signs of life.

Spring is coming.

INDEPENDENCE OR WAITING FOR A MIRACLE

When I left the ministry and the church in March of 2010, I had the very distinct impression that my next stage of learning was going to be about becoming responsible for myself.

Let me explain what I mean.

One day I was watching *3:10 to Yuma*. The sheriff calls for men to form a posse to deliver a dangerous convict to the train station in Yuma where he will be hanged. A farmer, Dan, who has been ravaged by harsh growing seasons, a lack of water, a leg crippled from an old bullet wound, and a growing sense of hopelessness, offers his services. There's good money to be made, and in spite of his wife's fear and protests, he's going to do it. At one point, when his wife's trying to talk him out of it, he says:

"I've been standin' on one leg for three damn years waitin' for God to do me a favor... and He ain't listenin'."

I remember the shock I felt in my heart when he said that. In a flash of insight, I suddenly realized I had been waiting on God to rescue me. Rescue me from what?

a ministry that was growing increasingly sad and meaningless;
a desperate financial situation that would eventually lead to personal bankruptcy;
a growing sense of frustrating confusion theologically;
a completely silent God;
and these all combined to make me feel worthless and hopeless.

At once I was reminded me of my fellow Canadian Bruce Cockburn's beautiful song *Waiting for a Miracle*. One verse goes like this:

"Struggle for a dollar, scuffle for a dime ;
Step out from the past and try to hold the line;
So how come history takes such a long, long time ...
When you're waiting for a miracle?"

Then this reminded me of another Canadian Leonard Cohen's song *Waiting for the Miracle* that expresses the same sentiment:

"Nothing left to do when you know that you've been taken.
Nothing left to do when you're begging for a crumb.
Nothing left to do when you've got to go on waiting,
waiting for the miracle to come."

All these piled together at once in that moment to make me realize this is how I was living my life. I was constantly waiting for a miracle. A miracle that never came. I was constantly waiting to be rescued. A rescue that never happened.

It struck me hard between my spiritual eyes that I was going to have to be like Dan and do something daring, something drastic, something dangerous… for myself. I had this keen sense that my next learning curve was going to be on the subject of self-care, personal responsibility, and spiritual and financial independence. Yes, I was scared. But something had to be done. Now!

I was trapped. I was seriously trapped. But something told me I had the means to escape. I had to stop waiting for a miracle. I had to make it happen. I had to stop waiting to be rescued. I had to save myself.

In 2010 I did it. The predicted learning curve began, and it was a steep one. I filed for bankruptcy. I quit the ministry. I left the church. I looked for a "real" job. I started learning the fascinating world of business. I had to get over my hangups about products and services, marketing and sales, revenue and money.

195

It's a tough school. But I'm passing.

To be honest, it went against everything I had been taught in the church… that I was to always and only depend on God and not myself. I could hear evil voices in my head saying, "If you try this on your own, then you're really on your own!" So I had to get over my fear of disappointing or even abandoning God. I had to get to the point where I knew that even if there is a God, if I was being challenged to be independent and achieved it, then either he didn't care, or he could handle it or was going to have to.

It was a moment of defiance. One that I haven't regretted.

Some might say I initiated the miracle, like Moses hitting the Red Sea with his staff and it opening up in front of him. My path has opened up before me and I believe it was because I took certain steps. I'm not going to presume God honored this by making a way for me because my belief in God has gone through a dramatic and traumatic transformation to the point where some think I am a heretic at best and an atheist at worst. All I know is that I'm doing well in this school and I intend to pass with honors.

I'm achieving my independence. I marvel at the independence of so many of you, and your efforts to achieve and keep it.

WE ARE WOUNDED FOR A REASON

I've come to the conclusion that The Lasting Supper is made up of two groups of people:

1. those who have been wounded by the church;
2. those who intellectually moved on from the church.

This is a generalization, but I think a pretty accurate one.

Actually, when I think about it, they both apply to me.

Then, when I think about it even further, they both may apply to all of us.

I'll share from my own perspective about myself, and see if this applies to you:

Yes, I got some pretty outstanding scars from the church. I've shown some of them to you. But, this is not what actually drove me away from the church. The scars didn't come out of nowhere. The wounds were delivered when people tried to confine me, constrict me, and control me.

If I had complied and conformed, things would have been much better for me. It was my root desire to be free to be myself that caused the problems. When I showed any signs of independent thinking or living, that's when the hammer always came down. It was when I challenged the centers of control or questioned the status quo that things got difficult for me.

But then, when I think about it even further, my desire to be free was rooted in my mind. My own mind. My desire to be me was my own thought.

So I can fairly say that it all began with a thought in my mind: I want to be free to be me! I want to be free to ask questions, explore, discover, and integrate what I learn that is true. I will do whatever it takes to realize this. This is really all I have, life is short, so I'm going to make it my priority to see this through to completion.

So... back to those 2 major determinants that would describe the demographics of The Lasting Supper members... people who are wounded and people who have moved on intellectually... can be boiled down to just one:

Independent thinkers!

In my case, and I think in the case of many here, the wounding is the result of this battle:

Who will control your mind?

The wounds are what you received for fighting for ownership of it.

I remember after one of the most devastating blows to me personally (we went through a church split in 1997 and experienced massive betrayal by our closest friends)… I got my whole leadership team and me to get group therapy. The therapist essentially concluded that we shouldn't identify ourselves by our wounds, but by our fierce desire to be free and independent. Just by a slight switch in perspective, it made us all realize that, as difficult and necessary as it was, we had done the right thing and had scars to prove it.

I eventually got to the place where I no longer identified as wounded, but as free.

So when people suggest that TLS is made up of a bunch of wounded people, I redirect their sight to what you really have been involved in… a bloody fight for independence!

And you're winning!

MY TRAP OF SELF PITY

I want to share with you all a very personal story of mine. Please bear with me. I think this will be a short but to the point letter.

As many of you know, I've had a very tough couple of weeks. It's been grueling actually. It threw me into a funk that was very difficult to get out of. I will tell you the story I've been spinning about myself:

"David, you suck as a person. You are a failure in helping others!"

This inner voice, this inner dialog and story, was confirmed by some unpleasant messages I had received. My own story and my fear of the stories circulating "out there" compounded to make me feel like I was a complete failure and that I should just give up and go back to being an artist only.

Then, the other night as I was just about to doze off to sleep, I heard the words, "David, self-pity is the greatest obstacle to your personal spiritual progress." Now, some might say that was God, or the Universe, or the Great Spirit, or Spirit, or whatever. I might say that it was my deepest, truest, yet unconscious Self communicating to my conscious self. If we were to believe there is a God, I would suggest that this is the part of me that That-Which-We-Call-God would commune with and nurture towards spiritual health, wholeness, and independence. I bolted up in bed and wrote those words in my journal because I instinctively knew them to be true.

Even though on one level I despise pity, I've had to come to realize that on another level I cherish it. It's delicious. Not only does it make my story feel validated, it also makes me feel soothed and comforted in it. We at TLS are really good at listening, validating, and comforting one another in our struggles. That's awesome. But there's more! There must be more.

I have also come to realize that my version of my story is not necessarily reality. I am discovering from brain science and psychoanalysis, which also agrees with philosophies like Buddhism, that me clinging to my version of my story, my attachment to certain thoughts or beliefs, or even any thought or belief, is the cause of suffering. My attachment to a thought is suffering. I had just read this the day before I heard the words above:

"Perhaps the most important revelation is precisely this: the left cerebral hemisphere of humans is prone to fabricating verbal narratives that do not necessarily accord with the truth... The left brain weaves its story in order to convince itself and you that it is in full control... What is so adaptive about having what amounts to a spin doctor in the left brain? The interpreter is really trying to keep our personal story together. To do that, we have to learn to lie to ourselves."

It was as if a pail of cold water had been thrown on me. I realized that I was clinging to a story about myself, that I was relishing a thought, and that it was causing me intense suffering. On the one hand, I want to stay attached to this story because it was evoking pity in myself and in others for me. On the other hand, I suddenly realized I simply could not continue in this vein because it would only perpetuate my suffering and therefore my need for pity. Pity can kill my motivation to move on.

It's a vicious, circular trap... the more I pity myself, the more pity I get, the more I need to stay in my suffering, then the more I pity myself and the more pity I get. There would be no possible way out until... until... I realized that this was all orbiting around a lie: a fabricated narrative that said I sucked as a person and that I am a failure as someone trying to help others. It is a lie that I suck as a person. It is a lie that I do not help people. It is not true!

As soon as the center disappears... the lie... so does its gravitational pull, its orbit, and its planets: my need for self-pity and pity from others. They are flung into the furthest galaxies.

It's not a one-time magic disappearing show. When I am inundated with negative press every day, not only from my own false mind as well as from those who don't respect me, it is a daily project for me. But it's not too difficult. It's just a matter of looking at these accusations and simply asking, "Is this true?" Is it really true? No, it's not. It's a lie.

This is what my progress looks like. It helps me escape from my victim mentality that would keep me bound in my own pity and the pity of others for the rest of my life. It helps me move on to really become healthy and independent. It helps me to become truly free. In fact, it sets me free to become a better person who truly helps others.

Thanks for listening, my friends.

STOP SABOTAGING YOURSELF

Lisa and I are getting ready to go on a little trip today for a week. It's our 35th wedding anniversary tomorrow… May 4th. I never realized until the day when someone said, "May the forth be with you!" that it is a cool date to get married.

Lisa and I were talking late into the night last night. Thirty-five years is a long time. We've learned a lot. One of the things I've been thinking about is how much or how many times I've hurt Lisa over the years. I think the hardest years for me personally, and Lisa suffered for it as well, were since I left the church in 2010. I went through a major kind of personal, emotional, and psychological deconstruction and reconstruction. I'm still under development in a big way.

I spoke with my counselor and spiritual director yesterday. While talking with her… she's such a good listener, very wise, and very helpful… but her greatest gift is just listening to me talk and talk and talk. In a way she helps me to be my own therapist. I came to some pretty major revelations yesterday about myself. In fact, I feel it was life-changing. It's like there was such a jumbled mess inside my heart and mind, and I honestly felt like I was going crazy. But yesterday's talk provided, in a flash of insight, a key to unlock it all. Suddenly, I saw the picture I needed to make sense of everything. It was like there were all these confusing, unrelated parts, but this revelation, this picture, suddenly melded them all together into a unifying whole that made sense to me and set me free. I actually felt better… not thought better, but felt better… after this talk. Now I just have to be patient and allow my self, my body, my mind, my heart, to integrate with this revelation, for me to become whole.

Here are three things I preached to myself yesterday. Maybe you can use this for yourself.

1. Forgive yourself: This is the first thing I have to do. I have to forgive myself. Not for all those years of ministry. I was a pretty good pastor. I don't have any major regrets there. My regrets come from when I left the ministry. I didn't kill anyone or sleep with anyone else or anything dramatic like that. Mainly, I was absent emotionally and mentally. I lived inside my own head and wanted to run away from everything. But I have to forgive myself. I have to let that go. If I were talking with anyone else who went through this, I would encourage that person to just empathize, understand, listen, and encourage them to forgive themselves. I have to take my own medicine.

2. Love yourself: It's not enough to just forgive myself. That almost has a cold feel to it. Something final. No further commitment required. I have to go deeper to not just say to myself, "It's okay." I have to move on even further than that to love myself. Appreciate myself. I need to get to the place where I actually care for myself, believe in myself, and even admire myself for who I am. A wise woman once said that humility is when you have an accurate opinion of yourself and you live that out. To have a higher than accurate opinion of yourself is pride. To have a lower than accurate opinion of yourself is false-humility. I'm a decent person. I'm a good person. I have excellent qualities. Sure, I have issues just like anyone else. But I'm intent on working through those. And I love me for it!

3. Embrace yourself: And it's not enough to just love myself. Love needs skin on. I need to get into me. Excuse the sexual innuendo, but I need to make love with myself. You know? It's not enough to forgive. It's not enough to love. Those are just feelings. Emotions. I have to be good to myself and show myself love. Pamper myself. That would mean talking nicely to myself. Being gentle with myself. Kind. Patient. Understanding. Encouraging. Edifying. Believing. Which would mean I would stop being mean to myself. This is the hard part because I've been harsh with myself in many ways. I've been encouraging to myself but undermining that by meaning harsh to myself. I realized that not only do I often sabotage myself in my business life, but in my emotional life. My negative talk was sabotaging my positive talk. Stop that! Just be honest but positive whenever possible.

3 STEPS TO TAKE WHEN YOU'RE MISUNDERSTOOD

I want to talk today about being misunderstood.

There have been many people on TLS who have felt misunderstood. I have felt misunderstood. In fact, we are all misunderstood at some time or another.

I won't attempt to describe how someone else felt misunderstood. I am the best and most reliable witness to my own life and experiences. So I'll share with you the three steps I take when I feel misunderstood. I'm going to use the episode that happened last week on TLS as an illustration. Some people said I did not empathize with their pain and that I wasn't a good listener for them.

So here are the 3 steps I take in the face of being misunderstood:

1. Step Inward: That is, when I feel someone misunderstands me and accuses me of something, the first thing I try to do is step inward. I try to understand what that person is saying and examine myself to see if their accusation is true or if there is even a shred of truth in it. Did they misunderstand? Or was I not understandable? So, for example, when someone says that I do not listen or do not empathize with their pain, I check myself to see if that's true or even possible. Even though I like to believe I'm empathetic, did I fail? After looking at myself for a good length of time, I do have to admit that I have weaknesses and faults. I know I could handle conflict better. I'm uncomfortable with conflict and anger scares me. Therefore, I recognize that sometimes I'm not a good listener and that I jump to conclusions and make hasty decisions, especially when I'm panicking. I want to prevent more people from being hurt as quickly as possible, and I am sometimes hasty in how I achieve that. I want to be a good facilitator of community. I really do. That's my promise to you. So I apologize for how I fall short or even fail. I want to listen. I want to empathize. I need to learn to do that even under extreme duress. This is an example of stepping in. I examined myself in the light of an accusation and saw how it could possibly be true, and I intend to grow from it and make TLS a better place.

2. Step Forward: It became clear to me through our ordeal, our conflict, that even though the vision and etiquette of TLS had largely worked up to now, that it was no longer working. I realized, while sitting on the beach during my vacation, that my vision and table etiquette for TLS was either not clear enough, not known enough, or not respectable enough. So I made up my mind that TLS's vision and table etiquette had to be more understandable, respectable, and communicable. I talked with a lot of people over the last couple of weeks. A lot of people for a lot of hours. On the one hand, I was trying to understand them. On the other hand, I was trying to make myself understandable. I tried to clarify what I meant. I tried to elucidate what TLS was about. I tried to apologize and make things right and try to shed light on my heart and what I hope for. I tried to articulate what its vision was and what the etiquette meant. Particularly, I tried to explain that I could hear them and empathize with them while at the same time hear and empathize with a person they may be angry with. This is the most difficult process because, well, it involves another person who may be in conflict with you. Will we reconcile or not?

3. Step Away: When it becomes readily apparent that the other person cannot or will not understand you, then it's time to step away. Some people give up during the arduous step #2 because it can get exasperating. I'm glad some people stayed in civil conversation with me as we attempted to understand each other. But it sometimes gets to the point when we realize that we are essentially on two different pages or even in two different books. We come to the sad conclusion that we simply cannot understand each other, or will not. Even though we speak the same language, it becomes obvious that we own different dictionaries. This can be frustrating and sad. But it can be relieving too. Some who misunderstand me and feel misunderstood by me are angry. Others are, oh well… we can agree to disagree and move on! So we do. I step away. There comes a point when you have to decide to stop investing in a conversation that simply is not healthy and is not working. I've lost more friends over the last week. In fact, I actively ended a couple of relationships that were toxic for me. That's a new development for me, and a good one! It's called self-care. I'm tossing that unhealthy Christian value that says I must be a friend with everybody, even my abusers. So, sometimes it means a change in relationship. Sometimes it means a loss of friendship. But at least we tried, and at least we'll be better for it.

In a nutshell, this is how it may work:

I have a great idea about community.
Someone tells me it's a stupid idea.
I examine it to see if this is true.
I work with it to make it better.
I try to articulate more clearly what I mean.
If it's still not understood, I may repeat the previous steps.
Eventually, I realize we may see things differently.
I move on because I believe in my vision!

HOW TO SPEAK COMPASSIONATELY

Today I want to talk about compassionate speech. It was inspired by one of our members posting this quote of Domo Geshe Rinpoche:

"There are many who are interested in gender-neutral language, as well as practicing open-ended statements in communication. These methods allow others to respond without trying to control them by selecting words with an agenda attached. Teachers of young students probably experience special challenges in their own use of speech because school children being taught how to use language skillfully will sometimes mimic a reprimanding style of communication from their teachers. What is compassionate speech? It is using non-inflammatory language. I attended a local township meeting here in Wisconsin. I did not intend to speak, but suddenly words became confrontational as tempers started to rise. Suddenly, I stood up, 'I am one of your new neighbors, sorry to interrupt… but please be careful, many of you are using inflammatory language and this is not going to help the situation. Thank you very much,' and sat down. Suddenly, the atmosphere calmed down, and people became aware of their word choices. By using words such as never, always, etc., others might feel attacked, blamed, or even wounded. If we think reasonably, there's really nothing that never happens, or always happens… such as blaming and shaming statements such as,

'You never do this! You always do that!' It will be hard to remember our vow to attain enlightenment for the benefit of all sentient beings while smacking others verbally. Instead, let's be alive in bodhicitta motivation to the best of our abilities!"

Let me tell you a couple of stories.

I'm Canadian. I live in Canada. Once in a while someone will be talking with me or a small group of people and they'll say something like, "Those stupid Americans! Especially those in the south!" I'll immediately speak up and say, "My wife's American. And she's from the deep south, southern Alabama." I'll say it with a smile and a sparkle in my eye, like a "Gotcha!" kind of thing. Most of the time they'll say something like, "Oh! I don't mean Lisa!"

Several weeks ago I was having a conversation with a few guys. One guy started talking about Heaven, saying that Heaven's like this and Heaven's like that. He was talking as if we all agreed because he assumed, I'm guessing, that I'm an orthodox believing Christian. His speech implied that if you didn't believe what he was saying that you weren't going there. I didn't say anything because, even though it was massively presumptuous, it wasn't insulting and he didn't ask me what I thought.

For me, both of these are examples of speech that is not compassionate.

To practice compassionate speech, I must remember a few things:

1. Not everyone is like me, nor should they be. As an example, when I'm speaking online, I must remember that not everyone is Canadian, liberal, progressive, carnivorous, etcetera. I am different than most of my family. A lot of my family in the states would be Republican, people who hunt, very conservative Christians, etcetera. A lot of my family in Canada would sympathize with them. Politically, we differ. Plus, I might not agree with them or appreciate their lifestyle, but it doesn't mean that I am better than they are. So when I speak, I remember this.

2. Generalities are usually wrong. We learn this in our personal relationships. "You never!" "You always!" kind of language is usually not true. Not all Americans are bad. Not all Southerners are narrow-minded rednecks. You know what I mean. So when I speak I try to avoid inflammatory language. Even though some of my cartoons are criticized for painting with too broad a brush, I try to indicate that I don't mean "all" or "every". I try to communicate that this certainly applies to "some". When someone says, "Believers are…" or "Atheists are…" or "Muslims are…" I know they may be smart but not wise or compassionate.

3. Compassionate speech is a universal expression. A universal door. I think this is a Buddhist expression. I want to be a universal door. Don't you? This requires compassionate speech that is open to the universe and everything in it. Of course, compassionate speech only emerges out of a compassionate heart. If my heart is not compassionate, then neither will my speech be. I want to be all-inclusive because this is an honest expression of reality. I truly believe we are united, one, joined, at an essential and fundamental level. Our various and diverse expressions are simply ripples on the surface of this deeper current of unity.

Of course, while we are diverse in expression, we can be united in justice. That is, we can be unequivocally opposed to racism, homophobia, transphobia, misogyny, hate, violence, sexism, Islamophobia, and so on.

I would like to share something more personal with you. Many years ago, when I was the pastor of my last church, we did a personality test on those who attended a seminar. I discovered, to my dismay, that many of the people were similar in personality types to me. A professional therapist who was there with us spoke to me about this because I was disturbed by it. She said something to this effect: "David, you don't want a church full of people with the same personality type as you, do you? A community full of INFPs just like their pastor isn't an indication of the diversity you desire." She was right. It was a shocking slap to my spiritual face. I think this ramped up my personal efforts to be more universally accepting of others, which of course meant being more universally accepting of myself.

207

The communities I find myself a part of now are incredibly diverse. Just look at TLS! We have believers, non-believers, agnostics, atheists, pastors, ex-pastors, Muslims, Buddhists, Jews, Nones, Dones, Pagans, Wiccans, etcetera, etcetera. Just the other day I got a personal note from Irshad Manji, who wrote, *The Problem with Islam Today*. She encouraged me by saying that we are both involved in the same project… what she calls, "Your work is very important. Keep up the 'ijtihad' [independent thinking—not to be confused with 'jihad']." It encouraged me to think that we are essentially united, not only at an essential level, but also on a practical one. This feels like TLS to me. And I think this is healthy because it is an accurate and honest reflection of reality… what is!

So when we speak, let's remember to speak compassionately… from compassionate hearts. One very practical, simple, and quick way to do this is, just before you post something, ask yourself: "Is this going to needlessly hurt or offend someone here?" Simple as that! This is what I do because I want to be a universal door, not a narrow or closed one. This is how a diverse community works well.

A QUICK WAY TO SELF APPROVAL

So, you are totally confused. Your journey does not make sense. You have difficulty understanding where you are and therefore even greater difficulty in loving yourself and articulating yourself. You're feeling a mixture of shame, frustration, and maybe even guilt.

Here's a simple little strategy I apply when I'm feeling this way:

I imagine talking with a friend. My friend Sue and I are meeting for a coffee. Sue says she is deconstructing and completely confused. She no longer believes many of the things she used to believe. She doesn't know what she believes anymore. She's even questioning the existence of God! In fact, she expresses fear that she might turn into an atheist. She wrestles night and day with her confusion, shame, and guilt. She says she really feels like a refugee lost at sea and wonders if she'll ever find solid ground again. She's in no-man's land, belonging nowhere and to no one. There doesn't seem to be anyone who can listen or who understands. To make matters worse, those who love her are very concerned and express this concern in meaning-laden comments loaded with ulterior motives that make her self-doubt loom large in her mind. At a few points in our conversation tears come to her eyes. She's embarrassed... not just by her tears, but with herself. I notice she seldom takes a sip of her coffee because she's so absorbed in her dilemma. I point this out, and she admits that this is what her life is actually like... she can't live life because she's stuck inside her own predicament, tangled up her own thoughts, and trapped inside her confusion. I recognize her impatience. She's desperate to settle down, find a home, and be fully and confidently herself again.

Then, I listen without judgment. I don't try to correct her or change her. Why? Because I'm not afraid of or surprised by what she's going through. I recognize it from my own experiences. In fact, I think she's in a good place. She's growing and it hurts. So I'm not going to say anything to endorse or fortify her negative feelings about herself... her shame or guilt. Although these are natural, these are negative, judgmental, and even destructive ideas, maybe even echoed by her concerned family and friends, that are attempting to drag her back to her former self. I love her and care for her and tell her that she's doing an amazing job and that if she gives herself time she will come out the other side of this dense fog where she will find confidence, peace, and even happiness again. I remind her that she's smart and will figure this out. I believe in her! In this tender moment, I just try to make her feel as normal, healthy, mature, and courageous as possible. Because that's what she is! She has rejected her conditioning and with full integrity wants to become a better, wiser, happier person. I'm not going to compromise that, but only encourage it. That spark I see in her dark passage... I'm going to fan that into flames so that she will regain her fearlessness and embrace the profound transformation she has already entered and embraced. She might not realize it, but she's committed, and I'm going to help her keep her resolve.

This is not imaginary. This has actually happened many times for me... face to face and online with many different people. True stories!

Finally, I apply that to myself. Aren't we often told that we are gentler with others than we are with ourselves? I know I am. But this is the trick. The same grace, love, and care I show to others I show to myself. As soon as I'm feeling ashamed or guilty for where I am in my journey, I immediately apply this simple technique. I treat myself like I would treat a friend like Sue sharing her journey with me. It only takes a second. That simple trick, in a split-second, immediately arouses the self-love, self-confidence, and self-care I need to be okay with where I'm at and to press on undeterred. It's a quick way to endorse yourself. It's an immediate way towards your own self-approval. It's a fast way of getting your confidence back and forging ahead with the courage you need to accomplish it.

HOW DO I DEAL WITH LOSS?

How do I deal with loss? Not very well. I'm human.

When I experience loss, I don't pull out my trusty roadmap for suffering and loss and follow the guidelines. No one has written such a book because each and every response to loss is unique to that individual. There's no one-size-fits-all approach to loss. Sure, there are books about the grief process, etcetera, but these cannot speak specifically to your own experience. They can help buffer the pain, but they will not eliminate it.

Even the most spiritually advanced people experience loss personally. I suspect people who claim they feel no pain and experience no grief.

I'm reminded of an old legend of a Buddhist monk whose son died. He holed himself up in his cave. After many, many days he emerged out of the cave where his disciples were waiting for him. They were bewildered that he was experiencing loss and grief… in a word, that he was suffering. They inquired, "But master, haven't you always taught us that suffering is an illusion?" To which he replied, "Yes, but this illusion was particularly convincing!"

In other words, it hurt. He experienced loss. He felt grief. A normal human reaction.

Let me tell you how I experience loss. Like, say, the loss of a friendship. As I've travelled my own spiritual path... because I must... I have gained some new friends along the way, but I have also lost some too. How do I deal with the loss?

First, I descend into a deep dark pit. I feel overcome with sadness. I feel powerless because there was nothing I could do about it. Sometimes I even question my own ability to have and hold a friendship. I'm inconsolable. Now, in the back of my mind I hear my truer, peaceful self, full of wisdom, encouraging me to be the peaceful, wise, enlightened person that I am (haha). But I resist this for a while because I want to feel sad. I want to feel this sense of loss. For me, it is an automatic, even involuntary expression of gratitude and honor for what I lost. It is paying my respects for what I had. So I just tell the illumined part of me saying "Get over it!" to get behind me. Let me feel this for a while.

Next, I start to allow my enlightened self to emerge. (By the way, I think we all have enlightened selves, so I'm not speaking boastfully here.) I begin seeing how this had to happen. Because it did! It is real. And I choose to love what is real. Reality rules! So the sooner I embrace this the sooner I will actually end my suffering. When I stop believing my negative thoughts and realize that I am well, that all is well and that all manner of things will be well, my peace reestablishes itself in my heart and mind. I also realize that the friend I lost is believing his thoughts as well, and that if I believed the same thoughts he was believing, I would unfriend me too. It's amazing how much peace this brings to my mind. This is the peace that abides, always there to take the throne.

Finally, I learn from it. Perhaps I do suck as a friend. Perhaps I have done things that give people no choice but to unfriend me. (When I say 'unfriend' I'm not necessarily only talking about Facebook, but friendships in general. Facebook coined the term and I find it useful to my experience.) I also learn a lot about people in general, the human race, humanity. It's during times like this I can look into my heart and realize that I really do have compassion for all living things because I can feel compassion for the person I just lost. I learn how to live as a more loving and compassionate person. I also learn that being a loving and compassionate person will not always be easy and that I may not always be understood or accepted. That's a lesson worth learning.

I don't think I'm naive to say I consider everyone my friend. At the deepest level we are all connected, one, united, and that it is only our thoughts that seem to apparently divide us. But these thoughts are illusions. They aren't reality. For me, the reality is that we are not separated or divided. So an ex-friend, in my opinion, and with genuine feeling I can say this, they are still my friend even though I might not be theirs. I wish them well.

Way back in 1997 I went through a massive church split. I was the pastor. Suddenly I had a whole boat load of enemies who just the day before were my closest friends. I've been around this block before and since. At the time I could not process it. Then, one might I had a dream in which I met with the leader of the split and I embraced him. I awakened the next morning no longer angry with him, no longer feeling estranged from him, no longer hurt or confused. He was no longer my enemy. I felt that dream was the emergence of my deepest and truest Self showing me what reality was: that even though we've never restored our relationship, that I could still love him and wish him well and not lose the real connection between us.

Loss hurts. But this is how I process it.

HOW TO DEAL WITH FAMILY

Last week, someone in our Facebook group brought up a question about how to deal with family and coming out to them theologically.

So in this letter I'm going to tell you how I do it. I hope these 3 steps are helpful for you.

1. You're no longer an evangelist. I don't know about you, but growing up in evangelistic churches, as well as an evangelistic Bible college, it was drilled into my skull that I always had to be on guard and ready to convert other people. I always had to be ready to give an answer for the hope I had within me. The pressure on me to constantly share my faith was enormous and unrelenting. I remember one beautiful Sunday afternoon being dropped off by our youth pastor at a beach and sent with bibles to witness to people there. Those poor people were just looking for a place and time to relax with their friends and family. But there I was to inject loads of my seriousness and intentionality into their day and get them saved. That kind of thing happened a lot. I'm glad to be free from it. I'm glad my victims are free from me too. Now, I don't have to change anybody's mind. I don't have to convert anybody. I just feel like I want to love everybody where they're at. So when I walk into a room of people who know me really well, there's no longer that pressure to perform or persuade anymore. I can just be with them. This is about peace.

2. You are your own pilot. Another huge breakthrough for me was realizing that I was in control of my life. I was no longer a victim of other people or their agendas or persecutions. No matter what my family was talking about I was in control of myself. They weren't in control of me. Even if you did grow up in a controlling, disciplinarian, or authoritative home, you're an adult now and they don't have to control you anymore. They don't have to control the way you think or speak or behave. In fact, maybe you realized early on that even though there was a lot of pressure to think a certain way, you only pretended to. You were always independent in your thinking. So, actually, it's embracing this reality that matters. I am an independent thinker! When I walk in that room with people all with different beliefs, I am still an independent thinker. They don't control my thoughts. They can't control my thoughts. It's impossible for them to. I acknowledge that and embrace it so I don't freak out inside when conflicting thoughts, ideas, and beliefs start flying around the room. I don't have to believe them. I don't even have to believe my own thoughts. I don't have to debate them or challenge them or present another side. It doesn't matter. This is about freedom.

3. You get to decide how to behave and respond. On the Facebook post, I said that I decide if I'm in wartime mode or peace mode. This might be a bit of a confession, but as a pastor I was often the center of attention. Not because I wanted to be, but because that's just how things were in the church. So at a gathering or something, I was often asked to say something. It's taken a while to get used to the fact that this is no longer the case. I can be in a room of people and frankly no one cares what I think. Actually, in the circles where people know I've gone through a dramatic change in my theology, they either think I don't think theologically anymore or, if I do, they don't want to know what I'm thinking. Often I think this is the case with some people who are close to me. They really don't want to know what I believe. So why burden them with it? A simple question I ask myself now when I'm in this situation is, "Is this about me?" Often it is not. And rarely when it is about me, when people really do want to know what I believe, then I give them both barrels. I don't hold anything back. If they want to be clear about where I stand, I will tell them as much as I can about that. It might even just be, "I just don't know anymore!" So wartime mode is when it's about me and people want to know what I think. Peace mode is when it's not about me and people want to just hang out. It's not a lack of integrity to choose to be quiet. Unless, of course, they start talking in nasty racist, Islamophobic, or homophobic ways, etcetera. Then, for the sake of those who are being attacked and my own integrity, I will often say something. Otherwise, nah. It's not worth it. This is about self-control.

Remember, most people don't want to change their beliefs. Therefore, you won't change them for them. But when they do want to change their beliefs, it often manifests as them seriously questioning their present ones. It's obvious. This is when I choose to speak my mind. Otherwise, it's a waste of time. I don't argue for entertainment.

So there it is. I'm no longer under pressure to change anyone's mind. I am in control of how I speak and behave. I will share my beliefs when asked or if I have no choice.

YOU DON'T ALWAYS HAVE TO DO SOMETHING

When I left negative beliefs and toxic relationships behind, I realized I was feeling a lot more peaceful. One of the things that religion likes to do is pound it into our heads that we have to change.

You have to change the world. You have to change other people. You have to change ourselves.

Now I realize, no I don't.

I don't have to change the world. I don't have to change other people. I don't have to change myself.

I'm not saying that change isn't good. Sure! Change is good and often necessary. What I'm laying emphasis on is the "have to". I don't have to! I'm free to do whatever I want. I'm no longer under the guilty weight of religions expectations on me.

If you feel like you have to change the world or other people or yourself, set time aside for it. Say, one hour a day! You can say to yourself, "I've got one hour, from 3 to 4pm, to change the world. Any other time I'm not going to worry about it." Or, "The last hour in the day, I'm going to focus on changing something about myself. Aside from that I'm not going to worry about it." About other people? Well, we could say, "I'm going to spend my lunch hour to try to help someone and make a difference in their lives. Aside from that, I'm not going to worry about it."

But, you know what I've discovered in my personal life? When I try to change myself it becomes unbelievably frustrating. Or trying to change the lives of others can become very disappointing. Or to try to change the world can be incredibly discouraging.

What I've come to realize is more beautiful and far more peaceful is just noticing these things as they are. Awareness.

Be aware of the world. Notice things. Be curious about it. Be aware of others. Notice them. Be curious about them. Be aware of yourself. Notice yourself. Be curious about you.

When you notice things as they are and, if your heart and mind is open, appreciating them as they are and even loving them as they are... here's the kicker: that's where the real dynamic change happens.

Scientists in the field of quantum mechanics are discussing this right now... how the observer projects unto the object... how change in the observer effects change in the observed. It's fascinating because this is what some mystics have talked about for years.

What I admire about you all is your willingness to observe. Honestly. Courageously. You don't have to do anything amazing (although you are). Just observing affects change.

This changes you. This changes those around you. And this changes the world. So get those religious voices out of your head provoking you to constantly do something and change things. Relax.

IS TLS SAFE?

I'm truly sorry for the misunderstanding about what "safe" means for TLS and how this misunderstanding hurt people. I accept responsibility for it since I was unaware of the very specific usage of that phrase "safe space" for abuse victims and survivors. So, out of respect for abuse victims and survivors (of which I am one), I am retiring the phrase "safe space" as a descriptor of TLS. I'm also going to be very diligent in keeping TLS on track for why it was created. I may use the word "safe", but only very cautiously when no other word can be found. Please forgive me for giving the impression TLS was something it wasn't. It's not a support group for survivors, although survivors, including me, can participate. It is a place for people to deconstruct. As one friend wrote me this morning: "TLS is a closed forum where people can be open - with open questions, open minds, open hearts—a place to privately be themselves to better publicly face their world."

TLS is an experiment. People aren't objects. They are living beings. TLS will continue to grow, stretch, fail, succeed, hurt, support... you name it. It's made up of people that co-facilitate the group. It's just like I've always said about the last church I was the pastor of: "There's no perfect church. Just perfect moments!" TLS isn't perfect, but it does have perfect moments.

I will also continue to write and cartoon about abuse, especially spiritual abuse, as well as the survival of it. I will continue to be an advocate for victims and survivors of abuse, and critique the people and systems that inflict it. Why? Because I've been doing this since 2005, and because I myself have inflicted spiritual abuse and I have been the recipient of it. I have firsthand experience in it, having over 50 years' experience in the church, 30 of those being in the ministry. I am committed to the spiritual health, freedom and independence of people, and to creating and helping to create healthy communities. I'm sorry where I've failed, but I promise to do better because I believe in it! I will persevere in using my art and writing, as well as facilitation skills, to this end because I am passionate about it.

THE 4 MAJOR PLAYERS IN MY DECONSTRUCTION

I think this letter will be short and sweet. I want to share with you what the four major players were in my relatively healthy deconstruction.

I say relatively because I did experience some major bumps and bruises, including hurting some people around me whom I love and who love me. I've written about those bumps before in previous letters.

Okay, here they are:

1. A good counselor: It took me a while to find one. I live in a fairly small city where everyone seems to know about the church I used to pastor and therefore me by default. I was commonly known as a pastor

217

who lost his faith and left the ministry and the church altogether. So it was impossible for me to find someone around here I could trust, who didn't have a preconceived opinion about me, and with whom I could divulge my deepest and darkest secrets to. After putting out some feelers online to a few trusted people, I was put in touch with a person who not only is a depth psychologist, but a spiritual director of sorts. This person also had a similar journey to mine and therefore "got" me. I was put in contact with this person when it was almost too late. Don't wait too long. My advice is that everyone should journey with a therapist anyway. But my advice is that you certainly should if you're deconstructing. This person saved me.

2. A few close local friends: Of course, my wife Lisa is my best friend. I'm eternally grateful to her for her love, support, and understanding. And patience. Oh yes, patience. Also, I have a few friends with whom I can talk about anything. Interestingly, most of them are my leaders from my last church where I was the pastor who had eventually left the church too. They aren't yes-people but honest, caring folk who let me say anything and everything to them, let me cry on their shoulders, and promised allegiance to me through thick and thin. They are still very close friends, and I credit my recovery to their undying love and friendship. One of the things that we have come to understand is that we should have friends. Find them. Keep them. Trust them. Let them help you as you help them. They saved me.

3. A few good books: I love books. My favorites are biographical and other non-fiction, although there are a few good fiction books that informed my journey. We've talked about important books before. I have a lot of them now… books that have been my traveling companions, road maps, encouragers, correctors, and informers of my journey. I will always treasure the wisdom that was delivered into my life from these wise people who wrote down their thoughts to help others like me. Books saved me.

4. A good community: One of the hardest things Lisa and I experienced was the sudden loss of community. After a couple years of despairing of ever finding one that understood me, would accept me, and that would support me, I started one of my own online… The Lasting Supper. Without you guys I wouldn't have made it. You made me feel sane, normal, healthy, and loved. It was a surprise to me, really, that a community formed around my idea of providing resources and support for people who are deconstructing. But it was a pleasant surprise. TLS became my family in a way. It certainly became my community. It became my go-to place where I could be totally me without fear, caution, or hesitation. I really don't know where I would be without you guys. You saved me.

What could you add to this list? What has been absolutely crucial to your healthy deconstruction process?

WHY I DON'T WANT TLS TO BE PERFECT

I have said in the past that TLS is perfect. But I want to explain what I meant by it.

*** Spoiler Alert: Do you remember the end of *The Last Samurai*? In it, the Samurai Chieftain is looking for the perfect cherry blossom. This is his life endeavor. Near the end of the movie when he lies dying on the battlefield, it is snowing cherry blossoms everywhere. He notices them and says, "Perfect! They're all perfect!"

That's what I meant.

However, TLS is also not perfect. But I want to explain what I mean by it.

If, as the founder and lead-facilitator of TLS, I claimed TLS was perfect, then this would mean a few things to others:

1. It would mean that TLS is controlled. It would mean that I was autocratic and that I expect people to conform to TLS… a group, program, or goal that I had pre-written and expect them to abide by. In my opinion, this isn't community in what I think is the truest sense but

219

an organization that people must submit to.

2. It would mean that TLS could not change. In other words, I had created something that people are required to fit into rather than be a living part of a living thing that moves, grows, and matures over time. It suggests that they really have nothing to contribute but only something to get out of it.

3. It would mean that TLS couldn't admit weaknesses. It couldn't admit its faults and even mistakes in order to actually change and become as good as it can get. This means that it would lack humility, an open mind, and the terrible lack of listening that would prevent it from learning how to do community in healthy ways.

4. It would mean that it couldn't improve. I believe in evolution… including spiritual and community evolution. I want TLS to be the best prototype for how healthy community works. A microcosm of a beautiful world. That's a worthy goal. And the only we can do that if we know we can make mistakes, learn from them, and progress.

It's like Apple releasing the iPhone, Elon Musk the Tesla, and Google new software or whatever. There are always bugs. It's because they listen to their clients, receive reports, and quickly maneuver to fix them that they become the iconic products and services they are today.

TLS is evolving. I'm learning a ton from my mistakes or lack of wisdom and experience. We as a community are learning a lot on how to function as a healthy community.

One of my driving convictions is that we are all one, undivided, not separated but united at a deep and fundamental level. I do not believe this unity, which already exists and therefore doesn't have to be created, is made manifest by propositional agreement, ideological conformity, or spiritual duplication but by personal integrity and dignity, mutual respect, and kindness. In other words, love.

I love you, as well as all those don't know it or believe it.

We're doing this together, and I thank you.

YOUR WEEDS AND YOUR WHEAT

Have I ever told you my analogy of the trellis? If I have, bear with me. I want to share it again because it's meaningful and helpful to me right now. First I have to tell you how I came up with it.

Many years ago, my spiritual director, Sister Marie, told me I should read a book by Thomas Green called, Weeds Among the Wheat. Being a good student, I got it right away and read it. It revolutionized my spiritual life.

He makes his essential point from the Jesus' parable of the weeds among the wheat. A farmer finds out an enemy has sown weeds among his wheat. His workers' first reaction is to go and pull out all the weeds. The farmer tells them not to. He advises that they allow the weeds and the wheat to grow together because if they pull up the weeds they will also accidentally pull up the wheat with them. He tells them that they will be separated at the harvest. Green suggests that this does not only apply to communities that want to separate the good people from the bad. It also applies to our personal lives. We should not try to eradicate those areas of our lives we are unhappy with by violently trying to overcome them. He says we need to be patient and gracious with ourselves because he believes there is a symbiotic relationship between what we perceive is good and what we perceive is bad about ourselves. In fact, to believe we can get to a place of absolute purity and doing things to ourselves to achieve it is impossible. I liked this because I used to be very brutal, relentlessly unforgiving, terribly impatient, and even cruel to myself.

I've kept a journal for decades. Thinking that I've progressed on the road to perfection, I would then glance back years in my journal and would be surprised to find that I really haven't changed at all. Oh, there were minor tweaks here and there, little adjustments to who I perceived I was. But I was still David, the same old me, deep down inside.

I have a friend who is one of the best guitar players I've ever met. Truly a remarkable player! In fact, he's famous in my city. And he knows it. He struggles with pride. I was his pastor for years and would hear is continuous confession that he struggled with his pride. On the other hand, he is one of the most humble people I know. It was then that I realized that it was his pride that was making him humble. It was his self-awareness that he was proud that caused his humility to grow. As his awareness of his pride grew, so did his humility.

So this is my analogy: what we perceive are our weaknesses behave like trellises up which what we believe are our virtues grow. Take away the pride and the humility goes with it because there would be no need for the humility to exist there. The same can be applied to any number of what we think are our weaknesses.

It's like our weaknesses are the shadows of our strength.

I'm feeling this right now. I have a deep passion for the unity of the human race to be made manifest. I want to work for the unity of all people. Of course, I know this starts with me. I think this is a strength. However, on the other hand, I know I have a deep need to be loved by everyone and keeping everyone happy. So here is what I think is a strength: bravely working for unity and peace. And this is what I think is my weakness: not being able to handle criticism, conflict, and personal attacks very well. As nakedpastor gets more and more popular, I get more and more afraid because of the personal attacks I receive. But if I tried to overcome this need to be loved and didn't care about the feelings of others, maybe I wouldn't care about peace or unity or love at all. Maybe it is in fact my need for love that drives me to see it in the whole world between all people. I don't know. It's just a guess.

Anyway, I hope you find this helpful. Be gentle with yourself. Be patient. Be gracious. We all have a dark side. We all have a light side. We all have trellises. We all have flowers. We all have weeds. We all have wheat.

Let's love ourselves for it.

IS IT POSSIBLE TO EVEN LIKE THEM AGAIN?

On Saturday Lisa and I, along with my sister, my brother-in-law, and our 3 nephews, went to the local Farmers' Market. It was a beautiful day and crowded with people. There was a steel drum band playing. The smell of fresh food being made was in the air. Lots of arts and crafts. Fun.

But there were some very special highlights I would like to tell you about.

We ran into several people who used to go to our church before the church spilt in 1997. Every one of them had left during the split and were, at the time, very much against me and my ministry and many of them were involved in efforts to take me down.

Now… this split happened 18 years ago. Lots has happened since then. But for most of these people we've either not or hardly seen them at all. And then all in one day we cross paths.

What do you think happened?

I'll tell you.

We met with smiles and "So good to see you!".

How did we get there? How did we get from mortal enemies to cordial acquaintances happy to see each other?

Time? Has the hurt dissolved over time?
Forgetfulness? Maybe we forgot how badly we hurt each other.
Life changes? Me no longer being a pastor takes the fun out of attacking me.
Ministry? Me no longer being in ministry (or the church) proves they won.
Forgiveness? Did we finally get to a place where holding a grudge no longer mattered?

Love? Maybe we've decided that love is best and resentment doesn't work.

Maybe it's a mixture of all of them. But here's my point: I've tried to get to a place where the process from animosity to amiable takes less time to practically no time at all. I've made it my intention to learn how to be able to process this faster. Sometimes I can. Sometimes I can't. But I'm learning. It's taken a long time.

A part of our deconstruction or change includes sometimes significant changes in our relationships.

Sometimes they stretch.
Sometimes they strain.
Sometimes they snap.

But sometimes they work.

Of course, there are some people who would like to hurt me. It would be foolish to pretend this is not the case. So respecting my own boundaries, taking care of my family and friends, and keeping a safe distance from those who mean harm to me and mine is wise.

RELIGION AND PARENTS

People are often confused about my views about religion. Some think I'm anti-religious. Some think I'm pro-. I'm neither. I hope I've come to a healthy place when it comes to my relationship with religion.

So I want to talk about the different stages of my personal relationship with religion in such a way that it might help anyone out there struggling with this.

Now, I'm talking about most of us who have been in religion, maybe even grown up in it, or have some kind of relationship with it. But even for those who claim to have no relationship or who have never had any relationship with religion, I hope the last stage might be helpful for you too.

I compare our relationship with religion with our relationship with our parents. Whether they were good or bad or average parents, whether or not we experienced abuse with them, whether or not they are perfect or bad people, I hope these stages help.

1. Dependence: As children, we are totally dependent on our parents. We need them. They give us everything we need. They help to shape our worldview.

It's the same with religion. We are totally dependent on it, it shapes our worldview and nurtures us in this world.

2. Codependence: This usually comes around adolescence when we start testing our boundaries and limits, and our parents' power and rule. We are stuck between needing our parents and wondering if we do anymore. They may still feel responsible and even assume they have total control, but our ability to challenge this and prove it wrong creates tension.

Again, it was the same with me and religion. I began to test its power and control. It thought it still controlled me, but I was beginning to prove that it didn't. There was a mixture of fear, love, anger, and resolution to find my way without it.

3. Independence: This came for me around the time I went to college. This was when I pretty much left my parents' home and never returned except for visits. Now and then, when I was in trouble, I would reach out to them for help. But I was pretty much on my own, liked it, and presumed the rest of my life would look like this.

Interestingly, and probably not by coincidence, it was around this time I started to explore my independence from religion. I began, painfully and joyfully, to discover that I didn't need religion. At least in the same way. Religion continued to assume I should do everything it said. But I had to make a life for myself.

4. Interdependence: Even though my parents and I are in very different places, I have come to the place where I can be with them, visit with them, and talk with them. I am independent now. But I do desire some kind of adult relationship with my mom and dad, and together we have achieved that. Of course, it does take two sides for this to happen well. I think we're doing our best. I've done a great deal of work to let my adolescent feelings go and move on to a new kind of mature and adult relationship with them. Relationships have to grow, including those with our parents.

When I read Louise Hay's book *You Can Heal Your Life*, I was struck by how, once she'd come to a place of profound wisdom, she felt it important to reconcile with her mother. I read the same thing in Byron Katie's biography about her relationship with her mother. For some reason, many people feel it's healthy to work through all the stages to come to a place of relating with all things, including the most terrible things in our lives, as adults. Sometimes it might even mean never seeing them again. It might mean giving it one more shot. It might mean reconciliation could occur. How it ends up looking is not the point. My point is that I come to a place where I can relate to them… together or apart… as an adult.

When it comes to religion, I do not hate it. I see its value. I no longer hold a grudge or wish it were dead. I know some people who had horrific parents, but they are not against parenthood. I know some people who have had terrible marriages, but they aren't against marriage. I have had some pretty nasty experiences with religion, but I'm not against religion. I can see its value, especially when it behaves. I appreciate it for what it is, but I will never let it control me again or negatively affect my life. I know it for what it is.

I can see the devil in the details. But, I can also see the better angels of its nature.

I'm going to relate to it….

Not like an infant.
Not like an angry confused teen.
Not like a prodigal.
But like an adult… who cares for himself and relates to it in healthy ways.

It took me some time to get here. But it's worth it.

WHAT ARE YOU GOING TO DO ABOUT IT?

Today I want to write about a sensitive topic. So I'm going to speak from my own experiences. I don't pretend to understand yours or to make light of your suffering. But I must admit I am incredibly interested in finding ways to help people feel empowered.

So here it is.

Once in a while my mentors will say something like this to me after I've been lamenting about a bad situation I'm in:

"Well, what are you going to do about it?"

This is usually my sequence of reactions:

1. Defensiveness: Why are you asking me what I'm going to do about it? I want you to hear me. I want you to listen to my pain and get in touch with my suffering. This hurts and I want you to soothe me. I'm the victim here! The people or the situation that are causing my problems… it's their fault. It's not my fault. They broke it, they need to fix it! Now… on the one hand I do need to be in touch with my pain, and empathy is good, but it can't end there. I wish there was more empathy in the world that can handle sitting with someone in their pain. It's called compassion… suffering together. It is powerful. But this is only the beginning. It's a good place to start. The most honest one.

2. Focus: After a while I begin to realize that even though I might actually be a victim here, that a bad situation was caused beyond my control, that I am not excused as an agent in the events or situation. If I keep looking with hope to my aggressors or initiators of my bad situation, then nothing will ever change. Because one thing I've learned is that perpetrators of pain, suffering, and abuse, often don't get it. They will continue their same patterns. Perpetrators perpetuate! So I have to stop hoping they will better my lot. It almost never happens. So while there is such a thing as perpetrators and victims, I can't rely on my aggressors to alleviate my suffering. I have to look away from them for help. I will continue exposing, educating, and reforming aggressors, as well as fighting to make communities safe. But that comes next.

3. Empowerment: Finally, and sometimes it takes a while (anywhere from the length of a phone-call to maybe hours, weeks, months or even years), I get past my defensiveness, refocus, and then start feeling empowered to actually do something about it. Now, I know it depends on the nature and severity of the suffering, but I always am able to come to a place of empowerment where I can actually do something about it. I mean, I might not be able to get out of prison, or immediately out of a bad relationship, or leave my job, or be relieved of bodily pain, illness or debt, but there is always something I can do in the midst of it. Even though I may be a victim, I don't have to think like one. I've been seemingly trapped in horrific situations, and sometimes for a long time, but then eventually I figure out a way to take back power and change it. It always begins with the change of my attitude within the bad situation. Then my perspective. Again... I embrace my suffering. I change my focus. This always has a way of transforming the situation from within even if the externals don't change much. But then, sometimes it goes further. I have ended bad relationships, quit jobs, moved, declared bankruptcy, and exposed my abusers. Etcetera.

In times like these I'm always reminded of one of my heroes, Nien Cheng, who wrote *Life and Death in Shanghi*, in which she recounts her harrowing experiences under the Cultural Revolution of China and ended up in prison for so many years. At first she was overwhelmed by the immensity of her suffering. But eventually she discovered how to be empowered in such a way that her guards and torturers were perplexed and even exasperated. Her resoluteness inspires me in times of suffering that no matter how tough things get, there is always some way to take back my power.

I know what it's like to need empathy.
I know what it's like to want to stay there.
I know what it's like to wait for the situation or the aggressor to change.
I know this often doesn't happen.
But I know the wonder of feeling empowered and getting my power back.
And I know what it's like to do something about it.

I was careful to frame it within my own experience because, like I said, I do not want to pretend to understand yours. Sometimes our circumstances can be so extenuating that we become completely baffled and confused and even unaware of any options and all possibilities. I understand this too.

I've experienced it. But then, at some point, a little flicker of light comes and I finally figure out a way to be empowered.

This is what I love about TLS. We are allowed to share our sufferings and receive empathy for as long as it takes. We are provided space to eventually be honest with ourselves that our situation or aggressor might not change. We are also given time, support and encouragement to empower ourselves.

I think that's cool!

ONE SAD REASON TLS IS THE WAY IT IS

I want to tell you a story that might help you understand what helped to build my philosophy behind TLS and why I do the things I do the way I do them, and why TLS is the way it is.

This story starts in the winter of 2007. Sarah is my friend. She was in her mid-twenties at the time. I was the pastor of the Vineyard church here, and she was a member of it. She had a boyfriend. They were close to being engaged. One winter's night I got a phone call. It was Sarah's mom.

She was hysterical. Sarah's boyfriend was found dead in his car on the highway. Sarah was, of course, at her mom's, beside herself! Lisa and I rushed over. They were both very distraught. Her boyfriend was such a wonderful young man. He seemed happy, smart, had a great sense of humor, and was very loving, especially towards Sarah. He was an all-around great guy. This just did not make sense!

We leapt to the conclusion that he must've been murdered or been involved in some kind of freak accident. The police were not very forthcoming right away. There was a cloak of mystery about it. But eventually we were informed that he had indeed ended his own life.

We couldn't believe it. We still can't.

We walked with Sarah through that whole season. The identification of the body. The preparations for the funeral. The funeral. The burial. Then the longest part, the grieving process.

I was just visiting her mom last night, and she said to this day Sarah still talks about that season and how grateful she is. She tells people that one of the key things that helped her survive was that I provided her with smokes and booze and listened to her process her grief out loud for a long, long time.

I'm not telling you this to get a pat on the back. I'm telling you this because this one story is indicative of how I did things as a pastor, how we did things as a church community, and that it is extremely informative as to why TLS is the way it is. I want to try to explain it.

Sarah was a part of a small group we had in the church. So after this tragedy she would come to group and just process. Sometimes she was completely silent. Other times she would question and question. Other times she would vent with rage. Other times she would pray and pray and pray. It took a long time. There was a lot of anger, hate, despair, doubt, fear, hopelessness, loneliness, depression, along with the tears and shouts and… you name it. The whole gauntlet of emotions. It was horrible to watch our dear friend go through this, but we went through it with her.

The small group was great. We never preached at her. We never quoted inspirational sayings. We never provided answers. We never tried to rush her or push her or stop her. We never denied her. We just listened. Oh, we'd occasionally say things, but never in a condescending or instructive or impatient or religious manner. Most of the time it was just repeating back what she was feeling and saying to show her that we were listening and that we were there for her. Sometimes we would just sit with her and cry. No words. What words could be sufficient?

It took a long time. In fact, it took too long for some people. A couple took me aside after a while and said something like, "When in the world are you going to tell her to get on with her life? This has gone on too long! She's stuck and needs to move on!" So I told them what I'm going to tell you now:

When people are given the space, they will heal themselves.

They lost patience and left the group. Sarah kept on sharing. I want to be clear. Sarah didn't dominate the group. She didn't take over. Maybe once in a while she did. But that's valid. We were all there sharing our struggles. But when Sarah did share, it was intense. Very intense! Of course! How could it be otherwise?

But I held to my guns. Sarah did come to a place of acceptance and peace. Even happiness. It's many years later and she's happily married and living a happy and fruitful life.

So last night I asked her mom how Sarah was doing. I told her the reason I asked was because one morning I was triggered into remembering Sarah's boyfriend. It was an overwhelming flash of sorrow and a flood of memories of that horrible season. Sarah's mom said she is doing great and that she still tells people about her pastor keeping her supplied with smokes and booze. It's kind of a joke. But what she's telling people is that she had people who were just with her, uncritically, non-judgmentally, patiently. That's what she's talking about. She was given space to process until it was all processed. That's what she means.

It's a proof to me that if we are provided a protected space to process, we will heal ourselves. It may take a short time or it may take a long time. It depends on our own inner resources as well as the intensity of what we're processing. But given the space, we will heal ourselves!

That, my friends, is why TLS is the way it is.

And you help to make it so. You guys get it.

THREE HUMBLE ADMISSIONS WE CAN MAKE

As I took my walk this morning, I thought of three humble admissions we can make with confidence:

1. I don't know. It's healthy to admit we don't know. We don't have all the answers. That we are swimming in a sea of mystery. In fact, I suggest this is really the most honest way to live. This presupposes a curious mind open to wonder rather than a closed mind open to nothing. Embrace it with confidence!

2. I don't feel perfect. It's okay to feel a little off. Even though you may feel you're progressing intellectually, philosophically, spiritually, personally… whatever… it's normal also to not feel perfect. It can be anything from a mild anxiety to full on depression. This doesn't negate our evolution or our progress. Sometimes it's just about being human. Embrace it with confidence!

3. I'm okay though. Even though we may experience confusion and even though we may experience feeling off, we can still be assured that at the root we are okay. We can love what is... even though we may not understand it or it doesn't feel right. Yet! You are okay. Embrace it with confidence!

FEELING YOUR FEELINGS

When we change our beliefs and our allegiances, it's also necessary to change our feelings about our feelings.

I don't know about you, but I was taught to not only distrust my feelings but to neglect them, ignore them, repress them, apologize for them, and even punish myself because of them.

Then I learned, kind of like a thorough conspiracy theorist, that religion demands total control over every aspect of our lives, including our feelings. That's when I decided, many years ago, to take ownership of my feelings, to respect them, honor them, feel them, process them, learn from them, grow from them and with them.

I know it's a hard lesson to learn. My religion was absolute lord over my entire life. But once I realized that I was free and didn't have to obey this master, I knew it was my responsibility to feel, and to feel honestly and authentically.

There's lots of talk about the lack of emotional intelligence today.

Religion is partially responsible.

The guilt, fear, and shame I was feeling about my feelings only made sense under my old master. They simply did not make sense anymore not that I was free.

Feel away. That's what I say.

EVERYTHING I S ASSIMILATED

I spent the day yesterday with two friends of mine, Brad Jersak and Peter Fitch, both theologians. Brad lives out in western Canada but comes to St. Stephen's University every semester to teach crash courses.

He was out this way and actually asked me to come and join him for the day! How cool is that?

Brad's wife was with him, so the four of us hung out. Lisa had to work, and Peter's wife was away. We sat around talking and drinking coffee. Then we went out for a walk and for lunch. Talking the whole time!

Usually I'm at home alone drawing, painting, and writing all by myself. But yesterday was a rare experience for me and I thoroughly enjoyed it.

I learned many things, but one thing has stuck with me: It seems I go as far as I can comfortably go in one church or denomination until I can't go any further and I have to leave.

From then on I'm lost in the wilderness.

First, I try to find a new home that will embrace me. Or, like now, I finally, like the desert hermits of old, settle in the wilderness and make it my home. I'm cool either way. I can visit churches. But the desert is my home now. I'm fine with that.

But what was neat about the visit yesterday is that Peter has loved me all through my journey. We met way back in 1995 and his love and respect for me has not changed. And Brad, even though we've just met this year, has a love and respect for me that I can tell will bridge time and change.

This was a very liberating experience for me. It made me feel like I can still call Christianity my home. I've always said, "Christianity is my home, but I have cottages everywhere!" And this felt especially true yesterday.

Even though I feel much of the church and Christianity has rejected me, I do not have to reject it. And I don't! And I won't! My understanding has gone so much deeper than that so that it embraces all of it.

I recently explained it this way:

I used to be inside a cup of belief. But now what I know fills the sea! I do not throw away that cup of water I used to believe. Rather, it gets subsumed into the sea. The sea embraces it all. I do not reject it. It gets absorbed into all that I am. All that we are. All that is.

So yesterday, as I was sitting and talking in the presence of love, all that had gone before was assimilated.

Things were added and multiplied. And the sum was grand!

ARE YOU RELAPSING?

I've not only observed it in others. I've experienced it for myself!

That is, I will go through a kind of deconstruction of a belief. Sometimes I react to a belief I no longer feel can hold up. I'll go long in the other direction.

Then, after my anger or frustration or sadness or disappointment or rebellion is over, I often come back to a more reasonable, rational, and less reactionary posture.

I think this is normal.

I've seen it in some, though, where they relapse to an even more conservative position than they were before... probably to protect themselves from ever approaching that line in the sand again. They don't like how deconstruction feels, so they avoid it at all costs.

But, this is a reaction too.

What I help people do is to experience and exercise their own freedom. They can end up wherever they want… without shame, fear, or guilt. That's the goal!

Your own personal freedom and your enjoyment of it.

Whether you end up a believer or an agnostic or an atheist… this is secondary to me. What is primary is your personal spiritual independence. That's it.

So don't worry if you're constantly ebbing and flowing in what you believe or don't believe. This is as natural as the tide!

Just observe. Just enjoy. Just relax.

Because you are not the tide. You are the ocean!

BUILD YOURSELF UP WHILE TEARING YOUR BELIEFS DOWN

I've been thinking a lot about deconstruction… that is, the changing of our beliefs, the loss of faith, the shift in our religious habits and behaviors, and the transformation of our inner and social selves.

This is what I help people do. I've been doing it for many years.

One of the things I have come to realize is that while we deconstruct, for many of us something else has to be happening at the same time.

That is, the reconstruction of our self-esteem and confidence.

For many of us, we've been exposed to a religion that is anti-human. Inhuman. Anti-human. It is what can be called worm theology… you know… that we're wretched and no better than a worm. Many beliefs ingrain into our minds that we are worthless sinners, broken and bad.

The only thing that can save us is the blood of a lamb that covers the sin but doesn't remove it. We live the rest of our days in a state of shame, guilt, fear, and lowliness. We despise even ourselves.

This is reinforced by our families, our friends, our churches, and even our God.

But what happens when we start to question, challenge, and even reject beliefs that teach us this about ourselves? Where do we go from here?

This is what I've come to realize: we need to edify ourselves. We need to start a new program of deprogramming our minds. We actually need to rewire our brains... and some claim this is actually physically as well... and train it to think positive thoughts about ourselves. We need to reconstruct (and for many of us it is construct for the very first time) a self-image that is positive rather than negative.

How do we do this? For example, how do we start feeling proud of ourselves when we've been taught to be ashamed of ourselves our whole lives? More than that, how to we feel proud about ourselves when we've been taught that this is the worst sin of all, initiated by Satan himself just before he was kicked out of Heaven for his rebellion and sent plummeting into Hell?

Well, I know for one that it's going to feel weird. It's going to feel foreign. It's going to feel... wrong! But I'm here to tell you that you must do it.

Here's where we can start: We can reverse the flow.

Negativity is reinforced by ourselves, our families, our friends, our churches, and our God. Instead, we need to start by positively reinforcing ourselves.

There might not be much we can do about our family, our friends, our church, and our God. Or is there? Yes!

As we boost our inner confidence, we can silence the negativity of those around us. Our inner voice can drown out theirs. We can distance ourselves from negativity if and when we can. We can surround ourselves with positive voices if and when we can.

Finally, as our new philosophy about life and ourselves is reconstructed, then everything else will eventually fall into place. It doesn't matter what kind of negative voices are around us, we've built ourselves up to the point where it doesn't affect us like it used to.

So, as you deconstruct, find ways to construct or reconstruct your positive inner voice and build yourself up, strengthen your inner being, fortify your self-esteem and confidence. Again, it might feel weird and even cheesy, but it works! I can testify to that.

YOU DON'T HAVE TO SUBMIT TO HARM

Suffering is built into the theology of many religions. The Christianity and the church know a lot about suffering. Unfortunately, my experience and the experience of many has been that this is often used against us rather than for us.

How?

I will share from my own experiences and observations: I believed I was worthless. I didn't feel I had much value. Then I was introduced to a Lord who taught me that suffering was my lot in life. You know: Take up your cross daily! Then I often found myself in churches that used this to manage me.

The more I suffered, the better I felt. The happier I was, the guiltier I became. Something was wrong if I wasn't suffering… if not externally then at least internally.

This theology became so engrained in my psyche that it's taken many years to pry myself free from it. I still wrestle with not feeling valued and slipping into the mentality that this is somehow the most noble attitude to have. As a result, this would cause me to allow myself to submit to being disrespected, hurt, and even abused.

Somehow I was a spiritual person by letting other people walk all over me. I used to think there was dignity in undignifying myself and, by extension, letting others undignify me.

No longer!

You deserve to be who you are! And you deserve to be happy!

You don't have to submit to harm.

TEN THINGS I COULD BE EMBARASSED ABOUT

This morning as I was catching up on the news online, I came across a video of one of the Brownsville, Florida, revival meetings. In case you didn't know, I was in the middle of the whole renewal movement. You know… that phenomenon that really began at the Toronto Airport Vineyard… what was called the Toronto Blessing.

My very first reaction to watching the video this morning was embarrassment. Man, did it ever throw me back! But, I relaxed, let my love and intellect engage, and then I felt something else other than shame. I'll tell you about that in a second.

But first, let me tell you some other things I did that I could be embarrassed about:

1. I was a born-again zealot and tried to convert anyone I met and even used Chick tracts.
2. I converted one of my brothers to Christ by terrifying him with the torments of hell.
3. I told my parents I was leaving high school to smuggle Bibles into communist Russia.

4. I faked speaking in tongues, as instructed, to kick-start the real speaking in tongues.
5. I continually despised my Presbyterian churches for not being on fire enough.
6. I walked 20 kilometers of the most populated part of the Annapolis Valley praying in tongues the entire way.
7. I was deep into the renewal movement and did strange things.
8. I faked being slain in the spirit at the Toronto Blessing because I was the only one left standing.
9. I constantly told my Vineyard congregation that revival was just around the corner.
10. I humbly believed the prophetic words that I was going to be world famous.

Oh man, I could go on. But isn't that enough? Yes, that one little video reminded me of all that. And, like I said, my first momentary reaction was shame.

But I thought again. I felt again. Then, instead of shame, I felt love for myself. I perceived in all that a man who wanted to know the truth, who was looking for connection, meaning, and love. I saw a man who was continually searching for what was authentic, trustworthy, loving and true. I saw a man going through stages, transitioning from one level of understanding to another, a man progressing and evolving spiritually.

Even if I was duped, it was because I was willing to be.

Because I chased any lead that presented itself to me. I was hungry! And that's okay!

I'm not saying I've arrived. What I am saying, though, is that that same obsessive search has come to an end. I've come to a place of peace of mind and spiritual contentment. I've come to a place of love where I can embrace myself and my earlier selves. I gather up all of me in my own loving arms, past, present, and future.

But another thing I feel is that I look at everyone else the same way. I don't laugh at those who are searching. I don't ridicule those who are progressing. Like me, they are all impermanent, moving, changing, and evolving into themselves… their truest selves. I do not shame them or feel ashamed for them.

And that's okay too.

VIKTOR FRANKL AND FINDING MEANING

Viktor Frankl, in his famous book *Man's Search for Meaning*, shares about a time he was participating in a group therapy session composed of a variety of people who were experiencing a variety of sufferings. As we know, Frankl's primary interest in logotherapy, which he developed, was that it is meaning that gives one a reason to live. The human is not given a passion for life by simply self-actualizing, but by self-transcending. We need to reach into our deepest resource, which is our untapped potential, to live a life of joy, passion and meaning.

During this session, the meaninglessness of suffering arose. Frankl's own life provides an example of how his life had meaning. When he was arrested and taken to a prison camp, he had a one out of twenty-eight chance of survival. That was the statistics. He had hidden in his coat the manuscript for his book he was writing. When this was confiscated, he lost all hope. Eventually, he realized that he simply must write this book, so he scribbled notes on anything he could find. It was his sense of mission to write this book that he believes kept him alive.

In this way, he didn't find meaning in the suffering. But he found meaning in the midst of his suffering. The suffering itself didn't have meaning that he could perceive. But he found a meaning for living while he endured unbearable suffering in such places as Auschwitz. He noted that it was those who had a reason to live that had a far better chance of survival. It wasn't that they had a reason to suffer that they could understand but that they had a reason to endure the suffering. You understand the difference.

So he gave a question in a story as an example to the therapy group. I quote:

"The question was whether an ape that was being used to develop poliomyelitis serum, and for this reason punctured again and again, would ever be able to grasp the meaning of its suffering. Unanimously, the group replied that of course it would not; for with its limited intelligence it could not enter into the world of man, i.e., the only world in which its suffering would be understandable. Then I pushed forward with the following question: 'And what about man? Are you sure that the human world is a terminal point in the evolution of the cosmos? Is it not conceivable that there is still another dimension possible, a world beyond man's world; a world in which the question of an ultimate meaning of human suffering would find an answer?'"

Please keep in mind that although Frankl believed in human spirituality, he was not religious. He believed in a transcendence that is within us all, and personal.

I think that it is important for us in our time of spiritual evolution, during our season of letting go of negative and harmful beliefs, of divesting ourselves of harmful behaviors and toxic people, of no longer taking upon ourselves unnecessary suffering just because it is expected of us, that we remember that even though we may not find meaning in the suffering, we can hopefully find meaning in the midst of it.

WHAT DO YOU DO IF YOU LEAVE THE MINISTRY?

This letter is especially for those of us who have left or are thinking about leaving the ministry.

If this doesn't include you, you might at least find it interesting because of the special challenges clergy face. Also, I think a lot of this applies to those of us who have left the church, especially if we were very active within it.

I know how difficult it is to leave the ministry. I wrote a post on why it is so difficult. But I've done it four times, and I've survived.

- The first time… a surprise to me… my contract wasn't renewed.
- The second time I was depressed and left cold turkey after I had a dream.
- The third time I was fired.
- The fourth time I could no longer live inside the box so I quit.

Each time I had to find employment right away. It was terrifying, nerve-racking, and depressing. I wish there had been someone who had gone through this before to give me encouragement, but there wasn't. I was on my own.

Here's how I felt:

1. **Ashamed:** Many people question why one would leave a secure career, a vocation, after so many years. Many times I wondered if they thought I was a child-molesting ex-priest, the way they looked at me.

2. **Unemployable:** What education did I have? What experience? Theology and ministry. That was it. What good is that in the real world?

3. **Unprepared:** The real world is real. In the church, the system supports the clergy. I was set for life if I kept within the lines. But in the real world I had to fight, compete and win at all costs. I was a virgin with these real-world skills.

4. **Desperate:** I have a wife and three kids. I didn't just want to find a job, I had to find a job. Quickly! I had five mouths to feed. As we all know, one week, even one day, without income can devastate a family.

I eventually found solutions:

- The first time I went to school full time with student loans and grants while Lisa worked.
- The second time I got a job at a donut shop, then as a door-to-door battery salesman.
- The third time I bought and renovated and flipped a house and worked at a call center.
- The fourth time I taught English as a Second Language at a university.

Now I am self-employed and make all my income online from home.

So I'm going to provide some advice to clergy who are leaving the ministry based on the four reasons I found it difficult above. Advice I never had but can now give!

1. **Shame:** You have no reason to be ashamed. There are lots of good pastors out there, and you were probably one of them. Leaving the ministry, I will assume, was for good reasons that reflect your integrity, strength and courage. Even if you were fired! I suspect you are looking for a job because you and the church just no longer got along, not a great fit, and you made the decision or the decision was made for you to go your own way. That, in my opinion and experience, makes for bright new possibilities. Also, being a clergy for many people is a respectable career. It's nothing to be ashamed of. As well, it's not like it used to be: one career for life. People are changing careers all the time. Welcome to normal!

2. **Unemployable:** One of the biggest lessons I learned after leaving the ministry the last time was that, in fact, I was very employable. When you are in the church your worldview tends to get constricted. Actually, many clergy are very well trained and experienced in skills the world needs. You just need to know how to re-imagine your education and experience, and how to present yourself. The last time I left the ministry I had a professional help me redo my resume to highlight my education and experience that was marketable in the business

244

world. Here's what I learned about myself: I knew how to manage volunteers, do a budget, raise funds, collect donations, speak publicly, counsel, coach, resolve conflict, mediate, lead teams, organize children, reach youth, comfort seniors, gather citizens, inspire people, master ceremonies, etcetera. I had no idea! Actually, the tweaking of my resume landed me a job as a facilitator at a university. Something I would've never expected. I know other pastors who have gone into selling insurance, real estate, non-profits such as The Heart and Stroke Foundation, charities such as World Vision, emergency, teaching, counseling, coaching, or they've used their hobbies such as carpentry to get into renovations, buy and sells, investments, landlords, on and on and on. I also know ex-pastors who have gone back to school to learn a new trade or develop their hobby into a marketable asset. The possibilities are endless.

3. **Unprepared:** In my opinion, clergy can have a very clear picture of the world as it is. However, I had serious problems with money and business and fending for myself. In fact, when I left the ministry the last time, I felt a very personal challenge to learn these arts. They are basic life skills I had avoided. What a learning curve! It's fun discovering and using the value of money, the quality of business, and the dignity of self in the business world. I've learned that money is nothing but an object in the value of exchange. I've learned that business is one way all human beings interact and relate. I've learned that taking care of myself is an adult responsibility that took me longer than usual to step into but that has been rewarding, dignifying and liberating. We are the captains of our destiny. This isn't to deny the possibility of being taken care of, for I feel this too. But I also feel I'm a partner in it, that I am a key player and that I am now responsible for myself. I'm enjoying the school of life!

4. **Desperate:** One of the admirable things I learned about myself: I will do anything to support my family. Yes, times were desperate, and I used connections and whatever else I could to land a job, even if it was minimum wage delivering donuts

to coffee shops. I clearly remember sweeping the coffee shop parking lot of cigarette butts while people flicked them at me snickering. It was humiliating. But I did it for the paycheck, which I got! I know it is hard to go from respected and revered clergy to humble laborer, but it's not my pride I was worrying about, but my family. And I provided! I also used these times as a spiritual lesson. I learned that while I was a minister I had a sense of privilege that was unhealthy. I allowed these menial jobs to beat that attitude out of me and to help me learn that I am just another human being along with other human beings on the planet. I let these minimum wage jobs teach me how to be a better person.

In the end, I believe that we are all ministers. I'm not talking religiously necessarily. But that is part of it.

What I mean is that at the bottom of it all is to love and serve humanity. We can do this no matter where we are. At each job I made connections with fascinating but normal people and enjoyed interacting with them. It was a lot different than church in some ways but very much the same in others. People are people no matter where we are. It was refreshing relating to people without the complications that church sometimes brings.

It was about learning a new world in a new way with new understanding, experience, and even language.

I know you can do it. I've done it four times! I'm nothing special. Seriously! If I can do it, so can you!

IS FREEDOM SCARY?

When you leave the church, you might feel a little lost.

You might feel that your spirituality, like water poured out of a bottle into the sand, is just spreading out in all directions with no focus. You may feel like your spirit has dissipated like helium in the atmosphere. Nothing is sure anymore. You can't feel anything solid under your feet.

On the one hand, the freedom is a good thing. Right?

The boundless freedom you now experience is positive and can be enjoyed once you learn how to do it. But, on the other hand, the freedom you now have might feel like you've suddenly been thrown into the deep end before you've learned how to swim.

One of the reasons this is happening is because when you are a part of a church, your spirituality had a kind of structure. There are services, small groups, instructions, and a network of relationships. Now that you've decided to be spiritually independent… whether you stay in the church or leave… these props to your spirituality are either lose their importance or are gone altogether.

Perhaps you need to establish new ones, at least temporarily.

Here are some suggestions:

Find time every day to be inward. Some people react to the term "spirituality" because it suggests a theology they may not agree with. What I mean by "spirituality" is our inner life. So, when I intentionally attend my spiritual life, the best time for me is when I wake up first thing in the morning. I begin my day with an expression of joyful trust. Trust in What Is. Blessing or Benediction. I also try to take a walk and exercise every day. Usually I take an hour after work to walk in this knowledge. You can call it a prayer walk, or a meditation walk. I just try to be present in the moment and breathe in What Is.

Keep a book on the go that encourages you. There are plenty of good books out there that give positive and encouraging information. In my opinion there's also a lot of garbage. So eat the meat and spit out the bones. Get encouragement every day from positive reinforcement. Read a book about studies in happiness, for instance. Read something that is going to make you feel better. It's not wrong to be happy.

Read a book that is way over your head. Deep theology or philosophy works for me. Something that not only stretches my mind but destroys it and makes total renewal the only option. Like Barth. Žižek. Krishnamurti. Read some mystics, like St. John of the Cross or Thomas Merton or Meister Eckhart. You will see you are not alone on your journey. This keeps my brain sharp, curious, and intelligent. Seeing how others think outside the box validates my own thinking outside the box.

Plan to get together with friends. Do this every week so you can talk about things that matter. Something other than sports, the weather, shopping, kids, or your next vacation. Make a deep connection with friends you enjoy every week. Otherwise, like Lisa and I have experienced… if you don't plan it, then it won't happen. Plain and simple. You need to plan to get together with people you can talk with on a significant level. This is a tough one, but try it.

Finally, if you can, find a professional you can talk to, like a counselor, a spiritual director or coach. They can help you find a way to self-advocate and self-validate. They can help you get better. Be willing to pay them! A good one can help you discover that the path you have chosen is not only valid but urgently necessary for you right now. I've paid for counselors, coaches, and spiritual directors… sometimes all at once. I figure I'll lay money down for a stupid car. Why not for my soul?

Those are just a few things I would suggest. They are easy to do. And they can help give shape to your spirituality. It will help you feel less dissipated and more intact as a spiritual being. Sooner or later you will learn to enjoy your freedom and some of these props will not be as necessary. Instead, they will become treats, as they are meant to be.

IT'S OKAY TO BE FLUID

I live on the Kennebecasis River. It's deep, wide, and beautiful.

It also changes every day.

No two days is it the same. It's constantly moving. It has a constant impact on its surroundings.

We've lived here for 13 years. Sometimes we consider moving. But then we realize how much we'd miss this river that we see every day.

Every day a different river. Every day the same river.

And never once is it embarrassed that it changes.

Because it always possesses its river-ness.

One of the things I've noticed in my unpredictable, constantly changing spiritual journey is that I confuse people. Heck, I even confuse myself.

People complain that they find it hard to peg me. They get frustrated that no two days am I the same. Some days I seem like a gentle believer, and some days I seem like an angry atheist. Even my dad confessed to me on my recent visit to see him, "I try to get inside your head to figure you out, but I just can't!" I said, "I can't either!"

But I've learned to not let that influence me. I'm not stressed about it. I've learned to not care. Because, like the river, I'm constantly transforming. Every day something different to behold. Sometimes as gentle as can be. Other days as tormented as humanly possible.

I don't care. Because I never lose my river-ness.

When we post our angry rants against all belief one day and then the next day mention our beliefs with affection… or whatever… I'm never alarmed by that.

Behind all the inconsistent beliefs is the consistency of a fluid you.

And besides, who is this "you"? Who is this "me"? I've come to question even this because it has become a very fluid, flighty, and impermanent thing. The "I" has become as slender as the letter itself.

Because what's most important is not consistency of belief, but consistency of freedom and independence.

Don't be embarrassed by your different manifestations that reflect your changing thoughts that express your transforming mind that display your fluid self.

Be the river that you are. Fluid!

You're terribly beautiful!

HOW TO BE FLUID

In last week's letter, *It's Okay to be Fluid*, I talked about how it's okay not to be one thing all the time, that we are constantly changing, nothing's permanent, and that we should embrace these beautiful transitions in our lives… like seasons… like a river.

Someone asked, "Can you give some examples?"

The first thing that came to mind was a little story that had a big impact on me several years ago.

As many of you already know, Krishnamurti has been one of the most influential mentors in my life. His book The Urgency of Change is probably the number one most impacting book in my life. I suppose aside from the Bible. Some time ago I picked up *Krishnamurti: 100 years*, by Evelyne Blau. It's a collection of a biography, photographs, and testimonials of people he influenced over the years… people like Bruce Lee, Aldous Huxley, Deepak Chopra, and Van Morrison. Another person he knew and influenced is a ceramicist and artist, Beatrice Wood. She shares a very poignant story I want to share with you. She went to speak with him because she was struggling with something:

"It had to do with jealousy. I am generally not jealous of other people doing art, but once I saw a glaze that I'd been trying to make. I juggled to get and hadn't. I went up to Claremont, and here was this glaze I'd struggled to get and hadn't. It was like a physical impact of jealousy, and I was horrified with myself. So I went and had a talk with Krishnamurti. These are not his exact words, but it's the impact of what he made me perceive. He said something like this— All right, we're all jealous. Don't try not to be jealous. Drop it, and go on to another thought— and that has helped me in ever so many ways. I was not jealous about art, but jealous, I'd say, about people. This thing of trying not to be jealous, but instead to touch the stillness of the mind."

Well, thanks Beatrice, because this has helped me in so many ways too!

Why this has helped me is because it is patient and gracious. Through this story I learned to be patient and gracious with myself. I learned to just observe myself and not be shocked by what I observed and to not obsess about it, but just to observe it and move on, to pass by, to drop it, and just move on to another thought.

I don't just apply this to feelings but to thoughts and beliefs as well.

Maybe today I notice I'm feeling a little religious. Maybe today I'm thinking atheist thoughts. Or believer thoughts. Maybe today I believe in a Divine Being. Or maybe not. Maybe I'm feeling in touch with the Universe or Mystery. Or maybe today I feel nothing at all. Or maybe today I'm missing the church. Or maybe I never want to darken its doors again. Maybe today I hear a worship song shuffle through my iTunes and I notice it brings a tear to my eye and a lump in my throat. Or maybe I quickly fast-forward. Yes, these all happen to me. Maybe many times a day!

Ripples! Ripples on the surface of the river of my life. All right, we're all jealous. All right, we're all religious. All right, we're all atheist. All right, we're all... whatever. At least some of the time.

So this is how we do it: we just notice what we're feeling or what we're thinking or what we're believing, drop it, and go on to another thought. We don't let it disturb us, upset us, or excite us. We just notice it. Drop it. Move on. Stop, drop, and roll!

Because deep down, beneath the wind and the waves, and even below the currents, there we are.

There we rest.

YOU DON'T HAVE TO BE ANYTHING

One of the more delightful things we provide at The Lasting Supper is the occasional video meet-up. It's just another way for TLSers to connect, and those who participate enjoy them very much!

A while ago when we had one I felt the usual stress to make people happy. I felt a lot of internal pressure to be an able facilitator, a good moderator, and an effective leader.

Note: This pressure was self-inflicted. The expectation was self-imposed. The stress was self-made.

Some people ask me how TLS manages to be such an amazing gathering of people and how we are able to be a peaceful community without much conflict. What makes TLS so special?

One day I want to sit down, reflect on it, and write down some points to eventually make into a book because I think our kind of community is going to be a necessary thing of the future, and I have something to say about how it is achieved.

But for now I can say this one ingredient is absolutely necessary:

I don't have to be anything. I am free to be me. You don't have to be anything. You are free to be you. And we mutually respect this allowance.

Here's a confession: When I first started TLS, it was called davidhayward. ca because I was going to provide resources from my own experience and knowledge to people who were experiencing a stressful change in their beliefs, a loss of faith as they knew it, or were struggling with their relationship with their church or religion. I was going to be a teacher! Some kind of deconstruction guru.

Instead, what happened pretty quickly is that a community gathered that was made up of people who no longer wanted strong leadership, a guru, or a pastor. The kind of community I tried to let happen locally here for years was organically developing right before my eyes at TLS! Whenever I tried to be a strong leader, moderator, guru, or anything like that, it was met was a bewildering lack of being impressed.

No one in TLS needed leading. What we needed was a place to learn to lead ourselves!

And I love it. I've always dreamed of such a place, and here it is. But it takes me, an ex-pastor, a lot of getting used to.

Here's an example. After a recent video meet-up we had, one of our members and I had a chat. I was feeling insecure because the conversation carried itself and the community members interacted without me needing to facilitate it. Plus, when there were silences, I felt like I needed to fix something. Was it a good meet-up? I felt uncertain and worried that people wouldn't be satisfied. She expressed concern that I not burn myself out. She insisted that it was a great meet-up. She said there was no need for me to feel that pressure to make things work. Just relax. Just let it happen. Just being me is enough. Don't worry about structure, content, or flow. Nobody cares!

Thanks! And thanks TLS!

You see, you can't prescribe or manufacture that attitude that is extended to everybody. But it's this kind of quality that makes TLS special. The same space provided for you is provided for me. It's thoroughly equal, level, and free. The space is the same for absolutely everyone.

I'm not sure what you call it, but I think this is the first item on the list of TLS ingredients!

HOW PEOPLE RESPOND TO MY FREEDOM IS THERE ISSUE

Hi Crazy Quilt!

I was pretty much raised in the church. One of the strongest teachings was that we were not to offend others and make them stumble. At first this made perfect sense to me.

I'm not sure when I realized I never believed smoking or drinking was a sin. Maybe it was because my mom and dad would drink. I was always around it so it wasn't a big deal. And many of my friends smoked. I never thought anything of it.

My youth leaders always used the verses about not offending people or causing them to stumble to mean that we shouldn't drink or smoke or chew or dance with naughty girls that do. Or something like that.

But at some point it suddenly dawned on me… and I was a teenager at the time… that this was being used to keep me obedient, to keep me in line, and force me to conform to the leaders' expectations. I frankly said to myself, "Heck with that!" and kept believing that drinking wasn't a sin, and that if it caused someone to stumble it was because they couldn't handle it.

I seemed to be amongst people who were increasingly unable to handle things.

This teaching about offending people and causing them to stumble, I came to discover, was not just a religious issue, but a common cultural one. It also dawned on me that our cultures, our societies, our groups, use this peer pressure to make us conform to the community standards and expectations.

But here's one of the biggest revelations I had while I was still a teenager: Paul, who wrote all that about offending the weaker brethren, was probably the most offensive person on the planet at the time. He was the one who said to be a slave to no man because we were bought with a price! The truth seems to be that I must live free, and how people react to that is their issue. It's their responsibility how they respond to my freedom. I can't be a slave to their sensitivities. However, at the same time, I should not intentionally intend to hurt someone. So... I concluded Paul was fierce about personal freedom, but he was also just as fierce about the quality of community. Paul was wrestling with what I wrestle with: How can I be free without violating the freedom of others?

This is why I think TLS is working so well. I think most if not all of us have come to a place where we are not offended by the beliefs of others. We've mostly come to realize that how I respond to the differing beliefs of someone else is my issue, not theirs. It's my response, not their belief, that is key.

Unless they believe I'm an idiot and need to be destroyed.

But you get my point. TLS is what I call a "crazy quilt". We are a mixed up non-pattern of beliefs sewn together in a mystifyingly diverse community called The Lasting Supper.

And we're keeping each other comfortable and warm with it.

I love you, crazy quilt people!

VACATIONS CAN BE CENTERING

My family is going on vacation tomorrow. In a rare opportunity, we are all meeting in Costa Rica to spend two weeks together. We haven't done this since the kids were little and we went camping together. We're very excited.

I'm looking forward to being able to relax and center myself. I enjoy getting away so I can think deeply. Several years ago when Lisa and I went on a vacation, I wrote some declarations down.

This is what I came up with:

I think it is very important to make declarations. Every once in a while, it is beneficial to sit down and think about what you really believe and write it down in your journal. I do this every once in a while. Not only does it document my progress or growth or development or whatever you want to call it, but it also helps me refine and articulate what I believe.

Four years ago Lisa and I took a vacation in the Dominican Republic. We had a fantastic time. It was so restful for me, and those hours of peace on the beach allowed my mind to rest and form its thoughts. I came up with several declarations early one morning. I was on the beach all by myself. Dolphins were swimming by as the sun rose. The sun was already beginning to warm the sand. And as I sat there taking it all in, I decided to write down in my journal what I really, really, really thought... as if no one cared and I wouldn't get in trouble. Here's what I wrote:

1. The love of all things. All beings. All life. My heart swells at the thought. My eyes get wet. The love. The benediction. Permeates all.
2. There is no god with substance, form, location, existence. Yet all is full of benediction, blessing. But even this confines. All-theism. A-theism.
3. Serve. Rescue. Liberate all! Faithful in little, faithful in much.

256

There are none in, none out. All are. Rules divide. Faith expressed through love.

4. Impermanence and transitoriness of all things. All things pass. Nothing is permanent. Change. Urgency. Now!
5. What we call the Christ is manifestation of all the above. He is, as we are, in whom all are and none aren't. To speak of him is not to speak of him. To not speak of him is to speak of him. This is a theological reality to me.
6. The mind's perception is the deception. The utter ego-centricity, self-serving, self-preserving, self-protecting, self-seeking, narcissistic obsession of the brain. See this and be healed of blindness.

I really do think this is what poised my mind to receive the z-theory dream. I also think this is what began to prepare me to leave the confines of the church and normative Christian theology.

What a liberating morning!

CARE BUT DON'T CARRY

So Lisa and I are in Costa Rica. We met our three children here, Joshua (29), Jesse (27), and Casile (23). Josh treated us with the airfare and some of the arrangements that made it entirely possible for us all to do. We're away a total of two weeks. What a wonderful and rare treat we are enjoying!

I've learned something very important for me, and I want to share it with you because maybe it'll help some of you as well. It's nothing new. It's just a realization that dawns on you when you get away. Here it is:

Care without carrying.

That's it!

I developed a terrible habit in ministry. I didn't just learn it from ministry but from the Christian culture I grew up in and lived in for so many years. The guilt that was pushed on me for not carrying people well, and then the shame for inevitably failing, was enormous. I'm obviously still learning how to deal with it.

How do I know? Because even just a few days after I was on this vacation I felt a huge burden falling off of my shoulders. I realized that I was still guilting myself into carrying people. It's okay to care, obviously. It's not okay to carry, obviously. One person can only carry so much. Perhaps I can carry one or two people for a little while, depending on how heavy their stuff is, but I cannot possibly carry many. The result is that I fail and then fall myself. Then everyone suffers, including me.

Many of us watched a Brené Brown video where she talks about the importance of setting personal boundaries because only then can we truly have compassion for others. If we allow others to invade our personal space and make unreasonable demands upon us, then certain things will almost certainly happen:

We will get exhausted.
We will become overwhelmed.
We will disappoint them.
We will get resentful.
We will feel ashamed.
We will feel like failures.
We will debilitate ourselves.
We will all suffer.

My best counselors, coaches, directors, mentors, leaders, and caregivers have been those who have cared for me but haven't carried me. Even refused to carry me. At first I would feel disappointment, hurt, resentment, and even uncared for. But after a while I realized they were teaching me to walk, ride my bike, swim, drive my car, or whatever analogy works for you... on my own. I had to learn to trust my own feet, my own sense of balance and direction, choose my path, take the initiative, and take that first venture on my own. It wouldn't take long before I realized that their care for me was teaching me to care for myself. The quicker the better!

The truth is, I'm learning, that I can be a better care-giver if I don't carry others. I'm a better helper when I don't handle every little problem. If I do feel pressure, external or internal, to carry someone, it's wisest to put my own oxygen mask on first rather than do CPR on another when I have no wind of my own. They have their own oxygen mask. Help them find it, put it on, and breathe their own air with their own lungs.

This might be simple for some of you. But I suspect it isn't for others. But I encourage you, as I encourage myself, to give it a shot. You might see just how much better you feel, more energetic, and even more compassionate, mainly because the negative feelings of trying and failing are gone.

I love you guys. I really do care for you. Sorry I can't carry you, though. But I will walk with you side by side!

THE HUNTER AND THE HUNTED

I want to tell you a little story of something that happened to me many years ago in the woods. I was thinking about this event in my life as a parable for my spiritual life. Maybe yours too.

I used to hunt. On this occasion I was hunting deer. At the time we lived in upstate New York in the Adirondack mountains. We lived in a church basement, using the Sunday school rooms as our living quarters with a male and female bathroom and the church kitchen for our facilities. We only had our first child, Joshua, at the time. It was a very remote church far back in the woods, miles away from our neighbors, tucked away on a secluded lake. It was late fall.

I took my canoe and paddled to a distant peninsula that had a ridge running down it. I figured it would be the perfect place to perch myself and wait until dusk when the deer typically start moving. My rifle was a .270 pump action Browning with a high-powered scope mounted on its top. I had a thermos of hot sweetened tea and some snacks to sustain me during my three- or four-hour hunt.

When I reached the peninsula, I dragged my canoe up onto land and tied it to a fallen tree then poked my way up through the brush up onto the top of the ridge. I found a good place to sit on the ridge, overlooking a wide valley of trees that had enough space between them that I could detect movement, organized my things around me so I wouldn't have to hardly move, readied my rifle to fire, and waited. I arrived quietly and waited quietly. Not a sound.

And waited.

I was used to waiting while hunting. You just sit there, possibly and probably for hours, waiting for the slightest movement to indicate the presence of a deer. I arrived there at around 2pm, and I saw nothing for a few hours.

Finally, when the sun had already gone down and darkness was setting in, I heard a rustling in front of me. I clicked off the safety and raised my binoculars to look. Nothing. But I definitely heard something. And it was very close. I lowered my binoculars and raised my rifle. I scoped the forest looking for any sign of movement. Nothing.

Then, and my stomach dropped when I saw it, right in front of me... about twenty feet... a small deer was rising from in front of a windfall of broken limbs and brush. He slowly scrambled to his feet and shook himself. He looked around but didn't see me. After I got over my initial fright, I raised the rifle and sighted it on his front shoulder right where his heart would be. But he was so close the scope was useless. I just looked at the beautiful animal. He started to move. Slowly. I noticed he was walking with a slight limp. Something was wrong with one of his hind legs. He walked to a small outcropping of green grass and nibbled for a while.

I wouldn't shoot him. I couldn't kill him.

This was a strangely mystical moment for me. I smiled. How beautiful a creature! And here we both were, in the wild, alone, with no one else around.

I kind of chuckled to myself. Here we were, the hunter, the hunt, and the hunted. And yet I felt a deep unity between us. Suddenly, I realized that in fact we were one. On a profoundly fundamental level, there is an essential unity that joins us. There was no me or he, no hunter and no hunted. I had been actively and aggressively hunting for hours, and this animal presented himself to me completely unaware of my active attempts to find him. Did the hunter find the hunted? Or did the hunted find the hunter? Who, in fact, was the hunter? Who was found?

He was me.

With deep love in my heart, I watched this lovely, limping deer meander slowly among the bushes and trees, completely unaware of my presence while I was completely aware of his. I watched him for about thirty minutes until he disappeared over the next ridge. When it was finally dark, I gathered up my things in my backpack and found my way back to my canoe to head back home.

In May of 2009, almost 30 years later, after years of aggressively hunting for peace of mind, I had a dream from which I awakened with that very peace of mind I so craved. It simply presented itself. Just like that deer popped up right in front of me, so did this peace of mind. Did my hunting procure it? Did I, the finder, find it? Or did it find me? Did my hunting have anything to do with it? Or was it a gift almost accidental?

I've always agreed with the scripture that says that it is not by effort. Yet what about simply being there? Didn't it take effort to be in the right place at the right time? No, my effort didn't fell it.

It was a gift. And the gift was this: that we were together the whole time, unaware, waiting, and then the surprise.

NOT DOWN. NOT UP. BUT ACROSS.

I can tell when I'm being talked down to.
I can tell when I'm being spoken up to.
I can tell when someone is talking to me as an equal.

Recently I ran into a pastor in a coffee shop. My first instinct was to hide. I know you know what I'm talking about. But I recognized that this was just a trigger, so I relaxed, stayed, and met him. He was nice. But there was also this strange attitude of pastoral care that rubbed me the wrong way. I call it the "ick of concern". It feels like pity. It feels like I'm being talked down to. Especially when the fact that I "used to be in the ministry" entered the conversation, then the concern ramped up and I felt I had been knocked down another notch or two.

You know what? I couldn't always tell when I was being talked down to. Why? Because it was so embedded in my religious culture that I didn't recognize it for what it was. Condescension. A very kind and gracious condescension, but condescension nevertheless. Don't get me wrong. I liked him. He is probably a good pastor. I don't know. I know his people love him. But I also see a cultural norm that everyone participates in that I no longer want to be a part of.

As a young pastor, I used to be condescending. But I went through a series of growths that eventually brought me to a place where I realized we are all equals. Our roles might be different, but fundamentally we are equal, the same, on the same level in terms of respect. I learned, by hard-earned experience, that I show people the respect they deserve by speaking not down to them, not up to them, but across to them and to expect the same from them.

This is offensive to people who think too highly of themselves.
This is dignifying to people who think too little of themselves.
This is authentic to people, all people, for they are indeed your equals.

How do I deal with being talked down to? I used to just be quiet and play along. I don't do that anymore. It took me some time to gain my self-confidence, my own personal sense of dignity and worth, to be able to talk to whatever person was talking down to me as though I was their equal. Sometimes they are offended. Sometimes they are surprised. Sometimes they get it. But in every case I maintain my dignity and self-respect. This is important!

I do the same when people try to talk up to me. I speak as though I'm nobody special and that we are equals. The same thing happens, though. Sometimes they are offended. Sometimes they are surprised. Sometimes they get it. But in every case I maintain my dignity and self-respect. I like to be affirmed (one of my love languages). But I don't like to be high and lifted up… if you know what I mean.

So, the first step is to get a healthy sense of self-respect and dignity. The next step is to project the same respect and dignity upon others. Then find the nerve to live this out in our relationships and conversations.

Peace my friends!

WHY WE WANT TO BE A GREAT TEAM

Google does a lot of research.

One of the most ongoing and intensive studies has been about teams. What makes a good team?

This is important to Google because they work in teams.

I was very pleased to read their conclusions that were released recently.

Before I tell you what they discovered is the key ingredient to a good team, I want to share with you what they found out was not a key ingredient.

It wasn't the perfect mix of individual traits and skills. There was no such thing as assembling a dream team of carefully selected experts.

They assumed this might be the case going into the study. But after hundreds of interviews with individuals as well as teams, it slowly dawned on them what made a team effective.

Here it is: psychological safety.

In other words, "Can we be vulnerable and take risks on this team without feeling insecure or embarrassed?"

I was so happy to read this because, having worked with teams for many years in the church and now with TLS for the past four, I've come to the same conclusion.

It's not who's on the team, it's how the team interacts.

As one researcher put it, "In short, just be nice."

I loved this research because it sheds light on why TLS works as well as it does. TLS is the kind of place where our intention is you can be vulnerable and take risks, and where you will not be ridiculed, humiliated, or silenced. Of course, slip ups have occurred in the past and we do our best to prevent that and to repair it if it happens. But I can say with confidence that TLS is a great team… because you guys show mutual respect and provide a safe space for us to express ourselves authentically and honestly.

So, kudos! I'm proud of you. I'm proud of us. I'm so thankful to be on this team. I'm so thankful that we have this space where we are safe to be ourselves.

WHY THERE IS SWEARING IN TLS

Last week I asked TLSers in our Facebook group for an explanation I can give to people who ask, "Why is swearing allowed on TLS?" Some people who are no longer with us found it either unnecessary, or rude, or indicative of immaturity or even sinfulness. Some others just found

TLS unbearably intense, and this is reflected, obviously, through our language.

Rather than promise them that I would police the words TLSers use, I bade them farewell and peace on their path because I think swearing is valid.

The responses I got from many TLS members were serious, hilarious, and poignant!

Here is a summary of the explanations for you:

1. Release: For lots of TLSers, they find using swear words incredibly releasing. Venting their anger or pain or whatever is more effective with swear words. In fact, some people found studies which showed swearing actually decreases physical and emotional pain.

2. Freedom: Many TLSers have come out of very controlling environments. Swearing is an easy and handy expression of their newfound freedom. Being liberated from a culture where even the words you can use is policed, saying a swear word is a radical and rebellious declaration of their independence.

3. Adulting: Several TLSers suggested that this is just the way adults talk. Adults swear because they can. It's a normal part of their everyday speech. I know people who use swear words liberally. It's just the way they talk. Some people judge those who swear by suggesting they are less intelligent and resort to lazy language when they swear. I know very intelligent people who swear and less intelligent people who don't, so... so much for that theory.

4. Word: Sometimes there's just no other word that expresses pain, anger, joy, frustration, confusion… whatever… than a well-placed swear word. We can use lesser PG-rated words, but they just don't convey the intensity of emotion like a strong swear word. The swear word is a verbal manifestation of the potency of what we're feeling or thinking.

5. Humor: The "F*** Threads" on TLS are, well, special. They are a mixture of seriousness because someone might be struggling with something, but they're expressing it in a way that makes us laugh sometimes. Or watching a video of a mystic guru using swear words… it's just funny! We all appreciate comic relief in the middle of a serious episode.

6. Spirituality: One of our members suggested that Jesus did the equivalent of swearing by calling his opponents names or suggesting they do this or that. Perhaps we have sanitized spirituality to the point where we're no longer truly human. Swearing is just a part of being real flesh and blood people rather than disembodied pure spirits.

There are probably a lot more reasons to swear. But, come to think of it, who needs a reason? Why do we need to police our words? Of course I want to only say things that are helpful, honest, and true. I want to speak in ways that build up the good and bring down the bad. And if a swear word helps me to do that, then I will.

Out of the fullness of the heart the mouth speaks. Swearing can be a healthy part of that process.

NO LONGER A VICTIM

This is short and to the point.
I notice a tendency in me to resort to a victim mentality. It's easy for me to feel victimized. Sometimes I feel the world is hostile against me personally and that the forces out there prevail against me and are determined to make me fail.
How did I adopt this attitude?
Was I born with it? Is it in my genes? Yes, maybe.
Was it instilled in me as I grew up that I was bound to fail, that I was to stay within my restricted limits, and that venturing out was careless and inviting disaster? Yes, maybe.
Did the church teach me that I was worthless, that I had to receive everything that came my way passively even if it was bad, that the only

things I could enjoy were those given to me miraculously by a Heavenly Father, that I had to take everything like a lamb to the slaughter, and to always hope for the best but expect the worst? Yes, maybe.

When I left the ministry and the membership of the church, I instinctively knew that my hardest education was going to be in taking control of my own life, of becoming the master of my destiny and the captain of my own ship. I just knew it!

I just knew my steepest learning curve was that I no longer had to be a victim, that I didn't have to take everything passively like a sheep, and that I could make decisions and take initiative without waiting for a divine green light.

Now, this isn't to negate the possibility of the Divine, but to challenge that I had no role to play except a sad and passive one.

Funny, isn't it, that the story of Jesus, whether we take it literally or not, narrates a man who was empowered, confident, and decisive. Even the passion narrative exposes a man who, even though he surrendered himself, somehow seemed to still be in control of the situation.

And the greatest saints and heroes we admire, even if they believed in God, show incredible courage, strength, and will to accomplish great things in this world.

I'm just sharing my journey with you. I'm not yet at my destination. But I've come a long, long way. There's no turning back because I just have a little further to go. And by "further to go" I mean deeper into this realization that I am not a victim.

Even though I find myself slipping into that mentality once in a while, I no longer live there. Not easy. But it's made my life easier.

Thanks for traveling with me.

AUTHENTICITY WITH ACCOUNTABILITY

This letter is going to be short.

I've been busy in many ways over the past 2 weeks. Lisa's been in Alabama taking care of her brother following his open-heart surgery. She returns tonight. I can't wait!

Today I want to write about something that TLS values very much. I coined this phrase many years ago when I was facilitating community at the last local church I pastored. It's this:

"Authenticity with Accountability"

I observed and therefore came to the conclusion this is a healthy way for relationships, and therefore communities, to function.

We all love TLS because, as many say, it is one of the only places we feel we can be truly authentic. We can be ourselves. We can express our deepest selves without being condemned or corrected. Authenticity rocks. We love being it. We love watching it.

The tricky part is when we allow ourselves to be accountable. But being accountable is the second ingredient in the recipe for healthy relationships and communities. Yes, I am allowed to be authentic. But if my authenticity is needlessly hurting Lisa, then she needs to tell me. I don't want to hurt her. So, I want to know when I do.

If we just valued authenticity, many of us would be very real but also very alone.

If we just valued accountability, many of us would be very careful but also very inauthentic.

We need the two.

Yes, there is real hurt and their is perceived hurt. But a healthy relationship talks it through to understand which it is and negotiates how to resolve it.

Mature people... authentic and accountable people... figure out a way to make the relationship and the community work well. Unless of course they decide it's not possible right now and go their separate ways. But that's a mature decision as well.

Conflict happens. It's the clash of authenticities.

But conflict resolution happens too. It's the ability of those involved to make themselves accountable to the higher good of love that integrates all.

You can't have one without the other.

Love to you authentic and accountable people!

CONCLUSION

Some years back when the nakedpastor blog first launched, a dear friend of mine posted one of his early entries on her Facebook page. I clicked the link and I immediately disliked him. Over the years I would continue to be critical of him. I would eventually bump into people that David and I both know, and they would tell me of the beauty of him as a person and The Lasting Supper. I was always dismissive. Yet another online community. Just what the world needs.

Then my life fell apart and things changed. I began to realize that the reason I disliked him was jealousy. The things he was saying were being heard, and they were the very things I felt and was never heard. Back then I wanted to be heard for ego sake (I was a minister). In my new life full of pain and darkness I wanted to be heard because I felt invisible. I did not have a place in this world to fit in because I did not think like anyone else, I just tried to love well.

Then one day I saw David give a voice as best he could to someone else who was invisible, and in that moment people from The Lasting Supper joined him and I began to see something beautiful. They were all willing to go to the mat for someone.

It was about that time that our circles were growing smaller and smaller and I found myself drawn towards him and his friends and something larger. The Lasting Supper is not Naked Pastor. It is not David. It is not a movement. It is something else.

When I was first asked to do this, I almost said no. The reason is I do not know quite how to describe it. What can I tell you? The letters are true. Our hearts are real.

The Lasting Supper does not slice and dice. It does not change the world. It is not a movement. It is a place of beauty because we are there together. In one day it can be funny, sublime, tearful, angry and empathetic. It is whatever we are in that moment and we are bound together by love and honesty and beauty.

All of us bring to the table whatever it is that we have with us, and we all feast together in the potluck of honest hearts and emotions. We are sometimes sad, giddy, angry, or just plain messed up. In that space we are surrounded by me too's, and we will stand with you.

I never thought that an online community could be so tangible. I never thought a virtual table could be such a feast. I never thought I could fit in and not have to believe in the same things everyone else does. I never knew I could love and be loved without the imagined fences and walls we build based on beliefs and non-beliefs in deities.

We fit in here because we don't fit in anywhere else. We are the exiled misfits and we are beautiful. You are beautiful too.

What you have just read in all the letters is a taste of what we are. You have seen our hearts. You have seen our wounds. You have seen the hope and the light in the darkness that we have found in each other. The difference we have made by simply belonging and having a space to be honest and not worry about it. If it has stirred you and if it has moved you, then there is something else I need to say.

I can write about what it feels like to fall in love, kiss someone, make love for the first time, experience a broken heart and a great many other experiences in life. None of it compared to actually falling in love, kissing someone, making love or having a broken heart. We can be stirred by beautiful words, but ultimately, it is the experience that changes us.

The Lasting Supper is in these letters and in the hearts of the composers of the letters. The Lasting Supper is even more real than the letters. It gets better when you are there with us.

I was reticent to join. I used the cost as a smoke screen. The truth was I had had my hopes dashed and heartbroken too many times. I had said the wrong thing in other spaces thinking I was safe and sent into exile. I had been lied to. There are only so many times you can hear all are welcome and find out that all does not include you. Eventually you stop believing that there is a space for you.

Not everything is for everyone. That said, if there was a letter in here that moved you. If there was something or someone that touched you. If you feel what they feel, then we have a chair waiting for you at the table in The Lasting Supper.

Each of us carries a story and together we are writing a new chapter. It is a beautiful one.

I hope to meet you again for the first time.

Pat Green

Dear Reader:

I hope you enjoyed the letters or at least found some of them helpful. Does The Lasting Supper sound like the kind of community you'd like to be a part of? Then please come join us at www.theLastingSupper. com. We always make people feel welcomed. See you there!

David

Manufactured by Amazon.ca
Bolton, ON